ISBN: 9781290600798

Published by:
HardPress Publishing
8345 NW 66TH ST #2561
MIAMI FL 33166-2626

Email: info@hardpress.net
Web: http://www.hardpress.net

D. A. THOMAS

VISCOUNT RHONDDA

J. Longstaff 21

Rhondda

D. A. THOMAS

VISCOUNT RHONDDA

BY

HIS DAUGHTER
AND OTHERS

WITH ILLUSTRATIONS

LONGMANS, GREEN, AND CO.
39 PATERNOSTER ROW, LONDON
FOURTH AVENUE & 30TH STREET, NEW YORK
BOMBAY, CALCUTTA, AND MADRAS

1921

PREFACE

I HAVE often felt that one of the problems to be solved in respect to biographies (those at all events which are written shortly after a man's death, when there is still something more than documentary evidence to depend upon) is that it may happen that those who can write do not really know, and those who really know are not skilled in setting down what they know.

It was only after considerable hesitation and consultation that my mother and I decided that it was best that I should make myself responsible for my father's biography. In the end we came to the conclusion that it was even more important to be intimately acquainted with the man than to have experience in writing. I did not, however, feel competent to deal adequately with his early political activities. Nor obviously could I speak of his work as Food Controller. I had not a sufficiently practised pen to write easily of phases and periods of which I had no direct knowledge. It seemed, therefore, that the best plan would be to ask able men who had known and worked with him to write. I was well aware that I was taking the risk of destroying something of the unity of the book ; it seemed to me worth while to do so if I could thereby achieve an accurate picture of my father taken from more than one angle. I decided to treat his business career in the same way, because although I was associated with him in many of his later enterprises I knew little of his earlier business life, and it would have been unsatisfactory to attempt to divide it.

In respect to his early political life unforeseen difficulties occurred. Two men who had known him in Parliament had promised me to write sections on this period, but unfortunately at the moment of going to press I found that one of these was unable to fulfil his undertaking. This section is therefore, I am sorry to say, less fully treated than it should be, having regard to its importance in his life.

My mother and I wish to take this opportunity of expressing our gratitude to all those who have helped in the making of this book, both to those whose names appear on other pages, to many whose names are not given, and in particular to Mrs. Mary Agnes Hamilton, to whom I am indebted for much literary help, and whose experienced advice and co-operation were largely instrumental in the final shaping of the book.

RHONDDA.

September 1st, 1921.

CONTENTS

PAGE

PREFACE v
Rhondda.

EARLY LIFE

CHAP.

I. ANCESTRY AND EARLY LIFE I
Rhondda.

II. ENGAGEMENT AND MARRIAGE 15
Rhondda.

III. HIS EARLY VIEWS 28
Rhondda.

IV. AMBITIONS, EQUIPMENT AND FIRST START . 40
Rhondda.

MIDDLE YEARS

V. THE CHIEF EVENTS OF HIS LIFE . . . 49
Rhondda.

VI. (1) POLITICAL LIFE 58
Llewelyn Williams, K.C.

VII. (2) POLITICAL LIFE (continued) . . . 69
Llewelyn Williams, K.C.

VIII. LLANWERN AND CARDIFF 84
Rhondda.

IX. THE SOUTH WALES COAL INDUSTRY . . 99
David Evans.

CHAP.   PAGE

    X. THE CAPTAIN OF INDUSTRY   122
          David Evans.

   XI. LETTERS AND PRESS CONTROVERSIES UP TO 1906   144
          Rhondda.

  XII. LETTERS AND PRESS CONTROVERSIES, 1906 TO
          THE END   163
          Rhondda.

EARLY PART OF THE WAR

 XIII. AMERICAN INTERESTS : THE ' LUSITANIA ' .   . 191
          Rhondda.

 XIV. THE MUNITIONS MISSION   201
          Rhondda.

THE FOOD MINISTRY

  XV. THE MINISTRY OF FOOD UNDER LORD RHONDDA   218
          Sir William Beveridge, K.C.B.

 XVI. LORD RHONDDA AT THE MINISTRY OF FOOD   .   249
          Sir Edward Gonner, K.B.E.

XVII. A SKETCH OF THE FOOD MINISTRY   .   .   . 258
          The Right Hon. J. R. Clynes, M.P.

XVIII. THE LAST YEARS   263
          Rhondda.

 XIX. HIS PHILOSOPHY   278
          Harold Begbie.

  XX. A CHARACTER SKETCH   291
          Rhondda.

CONTENTS

APPENDICES

PAGE

A. To Chapter I 305
  Professor R. J. Knaggs.

B. To Chapter VIII 307
  Miss Evelyn Salusbury.

C. To Chapter VIII 309
  Mrs. M. E. M. Walker.

D. To Chapter XIII 313
  David Evans.

E. To Chapter XVII 317
  Leonard Rees.

F. To Chapter XVIII 322
  F. L. Turner.

G. To Chapter XX 325
  H. O. Hughes.

Index 327

ILLUSTRATIONS

PORTRAIT (*Photogravure*) . . . . . *Frontispiece*
    From a Pencil Drawing by J. Longstaff.

AS A SCHOOLBOY . . . . . . *To face p.* 10
    From a Photograph by H. J. B. Wills, Cardiff.

LLANWERN FROM THE SOUTH . . . . ,, 52
    From a Photograph by H. J. B. Wills, Cardiff.

THE MEMBER FOR MERTHYR . . . . ,, 69
    From a Photograph.

HIS WIFE . . . . ,, 84
    From a Photograph.

CHECK ! . . . . *Page* 115
    From a Drawing by J. M. Staniforth in the ' Western Mail.'

A GIANT AT PLAY . . . . . ,, 177
    From a Drawing by J. M. Staniforth in the ' Western Mail.'

' LUSITANIA ' SAILING NOTICE . . . ,, 197
    From the ' New York Herald.'

AT THE MINISTRY OF FOOD . . . *To face p.* 218
    From a Photograph by J. Russell & Son.

THE GREAT UNCONTROLLED . . . *Page* 235
    From ' Punch,' Nov. 21, 1917. Drawn by L. Raven Hill.

AT HOME—A PHOTOGRAPH TAKEN DURING HIS
    LAST YEARS . . . . . *To face p.* 263

LORD RHONDDA WITH A PRIZE BULL . . ,, 303
    From a Photograph by W. H. Bustin, Hereford.

LIFE OF LORD RHONDDA

CHAPTER I

ANCESTRY AND EARLY LIFE

OF my father's forebears on his father's side very little
is known. His grandfather came to Merthyr as a young
man, set up in business as a contractor, and did well in
a small way. He had run away from his own home. He
came of small farmer folk, and tradition has it that he
fled from his home near Magor, in Monmouthshire, because
he had been caught playing football on a Sunday. My
father always averred that it was much more likely he
had been wanted for sheep-stealing, but this aspersion on
his poor grandfather was, I think, a pure figment of his
imagination.

My father's own home, Llanwern, was within five miles
of Magor (in later years he owned most of the land adjoining
that small country town), and he took considerable trouble
to find out more about his mysterious grandfather; but
although many inquiries were made and every possible
source of information was followed up, we never met any
certain information as to which of the small white farms
dotted about that green and fertile country-side had been
the home of his ancestors. His grandfather, who was born
in 1770, had gone to Merthyr, probably about 1790, and in
the life of a farming community who keep but few and
imperfect records a century is a very long while. Comparatively few years can and do obliterate every trace of
a family. It was always a source of pleasure to my father
to feel that he lived in the same country as his forebears,

probably indeed owned the very land which they had tilled, and he often referred to it with satisfaction.

On his mother's mother's side he came of a stock of small yeoman farmers, the Williamses, who had long owned and lived at the same farm (the Forest Farm), which is still in existence (and still a family possession) to-day, up on the hillside in Merthyr Vale, though the mining tide has swept very near to it. They could trace their direct descent back for several centuries. Merthyr Vale, though it is beautiful, or rather was beautiful before the days of collieries, is poor mountain land, bleak, and not very profitable to till. One imagines the Williamses must have been hard put to it to live at times during those centuries.

His mother's father was one Morgan Joseph, a mining engineer in Merthyr, who married Jane Williams ' of Forest Nest in the Parish of Merthyr.'

There is no similarity between the two stocks of Thomases and Josephs : the Thomases, hard-working, stiff-necked, intellectual, sincere, religious folk as a rule ; the Josephs, the very opposite, generous, extravagant, superficial, quite unintellectual, of the ' easy come, easy go ' type. But on both sides my father came of small farmer stock ; it had, I think, some bearing on his habits, preferences and character.

John Thomas who fled from Magor to Merthyr [1] made his living as a contractor, hauling at Cyfartha for the Crawshays, and was moderately successful. He was, we are told, a man of ' exceptional piety, and was remembered for the power and fervency of his prayers.' He had four children, three sons and a daughter. The sons received an education which was for those times, and considering their father's income and standing, exceedingly good. The youngest, David Thomas, afterwards became a Congregational minister at Clifton, and was one of the best-known Non-

---

[1] South Wales, known in those days for its iron, as it is now for its coal, was then in a full tide of prosperity. ' In 1758 the Dowlais Iron Works were started, followed seven years later by Cyfartha . . . the great want of the ironmasters was labour ; to attract this, wages were offered considerably higher than those obtained in agricultural work. Merthyr became the Golconda of South Wales and Monmouthshire ; and farmers, labourers, and shopkeepers poured in to secure some share of the prosperity.' From the *South Wales Coal Annual* for 1907.

conformists of his day. The eldest, Samuel Thomas, my father's father, born in 1800, was educated at Cowbridge Grammar School. He very nearly became an official of the East India Company, but for some reason decided against this course and remained in Merthyr, where he started a small grocer's shop, which he owned for many years. He gave this up, however, about the year 1851, and devoted himself exclusively to mining propositions from then onwards. The South Wales coalfield, the last to be developed in Great Britain, was in its infancy, and to men of enterprise and imagination a veritable Eldorado was opening. Mining, however, then as now (even more than now, since it was a new trade to most of them, and it is by failure that we learn), was a risky business. My grand-father showed great courage. He died a comparatively rich man; but there were times in his life (certainly one, probably more) when he came very near to bankruptcy. It is said that at the time of David's birth had the Brecon Old Bank known of the state of Samuel Thomas's affairs he would have been made a bankrupt. He was saved on this occasion, I believe, by his old friend John Riches.

He married young. His first wife was a daughter of Benjamin Williams of Twfwyrodyw, by whom he had one child, who died in infancy. His wife died when he was still a young man, and when he was about forty years of age he married my grandmother, Rachel Joseph, then a girl of eighteen. If my grandmother was to be believed, his first wife had been the romance of his life, and he had cared for her as he never cared for her successor. By his second wife he had seventeen children : the elder children, however, all died in infancy, only the last five surviving. Of these my father was the third. The living children were Mima Williams, who married Frederick Robert Howell and had a large family ; John Howard, who married Rose Helen Haig, a sister of my mother's, and had one son ; David Alfred, my father ; Samuel Moreton, who married Mary Hamilton Evans and had one daughter ; and Mary, who died unmarried.

They are all dead now. John Howard, the only one to survive my father, was the last to go. He lived to be sixty-six, and died in 1919. Of the others, my father lived to be sixty-two, another died under sixty, and two under fifty.

David Alfred Thomas was born at Ysgyborwen,[1] during a stormy night, on March 26, 1856. His father was down at the Ysgyborwen pit,[2] about half a mile from the house, at the time, and one of the maids ran down to tell him of the new arrival. My grandfather, who was a taciturn old man (he was fifty-six at this time) and just then in the midst of a severe financial crisis, made only one comment : ' Well, I see nothing for him but the workhouse.'

It is not altogether easy to picture the atmosphere of little David's early youth. On the one hand there was his mother, still young or youngish, pretty, charming, very sociable, generous, popular, affectionate, rather inconsequent, and, though shrewd in her way, quite unintellectual. Caring considerably for appearances, anxious always to make a good show, anxious that her children should make a good show—she was friendly and popular with all her neighbours. She was by no means without instinctive taste, as she showed later when, mistress of a considerable income, she spent extravagant sums on beautiful old lace and china. Devotedly fond of all her children she assuredly was ; one questions whether her husband ever really meant very much to her. She was a kind and a nice woman, but never probably a very interesting one. She brought up her children with much affectionate spoiling and exceedingly little discipline. I remember her only as an old lady in spectacles (very nearly blind), with a kind face and a pleasing habit of tipping me ten shillings whenever I visited her. So far as I can recollect, the ten shillings was the one feature which redeemed the visits from dullness. She died in 1896.

His father, on the other hand, an elderly man, a hard worker, taciturn, a trifle grim, decidedly stern, clever, intellectual, enterprising, a man who dared risk his all not once but several times in the course of his life, was a

---

[1] Pronounced Skibborwen. A house which stood on the hillside about a mile and a half above Aberdare, close to the Ysgyborwen Collieries.

[2] Samuel Thomas, with his brother-in-law Thomas Joseph, had started the Ysgyborwen Colliery in 1849.

man of imagination, a man to whom life outside his home held the greater possibilities. He valued education highly, had had a fair education himself, and proposed giving his sons a better one. Unsociable in private life, a bit close-fisted, hating any form of show or ostentation, Samuel Thomas was a strong Nonconformist and disciplinarian, who gave to his household order and simplicity and stern religious observance. Like his brother, he was a Congregationalist. A man who was, as the saying goes, ' Master in his own house,' he was more feared than loved perhaps, but always respected, and undoubtedly interesting to talk to, shrewd, intelligent, with a good deal of dry humour.

The two, as might be supposed, formed a not very well-assorted couple. My grandmother's extravagance infuriated my grandfather, who had that Puritan horror of waste common to the self-made man of the nineteenth century.[1] He once went so far as to burn a new fur coat which she had bought without his permission and paid £60 for. My grandmother, however, showed a very proper spirit on this occasion ; she bought a new coat for £60, and told him she would go on buying till he stopped burning, which he did immediately.

Samuel Thomas disliked his wife's sociable instincts, hated her attempts at show and ostentation. On one occasion he walked in wearing his oldest clothes (and legend has it that his old clothes *were* old !) to a smart evening party she was giving, without speaking to a soul, took a stool and sat down in front of the fire with his back to the whole party, which, under the influence of

[1] Mr. Keynes' description of the nineteenth century was certainly applicable to old Samuel Thomas, as indeed one suspects to many others unjustly called ' close.' ' The new rich of the 19th Century were not brought up to large expenditures and preferred the power which investment gave them to the pleasures of immediate consumption . . . the capitalist classes were allowed to call the best part of the cake theirs, and were theoretically free to consume it, on the tacit underlying condition that they consumed very little of it in practice. The duty of " saving " became nine-tenths of virtue and the growth of the cake the object of true religion. There grew round the non-consumption of the cake all those instincts of Puritanism which in other ages has withdrawn itself from the world and has neglected the arts of production as well as those of enjoyment.'

his gloomy figure, shortly broke up. The marked discrepancy in their ages tended to accentuate temperamental differences. One pictures the children growing up spoilt and indulged to the top of their bent in all the small things of life, but always retaining a wholesome respect for their stern old father, who laid down the main rules of the house. Sunday was apparently a day of the deepest gloom. I remember that in later years, when we went to see ' Bunty pulls the Strings,' in which a Sabbath so severe is portrayed that the very blinds are kept down all day, my father said, ' That takes me back fifty years. It was just like that at home ; we never pulled the blinds up either.'

The fact that the father and mother often failed to agree was, of course, common knowledge to the children, and probably affected their home life unfavourably, as such things must. My father remembered on one occasion actually rushing to protect his mother, under the impression that his father was going to strike her. Of his early home life he did not generally talk very much in later years ; though as a younger man he told my mother something of it. He used to play about a great deal with the little boys belonging to the colliers living in the neighbouring cottages, probably the sons of the men who worked at his father's colliery Ysgyborwen, and in those early days on the mountains behind Ysgyborwen he acquired a love of bird-nesting which never left him. Another lifelong habit formed as a youngster was a fondness for taking long walks. He and his brother Jack and his cousins, the Josephs, would walk over the mountains to Brecon searching for parsley ferns, nests and fossils.

One of his favourite haunts in very early days was Ysgyborwen farm, not far from the house. The old man who lived there (a grand-uncle, or possibly cousin of his father's[1]) had been a soldier and had fought at Waterloo, and my father never tired of listening to his stories of the wars.

A tale that comes back to me is that on one occasion

[1] The Welsh fashion of calling cousins ' uncles ' makes the relationship a little difficult to ascertain.

when his mother was giving a party he was brought in to recite some verses, instead of which he insisted on asking the leading lady a riddle : ' Can you spell Mad Dog backwards ? ' The innocent lady did so. My father was subsequently spanked. All the descriptions that have come down of him in these years picture an eager, cheery, very keen and active little fellow, rather small for his years. His mother took special pride in his unusually small feet, his well-shaped ears, and his rosy cheeks, but it seems probable that to the outsider his attraction—and all are agreed that he was noticeably attractive—lay rather in the very human twinkle in his very bright blue eyes.

Undoubtedly Dai [1] was fonder of his father than his mother (although I doubt whether this would be true of any of the other children). He was his father's favourite son (Jack, the eldest, was his mother's), and he was very proud of his father. It was usually, though not always, the case with him that his affection went to the person who interested him intellectually ; certainly he often spoke of his father, and was fond of quoting his opinions and sayings.

One remark of the old man's which he often quoted ran : ' Money like manure does no good until it is spread abroad ' —not, one would feel, the saying of a miser.

He told my mother that though his father was sometimes said to be close-fisted and stern, he had on the contrary always found him most generous and kind and affectionate. I have heard him regret that his father was so much older than himself (he died when he was still at college) that he did not, as he might have done, pass on to him all his experience of life and affairs : in later years too, I think, he regretted that his father could not be there to see and take pride in his own success.

Dai was nine years old when he was taken by his father across the Bristol Channel Ferry to Dr. Hudson's, a large private school at Clifton, at which he remained (except for one occasion when he overgrew his strength and was kept at home for a year) until he went up to college.

---

[1] Welsh for David. As a boy D. A. Thomas was always known as Dai.

I am indebted to Mr. Algernon Warren for the following description of my father's schooldays :

'My recollections of the late Viscount Rhondda extend back to 1866.   In 1865 I went, as a nine-year-old boy, to Dr. C. T. Hudson's school at Manila Hall, Clifton.   One of the first boys that I noticed, when introduced to the fourth and lowest class, was the subsequent " Thomas Primus," Lord Rhondda's elder brother John.   He was a stoutly built, well-grown fellow of good-humoured countenance. He did not stay long in that class, and I had reason to bless his industry.   For Dr. Hudson gave a prize for each subject, but no boy might have more than one.   If he came out top in three things, he got one prize and two certificates.   I came out second in Bible, while Thomas was first.   But fortunately for me he was also first in History and Geography, so I got the prize for Bible.   I have it now.   It is " Gleanings in Natural History," by Edward Jesse.

' " Thomas Secundus," the embryo Lord Rhondda, came to the school in the following year ; for a short time I was in the same class with him.   He was a bright, good-natured little fellow, very much all there.   He had light brown hair and a fresh complexion—altogether a healthy-looking boy. But recently an " old Hudsonian," harking back to early recollections with me, said how he remembered Thomas as peculiarly " cherubic-looking," and always friendly, affectionate, in fact, to his chums.

' His brother grew to be quite a big fellow, but Lord Rhondda did not broaden out to the same extent, and for a while was, if anything, rather small for his age.   He and I were friends from the outset.   He used to sit opposite to me at the dinner-table, and had much more to say for himself than most boys of his age.   "Little Tights," [1] as he was often called, was certainly popular.   There were several Welsh boys in the school, including three of his cousins, namely, the two Josephs, and Tom Lewis, the recently knighted Stipendiary Magistrate at Cardiff.   The last named was an exceptionally powerful fellow, and a good gymnast (he won the gymnasium prize in my time) and freely addicted to pugilism.   I remember his being adorned with

[1] The nickname ' Tights ' was originally given to his elder brother Jack, on account of a pair of very tight trousers which the latter was said to have brought back to school on one occasion.   When the younger Thomas appeared the nickname descended to him, and he became known as ' Little Tights.'

a terrific black eye after a desperate encounter with a "cad" much bigger than himself. He came off the victor, although the defeated one gave him something to remember him by. Lord Rhondda had intense admiration for this cousin's fistic powers.[1] There was the son of an Army Colonel at the school, who was a graceful athlete and a particularly fast runner, and considered more than a match for most boys of his size, but I recollect Lord Rhondda's telling me subsequently across the dinner-table, after both this boy and his cousin had left the school, how X—— had "funked" Lewis. He had agreed to fight him in the playground before breakfast, but failed to keep the appointment.

'Lord Rhondda had too sunny a temperament to be quarrelsome as a youngster. But he had plenty of pluck. The Rev. J. V. Morgan says of him that he suppressed a robust bully of whom all the other boys were afraid. If he really did so, it was not in my time (though there was bullying then), for he was my junior by about six months and I was not much over fourteen when I left.

'But when he was still in his first year at the school I once saw him fight one X——, an Irish boy older than himself. The encounter was neither prearranged nor carried to a complete finish, as it took place in the Fourth-form room just before morning school. X—— attempted some baiting and Lord Rhondda resented it. Then X—— hit him, and rather to the surprise of some present was hit back again. Sympathy went generally with the younger boy. Up rushed Edwin Hughes, a vigorous young Aberystwithian of legal stock, with "Go it, Thomas; keep your head up!" and it was soon apparent that Thomas would make a good fight. He was the more encouraged when he drew "first blood," and the general pronouncement was that he had got the better of it. But let his own version stand as testimony. When he became elected to the peerage, I wrote my congratulations. Fifteen years earlier, when I applied to Lord Rhondda for some coal intelligence, he had furnished what served my requirements for an illustration in a Chapter on "Supply and Demand" in a Commercial Text Book for which I received a commission. But we had not corresponded in the interim, so, recalling early days, I hoped that "Warren Secundus" still dwelt in his memory, and said in

[1] To the end of his life my father entertained a strong friendship for Sir T. W. Lewis.

jocular strain that his Peerage had not been anticipated by the French master, who, irritated by some restless outcome of his mercurial temperament, had asked angrily, "What are you about, Thomas?" To which straightway came the cheeky answer, "About eleven, Sir." Furthermore that X——, when he began to fight in the Fourth class-room, little thought that he was milling a future member of the House of Lords. His answer thus reads in entirety:

"My dear Warren,

"Many thanks for your kind congratulations and good wishes: they are very much appreciated.

"It is very curious that you should have remembered my great fight with X——; I have often thought of it since. I remember 'Warren Secundus' and your two brothers very well [Herbert, the present writer's senior by two years, and Edward, his junior by a year, otherwise the Hudsonians, Warren Primus and Warren Tertius]. I travelled down from London once or twice with your younger brother.

"X—— was a stronger boy than myself, and inclined to bully. When I attempted to wrestle with him, he invariably put me on my back. It was on one of these occasions that T. W. Lewis, my cousin, who has been Stipendiary at Cardiff for the last thirty years, said: 'Don't you wrestle with him, Dai: you hit him with your fist.' On the next occasion I adopted the suggested tactics, and gave him a good licking.

"With kindest regards, believe me,

"Yours very faithfully,

"D. A. THOMAS."

'Trusting that it may serve as a testimony to the late Lord Rhondda's modesty, my brother Edward has since mentioned how he happened to meet him in the Reform Club some time afterwards. Lord Rhondda mentioned my letter, and, said my brother, "seemed to think more of his fight with X—— than of all he had done for the country in the way of rationing."

'Lord Rhondda, as a small boy, did not evince any particular athletic propensities. He was not good at short or long distance running, nor yet much of a cricketer. He used, on occasion, if memory serves aright, to go with other

AS A SCHOOLBOY

boys to the now long non-existent Bolton's Swimming Baths at the Hotwells, but did not then give much promise of the aquatic proficiency to which he had attained when a Cambridge undergraduate.

'As regards school work, he showed a mathematical tendency from the outset, but did not go up from class to class as quickly as his elder brother. I got to know something of him out of school as well as in. We used to have "monthly holidays" at Dr. Hudson's. These could be forfeited by slackness, involving what were called "detentions," or by other misdemeanours, but their losers were usually in a considerable minority. I recall one pleasant one when the two Thomases and Derwent Norton, a Carmarthen boy, whose father had been a chum of our father (likewise Carmarthen born), came to spend the day with us at our home in Great George Street. We had some croquet in the afternoon, and some rattling good games of blind man's buff, etc., in the evening. My mother said afterwards what a nice bright little fellow Lord Rhondda was. In the summer, too, of 1867 our two families were at Tenby for some weeks together, and foregathered to an extent. Nor did we lose sight of the Thomas brothers when I and my younger brother Edward left Dr. Hudson's at the close of 1869 to go to Clifton College, whither my brother Herbert had preceded us some two years previously, for we still used to meet of a Sunday. Alike of Nonconformist stock, we attended the same place of worship, namely, Highbury Chapel, Clifton, where Lord Rhondda's uncle, the Rev. David Thomas, was minister, as is his cousin (also an old Hudsonian of the Park Row era), the Rev. Arnold Thomas, at the present day. Now it often happens that when boys leave one school to go to another in the same town they drift apart. Not so, however, in my case and the two Thomas brothers. They used to sit up in a side gallery, while our family pew was in the middle aisle. We would wait outside for each other at the close of the service and walk back together to the corner of the Oakfield Road leading into the Pembroke Road, whence our ways deviated.'

The President of Magdalen, who was at Manila Hall with his younger brother, Mr. Algernon Warren, has given me an interesting account of the School and of Dr. Hudson, who was, he says, a remarkable man :

'A good-looking clever man, with much intellectual interest, he was especially devoted to Natural History, and in particular he wrote a monograph on the Rotifera, by which he made a name, and which led ultimately to his becoming a Fellow of the Royal Society. He was also fond of drawing and music, and he pleased us boys by his keenness about games, especially Fives.'

Sir Herbert, who left to go to Clifton College in 1867, does not, however, remember much of my father at that period beyond the fact ' that he was a bright and agreeable small boy.'

My father was very fond of talking about his schooldays, which he had obviously much enjoyed. He had a very great admiration for Dr. Hudson, whom he specially revered for being a first-class mathematician. Chief among the impressions left on my mind from his description of those days is that of the overpowering personality of Dr. Hudson. I remember also many descriptions of the joys of catapults and the thrill of using them without being found out—not always without being found out. 'What have you got there, Thomas Secundus ? ' inquired Dr. Hudson on one occasion when catapults had been declared contraband, as he watched my father scurry across the playground carrying as unostentatiously as might be a parcel. A rapid mental calculation to the effect that Dr. Hudson probably already knew, and would certainly in any case know within the next three minutes, produced the frank and ingenious answer, ' Some catapults, Sir.' The candour of the reply disarmed the Headmaster. My father (who was I suspect a favourite) got off without severe punishment. The moral of the tale as expounded to me in my early youth was perhaps scarcely up to copy-book standard, ' Always confess freely what is already known.'

Another vivid impression was that of the amazing fascination of mathematics and the infinite satisfaction of coming out top in an examination. I doubt if my father really worked much at anything but mathematics in his school-days, but at this one subject, which he loved, he worked hard. He once told me that he first came to like it because Dr. Hudson did not let the Junior forms do any preparation for this subject, so it stood out as involving less trouble and work.

But I believe the strongest impression he retained of school was of a place which afforded a perfect opportunity for long birds'-nesting expeditions in distant woods, salted by the evasion of many keepers. Looking back on his tales of life at Clifton, it scarcely seems possible to believe that birds'-nesting was a sport only possible during a few weeks of the year. During the last year of his life my father was able to spend one Sunday down at Clifton. We drove him round to his old haunts, bumping across field roads and over rutty tracks through many woods. It seemed to me as if fifty years ago almost every tree had sheltered some rare bird's-nest and every copse concealed an irate keeper's form. This passion for birds'-nesting lasted all through his life. In earlier years when I was a child the ensuing collection was for form's sake called mine ; later it became frankly his own again, but every May saw it added to.

J. W. Welsford was his greatest friend and rival both at school and later at college, and although they came to differ considerably on many public questions in later years, they remained friends till the latter's death in 1909.[1]

Of his uncle, David Thomas, the Congregational minister, mentioned by Mr. Algernon Warren, my father always spoke with great pride and affection as one of the big men he had known, and to the end of his life he kept in touch with his cousin Arnold Thomas, David Thomas's son. He would relate how when David Thomas died several Bishops came to his funeral.

My father and his brothers went from school to college as a matter of course. My grandfather, who by the time they were of an age to go had made a considerable fortune, would probably have sent them even had it been a hard struggle to do so. He looked upon education as of the first importance.

My father was much frightened just after he left school by being told by some specialist that he had Bright's disease

[1] J. W. Welsford also took the Mathematical Tripos at Cambridge, and was Seventh Wrangler. He was made a Fellow of Caius College. He afterwards became a House Master at Harrow. He was a strong Imperialist and Tariff Reformer.

and could not expect to live long. Other experts disagreed with the verdict ; nevertheless its shadow hung over him for some years and was probably partly responsible for the fact that he did no work whilst at Cambridge. He was ordered to go abroad for a year for the sake of his health before going up to college, and set off by himself with £300 (a large sum in those days) in his pocket, to see the world. His father, always generous to him, told him to write for more if he needed it. As a matter of fact he did not spend the whole £300. He visited amongst other places Naples and Egypt, and was immensely impressed by the latter, which he always intended to revisit, but never did.

He was twenty when he went up to Caius College, Cambridge, in 1876. He had won a scholarship for both this and Jesus, but for some reason, probably because a number of his friends were there, chose Caius. His scholarship was, I believe, afterwards taken from him because he did no work.

His life at college seems to have been spent mainly on the river. At least his later accounts related chiefly to boating exploits. He rowed for his college and did a good deal of pot-hunting sculling, but he never achieved any outstanding distinction. It is probable that his light weight, which was considered a greater drawback then than now, told against him.

He went in also for boxing—he was the Champion Amateur Lightweight of his day, and I believe he held the record for long-distance swimming under the water.

He made a host of friends (chief amongst these were J. W. Welsford, Professor R. L. Knaggs of Leeds, R. F. Cobbold, and W. Ridgeway) and of course spent many hours in discussing everything in heaven and earth.

He did practically no work. He always declared that he knew far more when he went up than when he came down. Towards the end of his time he began to be afraid of what might happen in his finals, and did a hard sprint during the last few months or so. He only achieved a Second in mathematics, however, a fact of which he was always a little ashamed.[1]

[1] See Appendix for an account of his college life by Professor R. L. Knaggs of Leeds.

CHAPTER II

Engagement and Marriage

DAVID THOMAS left college in December 1879 and studied law for a short period, but soon decided to abandon this and spent most of the following two years up at Clydach Vale studying mining conditions on the spot. In July 1881 he became engaged to be married to Sybil Margaret Haig, one of the ten children of George Augustus Haig of Pen Ithon in the county of Radnorshire.

Her brother, A. W. Haig, was a college friend of both John Thomas and of David. Both brothers had on several occasions been invited to stay at Pen Ithon, and John had accepted the invitation and had there met and become engaged to Rose Helen, Sybil's elder sister. In the summer of 1880 Mrs. Haig was asked to bring her daughter Rose, with another sister, to stay at Ysgyborwen. Sybil was chosen—so family tradition has it—because she was the one member of the family who could be trusted to be always polite to strangers. If this throws an unduly hard light on the family manners it must be admitted that their record in respect of the treatment of impending brothers-in-law was and remained a bad one.

It was during this visit to Ysgyborwen that David and Sybil first met. I give the description in my mother's words :

' I first saw David at Ysgyborwen in the small drawing-room. He came home late from some meeting or business he had been attending. He had a frank, fresh face, and a very attractive one. I had come down with my mother and Rose to make the acquaintance of Jack's people. Alexander [A. W. Haig] had very often talked of David and praised him for his ability and good qualities, as he admired him very much and had always wanted to get him to Pen Ithon, but had not succeeded.'

The visit was a short one, but its result was that when David was next asked to Pen Ithon (for the shooting the following September) he came. He came again in November when Jack and Rose were married. On this occasion he and Sybil came to an understanding which amounted in both their minds to an engagement. Its exact terms (they were an inarticulate couple) were that she was to let him know if she got engaged to anyone else. The actual engagement did not take place till June of the following year, when Sybil and her younger sister Lotty went to stay at Ysgyborwen for a dance.

The Haigs were a vigorous set—full of vitality, energy and high spirits. Like all large families they possessed a strong family atmosphere. They might and did quarrel amongst themselves, but they were certain that they, and in a lesser degree their endlessly ramified cousins (whom they counted to the third degree, for like most Scotch families they were very clannish) were collectively infinitely superior to the rest of the world. At the same time they were quite prepared to see faults in individual members of the family, and usually ready to admit that any one of the sisters who was so foolish as to decide to marry was quite past praying for.

They have been described by a casual visitor of those days as an overwhelming family : ' The Haigs were a family that absorbed one—it was a regular maelstrom. If you went to stay at Pen Ithon you had to see life from the Haig point of view, and if you entered into friendly relations with them you had to become a Haig.'

Sybil Haig was by common consent held to be the best-tempered, the most unselfish and gentle of the girls. (I remember my grandfather on one occasion many years later saying to me, ' Your mother was a most amiable girl before she married your father, and he spoiled her by turning her into a Liberal.') The family were afraid of their father, who indulged in the uncontrolled fits of temper which so many early Victorian gentlemen permitted themselves.

They adored their gentle, humorous mother, the one comparatively conventional member of the clan. It would, however, have taken more than either father or mother to have a permanent marked effect on the views and behaviour of that large, vigorous, and united family.

Into such a group did David Thomas enter when he became engaged to Sybil Haig in June 1881, and this somewhat formidable family was decidedly prejudiced against him as a brother-in-law.

Old Mr. Haig found nothing to object to in this perfectly suitable son-in-law except his politics, which he much regretted and occasionally wrote rude letters about. Old Mrs. Haig liked him and was quite content, provided her husband and daughter were content. The family, however, more especially the girls, were distinctly troublesome. In the first place they objected to brothers-in-law on principle. In the second place, since Sybil was one of the younger ones, the elder ones placed no confidence whatsoever in her judgment, but anxiously desired to save her from ' making a fool of herself.' Then they had objections to David Thomas in particular. His own brother Jack said he was selfish, so he would surely make a selfish husband. They were certain he did not really care for Sybil. He was more interested in his business than he was in her (he was probably one of the few men they had ever met who did take business and his career seriously, and they mistrusted this new type). Incidentally he did not know how to tie his ties properly.

Had Sybil been one of the elder ones she would probably have told her family to go to the rightabout. She was one of the younger and moreover the mildest member of the family. The family atmosphere was too strong for her to ignore ; it is clear that the constant criticisms and forebodings were a source of trouble and worry to her, and consequently to some extent to David all through their engagement.

The engagement lasted for just a year. During the greater part of the time David was working up at the Cambrian Collieries at Clydach Vale. Sybil was up at Pen Ithon or staying at St. Leonards or in London or on visits,

c

often to newly married sisters. They wrote about three times a week.

There is after all a similarity about these things. All healthy normal couples are occupied during the period of engagement and early years of marriage in groping by the light of a strong affection towards understanding each other and in trying to adjust themselves to one another. The process is for the time being enthralling : it is not infrequently slightly painful. These two formed no exception to the rule. All through the year's letters it is easy to follow the gradual progress of understanding and adjustment between two shy and sensitive people very normally in love and anxious to make themselves and each other happy. If they differed in any respect from the average it was in that each—he especially—was shyer than most, more reserved than most ; and they were both unusually inexperienced and unversed in such matters.

They were fortunate in that they possessed the essentials in common : kind-heartedness and goodwill towards mankind, simplicity and a distaste for tight-laced conventionality, a certain unworldliness and a dislike—in his case amounting to horror—of ostentation. Beyond this their differences were as marked as those of the average couple.

Several distinct threads run through his letters. He is very much the more self-conscious—in every sense of the word—of the two. He is—especially in the earlier letters —trying to explain himself to her. He is trying to get to understand her. He is commenting—sometimes halfamused, sometimes distinctly irritated, occasionally a trifle anxious—on the family attitude towards the engagement. He is trying to please her in various ways, but especially, the while he enjoys teasing her about them, by his religious observances.

It is clear from his letters that Sybil Haig, brought up moderately conventionally in the Church of England, is troubled by his lack of definite faith in matters which to her are beyond question. Slightly troubled, too, to find that he has never been baptised. My mother, always an optimist, felt that these lax views would surely soon right themselves if he went to church regularly ; hence her efforts.

On August 28, 1881, in the course of a letter, several portions of which would scarcely commend themselves to the strictly orthodox, he remarks :

' I'm going to be christened next week, and the old vicar tells me he knows me so thoroughly and is so satisfied that he won't have to ask me any questions. He flatters himself that he has brought about this reformation himself, but it is really owing to your influence and a little bit perhaps, but really not much, to the fact that he will give me a good lunch without any extra charge at the same time.

' . . . I shall go to Church this evening and pass a weary half-hour listening to ———, of whom I entertained the meanest opinion when at Cambridge, asserting his superiority by maligning me. I have explained to you before that when I make a martyr of myself and undergo all these humiliations for your sake I like it to be thoroughly understood and, I sincerely trust, appreciated.'

On September 10 we get the account of his christening. He begins his letter (which is dated Cardiff) :

' I was christened yesterday and I feel exceedingly bad to-day—not in a moral sense—but I attribute this very largely to the lunch. Such an important event in my life, however, deserves to be described more in detail, and must not be dismissed in this summary manner. After some negotiation I chartered a hansom and drove out five miles to Dynas Powis, but from the intense respect with which the cabby regarded me I felt I had commenced the day badly. I entered the rectory with little spare confidence, which was not increased when the Reverend X—— put a prayer-book into my hand with the page turned down at the baptism of those of riper years, and I had read it through. I don't care for the phrase " riper years," I must confess, although I suppose it is inspired, for it sounds so much as though one were on the eve of decay. Then I had a momentary (?) scruple whether I could conscientiously say " I stedfastly believed it all," but this difficulty was at once dismissed when I remembered you had told me it was quite true. And you never say stories, so it did not trouble me further. After this I was conducted into the Church by the rector and his nephew, a stout young clergyman (who always pays his uncle a visit when the fruit is ripe), and followed by the old gardener in case I should change my mind and bolt ; he carried in his hand a slop basin. The Reverend Isaac read the ceremony in his usual impressive manner and I promised " to renounce them all " with a mental reservation " until the next time." He then took me by the right hand and with the left pushed back the hair from my massive brow, exposing thereby the beauty spot,[1] which you may remember. I couldn't help giving just half a little smile when I thought of the unnecessary trouble I had been at that morning in trying to conceal it. I was then soused with water which ran over and stained a nice black coat, and a cross was made on my forehead. . . . The rest of the service I passed in a high state of discomfort. The water was tickling me, though I managed to give it a surreptitious wipe a little time afterwards. It left a couple of dirty streaks, and though from a casual remark dropped some time afterwards I know the nephew thought I had not washed after coming up from the colliery, I assure you that this was not so, but that it was some peculiarity about the water.'

'Ysygborwen, Aberdare, October 4th, 1881.

' I haven't been to Church since I was christened, but I have shaken hands with several clergymen, taken the plate round in chapel, helped to sing half a dozen hymns in a private house, expressed pious indignation at several bits of scandal and passed them on with a few thoroughly Christian and uncharitable additions of my own, and mastered the marriage service, so altogether . . . I show signs of improvement, don't I ? '

On October 30 more about church-going :

' I'm going to a Church three miles away to-morrow morning to hear the rector of Merthyr, who generally preaches more stirring sermons and in less studied terms than the majority of those who employ themselves in the cure of souls. There is a Church only about a mile from here, but the incumbent is a man I have very little respect for. I'll promise to come with you when we are married ; promises are easily made ! '

[1] A bad bruise he got when down the colliery.

'Ysgyborwen, 18th January, 1882.

' I'm afraid I haven't got much more faith now than I
had before I went to Church so regularly ; perhaps it is
because I have so much in you . . . that I haven't any to
spare for anything else. . . . Never mind, it will be all
right when you are able to take the care of my soul in hand
yourself. I wish the time was not so far distant, for I
do want to have my religious welfare looked after by
you. . . .'

In response to pressure he was evidently at this time
attending a service of some sort fairly regularly (my mother's
view doubtless being that Church was likely to do him most
good, but that a Nonconformist place of worship was a
great deal better than nothing). In doing this he was
in fact doing a big thing ; he was allowing himself to be
utterly bored once a week for at least an hour. To allow
himself to be bored was with him the ultimate and (it must
be admitted) the rarest proof of affection, and as he said in
one letter he had no intention of allowing Sybil to forget
his self-sacrifice.

In considering the extracts it must be borne in mind that
the tone of his comments was dictated by three considerations. He always disliked taking things seriously ; it em-
barrassed him. He would have objected to my mother
supposing that his baptism and course of church-going was
instilling one jot more faith than it actually was. Finally,
he had then what he retained for the whole period (close on
forty years) of their acquaintance, an irresistible desire to
tease and half-shock her.

His attempts at discussion of personal matters were not
always entirely successful :

'Ysgyborwen, 31st July, 1881.

' They say people never thoroughly know each other
until they marry, and that no man is a hero in the eyes
of his valet.'

'Ysgyborwen, 7th August, 1881.

' What rubbish, Sybil . . . you couldn't possibly have
construed anything I said into putting you " on a level
with a valet." At the same time they are human beings

like ourselves : they have their good points, which it is
no disgrace to share in common with them.   The expression of this last fine sentiment is the result of regular
Sunday evening attendance at Divine Service and is hence
indirectly due to yourself.

' I had a long letter from Mr. Haig the day before yesterday.   I don't think his breakfast can have agreed with
him.'

Mr. Haig's letter seems to have troubled my mother
more than it did him.

From Sybil Haig :

Pen Ithon, August 5 [1881].

' I do hope it is all right with you and my father, and
that he sees things in the same light as you now, David . . .'

' Pen Ithon, August 9th [1881].

' I'm very sorry that Papa wrote a nasty letter to
you.   He has a habit of writing nasty, very nasty letters
sometimes.'

Whatever Mr. Haig's annoyance may have been due to,
it appears to have blown over pretty quickly, for there is
no further mention of it.

My father always laboured under the delusion that he
was very thick-skinned, and much prided himself on this
fact.   Perhaps in one sense it may have been true.   It
would seem that he developed the theory early in life.

' August 30th, 1881.

' Don't talk about hurting my feelings, I've told you I
haven't got any, and that is why I appear good-tempered
and possess all the other good qualities with which you
credit me.'

' November 15th, 1881.

' If you expect me to be perfect to you—whatever that
may mean—I wish you would explain fully—you know that
it is more than I am ever now, don't you ?   For I never
talk when I should, and say too much when I oughtn't to,
and there is no health in us.   It doesn't matter much
whether you do things right at first or not, as long as you
try, does it ?   We shall be able to laugh at each other's

mistakes, shan't we ? It's the will to do the deed, and not the result that we must judge by in such cases.'

'My dearest Sybil,
    'I have put it in the superlative degree in imitation of you, than whom I couldn't find a better model ; but I must explain that though you are so very dear, you are the only Sybil of my acquaintance, saving a steamer we once loaded last Spring and which was supplied with a cargo of superior quality on account of the association. I must be satisfied, I suppose, with being the dearest of all Davids and not grudge the rest of them a little bit of the affection I am so happy in possessing. . . . I don't count these scraps of things letters at all, though I do like getting them, even when they are full of grumbles, like the one a week ago was.'

This last extract is very typical. He had a pedantic dislike of using the word ' dearest ' at the beginning of a letter. I remember as a schoolgirl beginning a letter to him ' My dearest father,' and receiving a reply to the effect that as I had only one father he could not be ' dearest,' a reply which I noticed the more because it was dictated purely by a dislike of a technical misuse of the word, for he was an affectionate father. He was always rather stilted in his letters and extraordinarily different from himself. To draft a business letter for him to sign was sheer pain and grief : often every other word would be altered before it would be allowed to pass. One got to know certain errors, which must always be avoided. No letter, for instance, ever left his office containing such a phrase as ' as regards ' or ' with regard to ' in it—they were his pet aversions, nor was one ever allowed (even in ordinary speech) to use the word ' mutual ' in a wrong sense. But there were hundreds of other pitfalls. I used to persuade him to let me sign the letters I wrote for him myself and just let him know the gist of them, though I am inclined to think I avoided explaining my reason.
    That he was suspected of caring too much for his business was probably due, in part at least, to family influences.

' 15th January, 1882.

'. . . . I thought unless I was careful perhaps you might begin to think again that I cared more for my business than I did for you. . . . I tell you, you have got a much better temper than I have, so please don't contradict me or I'll very soon prove it to you.'

The family attitude towards the engagement leaves him on the whole very placid and undisturbed—perhaps slightly interested and amused, for he always loved anything that savoured even in the remotest degree of a fight.   Now and again, however, he would feel some anxiety as to its effect on my mother.

Reference to family rudenesses and coolnesses are frequent.   I have selected a few.

' Clydach Vale, 30th October, 1881.

' X—— didn't make herself particularly unpleasant to me, though no doubt she was annoyed about something. I think she is rather a sport because she is such a good type of a certain class of character.   I have an unhappy knack of quarrelling with my own relations so don't fall out with X—— on my account or else we should be isolated from our relations altogether.   I want you to mend the quarrels that I make.'

' Glamorgan Club, Cardiff, 6th November, 1881.

' I do trust you won't put J——'s tips on " clearing the atmosphere " to the test with me.   You couldn't get in a rage if you wanted to—Yah !   I'll promise to give you plenty of opportunities ; you needn't fear the lack of them. I hope you haven't been " very untrustful and unbelieving " lately, Sybil.   I know it is very difficult not to doubt, when everybody is constantly driving fears into one's head.   I have more than once sold things which I felt convinced myself were good holding because people have expressed a pessimistic view of them to me ; I have afterwards regretted disposing of them.'

' 28th December, 1881.

' I. know J—— would only do it because she thought it was for your ultimate happiness, but don't let her say anything to my detriment without giving me an opportunity of explaining it, will you, Sybil. . . . ?

'24th (January) 1882.

' I don't see what difference it makes what other people think of me as long as you are satisfied yourself, and I don't know that it would be a bit better for us if no one had run me down to you. You have had a much better opportunity of judging my character than anyone who has told you anything ; besides I have a very good opinion of myself, and I ought to be an authority, while also it is your duty to respect my opinions. No, what I meant when I said you did not understand my character yet, was that I am not quite so slow as you would naturally think from what you have seen of me. I am, I fancy, about up to the average in moral qualities, but I should have to be a good deal better to be worthy of you. . . .'

It would appear that the wedding, originally fixed for June 8, was once (and very nearly twice) postponed to suit the convenience of other members of the family. The following letter shows him in a more ruffled mood than does any other :

'19th May, 1882.

' I do rather object, I must say, to having my destiny disposed of by R———. In a letter J——— wrote to the Mater he said something about our wedding being postponed till after Henley, or because his coachman wanted a week's holiday in June, or the neighbour's cat was expected to have kittens or something of that sort, I forget exactly why, and I'm too sleepy to remember, but I know it was for some such important reason. I hope you won't consent to put it off, Sybil ; they say it's very unlucky.'

There are several references to their fear of the marriage ceremony. It would appear that my mother was really dreading it very much, but felt a little afraid that he might be hurt at her fears. She was no doubt also dreading the impending separation from her family and the plunge into a new and unknown world. He seems to have understood and sympathised.

'Ysgyborwen, 1st April, 1882.

' I wish it were over, but it has to be gone through, we must set our teeth, make up our minds for it. It isn't a very terrible ceremony although it is such a solemn one in a way, after all.'

'April 27th, 1882.

' I don't think you told a lot by any means. You wrote a good deal and left me about as wise as when you commenced. You are as bad as . . . a Prime Minister at a Lord Mayor's Banquet.'

'15th May, 1882.

' If it's silly to show that you are sorry when you see other people unhappy, I hope, love, you'll never be wise, and as for being hard for a moment only, you know you couldn't if your whole future happiness in this world and the next depended on it.'

'June 14th, 1882.

' What a little duffer you are to apologise for giving me advice. . . . It is only when people remotely interested in me insist on advising me instead of minding their own affairs that I get annoyed . . . that, among many others, is one of the great objects I have in marrying you—that you should give me the benefit of your taste, tact and good sense, and that by combining our wisdom (! !) we shall be able to breast the hill of life with more success than we should individually.'

As a young man he dressed exceedingly carelessly, regarding clothes as one of the minor details of life which might be neglected with impunity. His clothes were good in themselves and well cut, but whether it was that he never bought any new ones, or whether it was that he treated them as one of his brothers-in-law declared : ' David always climbs two trees in a new suit and then sleeps in it for three nights just to take the edge off it, after that it's ready to wear ' ; it is certain that no suit of his ever looked less than five years old.

His letters about his wedding garments are characteristic :

'12th June, 1882.

' I haven't bought the trousers yet for the eventful day . . . but I have the coat and waistcoat which I have only worn *once*, so it isn't necessary to get a new one, is it ? Tell me what you think yourself. . . .'

From my mother :

' Pen Ithon, June 14th, 1882.

' I think I should like you to have a new coat . . . if it's a good dark green or blue (green for choice) it does quite well to wear on Sundays afterwards. I don't want to [be ?] put off with Jack's and Rose's old coat (though it is quite good). And David, please will you ask a friend, I daresay there are several for you to choose from up at Cambridge now, please . . . do ask some one. I'm sure the rest of your friends won't be offended really. . . .

'And don't let it be X——, though I know he is very worthy; however, I should not have bothered to mention him as I know he is not a particular friend of yours, only I thought you might perchance ask him on purpose to play me a trick.'

'Caius College, 15th June 1882.

'I am writing to order a coat and waistcoat. I debated some time in my mind whether I should or not . . . as I thought perhaps you would prefer my doing so, and that is why I asked you. They are coats that one is not likely to wear again, but we mustn't have our wedding altogether a re-shuffle of the fact [?] of Rose's (oh no, it was a *re-chauffé* (?) she called it, wasn't it ?). I have ordered it of a green shade, as you consider it more appropriate. I am also writing to Y—— [a friend whom he asked to the wedding] by this post. . . .'

They were married by special licence in the billiard-room at Pen Ithon on June 27, 1882.

It was characteristic of the Haig family that once the wedding was accomplished they entirely forgot all their previous objections and rudeness and made him welcome in perfect amity and affection as their brother-in-law.

It was characteristic of him that he forgot the matter as completely as they did, and accepted them entirely on their merits, regardless of past behaviour.

CHAPTER III

His Early Views

My father often spoke of his college days; they had been amongst the happiest of a very happy life.[1] One had the impression that little as he had worked they had counted for a great deal in the making of him. He had loved the whole atmosphere of the place and had imbibed the traditions of the University (and many of the intellectual prejudices of the period), possibly the more whole-heartedly that he had lived so little with his books and so completely in the sociable undergraduate world.

During college years, or those immediately following them, his views crystallised on three big aspects of life —economics, politics and religion. They remained practically unaltered to the time of the war. His views on all social problems, though modified by the originality of his own mind, always bore visibly (certainly up to 1914) the hall-mark of the advanced Liberal thought of the 'seventies. In economics he was a follower of the Mill school of thought. It is from his college period that may be dated his love of economics, and his admiration for the writings of John Stuart Mill. Although this admiration was tempered somewhat of later years, it remained with him to the end. ' Mill was perfectly right so far as he went,' he would say; ' but he sums up Political Economy as a static problem, whereas it is really dynamic.' It was a subject which interested him enormously. He began to read, think of it, and discuss it at college, read widely on coming down from college, and came to a number of definite conclusions about

---

[1] Proof of how largely his own college had continued to bulk in his mind lay in the fact that he left a legacy of £20,000 to Caius College to be used for scholarships.

that time which he never seriously altered. In later years, though always much interested in such questions, he seldom gave himself much time for study or reading which was not devoted to some definite and practical object.

Whilst he had the bent of mind that lent itself with eager readiness to the consideration of any economic problem, he naturally made a special study of the economics of the coal question. I think he knew Jevons'[1] book on coal nearly by heart, and regarded it as the finest book of the century. He always declared it was his Bible, and never wearied of quoting from it. He was from early youth convinced that the average person was quite unaware of the supreme importance of coal. ' Coal,' said Jevons, ' is the mainspring of modern material civilisation . . . coal in truth stands not beside but entirely above all other commodities. It is the material source of the energy of the country—the universal aid—the factor in everything we do . . . without it we are thrown back into the laborious poverty of early times.' And again, '. . . the peculiar material energy of England depends on coal ; we must not dwell in such a fool's paradise as to imagine we can do without coal what we can do with it.' No one who knew my father well was allowed any opportunity of dwelling in any such fool's paradise. That the British Empire as we know it to-day could never have existed in its present form were it not for the fortunate fact that Great Britain was peculiarly rich in coal supplies was a theme on which he never tired of dilating.

His political views were formed at the same time and under the same influences. He was a Liberal[2] of the school of Cobden, Mill and Gladstone, a convinced Free Trader, above all, an individualist. His strong individualism was so eminently characteristic of the man that it is difficult to believe he could in any circumstances have held other views, but it was undoubtedly fostered by his early soaking in the Mill school of thought. He was sometimes accused of becoming more Conservative as he grew older. I do

[1] *The Coal Question ; an Inquiry concerning the Progress of the Nation and the Probable Exhaustion of our Coal Mines*, by W. Stanley Jevons, M.A., LL.D., F.R.S.

[2] He was the only one of his family who adopted the political creed of his father—a strong Nonconformist Liberal.

not think he ever did. What actually happened was that while other people's conception of Liberalism altered, his remained what it was when he first knew it. Modern Liberalism is tinged with Socialism as Gladstonian Liberalism never was. In so far as he found this to be the case, he never hesitated to criticise the new tendency forcibly and freely. Socialism was to him abhorrent—the negation of all progress, the grave of all hope of success. He fought it laughing (' ridicule,' he would say, ' is the strongest of all weapons '), but he fought it from the deepest conviction.

Except during the year that preceded his marriage he was never a good correspondent, and few testimonies to his early views remain, his letters to his future wife being naturally but little concerned with politics. One mention of the House of Lords is, however, perhaps not uninteresting :

To Sybil Haig :

' We lost our cause in the House of Lords, that is to say, the Committee pressed the preamble of the Bill which we freighters were opposing ; and really if the intelligence displayed by their Lordships is a specimen of that possessed by our hereditary Government, I shall certainly feel inclined to vote for some substitute for that branch of the legislature when the question is raised, as it probably will be some day.' [1]

He was a Home Ruler, but rather one suspects because Gladstone was a Home Ruler, and possibly because he disliked the type of mind which adopted the Anti-Home Rule position, than because he was deeply moved by Ireland's desire for self-government. Nationalism was not a conception he ever really understood—to him it was based on sentiment rather than reality, and he had a horror of sentiment. Intellectually, logically, one could make out no case for nationalism, thus he failed (at all events up to the time of the war) to understand it. As a Welsh politician

[1] When the question became practical politics in the election of December 1909 he was doubtful of the desirability of limiting the veto of the House of Lords, but stated in his election address: ' I am myself in favour of a Second Chamber, but I regard the continued existence of a legislative body constituted on hereditary lines not only as an absurdity, out of keeping with the spirit of the times, but as a reflection on the intelligence of any independent and self-respecting community, and I would heartily support a well-considered proposal for the entire abolition of the hereditary, and the substitution therefor of the elective principle in the formation of a Second Chamber.'

he would have had a very much greater chance of success if he could have thrown himself with enthusiasm into the Welsh Nationalist movement. The thing, however, really struck him as sentimental, unreal, and, as a policy, unwise, and he was too sincere intellectually to be able to pretend an enthusiasm he did not feel. When 'Wales for the Welsh' was the great cry of the Cymru Fydd, he would laugh and say he preferred as the Welsh motto, 'The world is our oyster.' He disliked the separatism of the Welsh movement. But he carried this to its logical conclusion ; he was no more biased in favour of Britain than of Wales. Holding such views he was, as may be imagined, never an Imperialist. He was, for instance, strongly opposed to the Boer War. He would say that he could not understand how a man could put his country before his sense of right and justice. His views of other nations were curiously little coloured by any sense of British partisanship.

In later years he would say sometimes that he could well imagine having emigrated to America had he visited that country in his early life. The immense opportunities of the new world fascinated him, and he found himself in very close sympathy with the American character. 'I believe I ought to have been an American,' he would say. The real fact was that nationality meant little to him. He was even during the war quite unable to understand how a man might sacrifice his honour or his friends for his country. To him honour was infinitely the bigger thing. Up to the time of the war he would have said that he had no strong patriotic feeling. 'My country right or wrong' was not a toast he could ever have drunk, and his attitude during the war was, he believed, dictated rather by the fact that Britain was in the right than that he happened to be British. I say ' he believed,' because I doubt whether this was really entirely true. Even if the justice of our case had been less apparent, I should have been surprised if he had sided against England. His temperament in this (as in religion) had a way, when it came to a big practical issue, of getting the better of his intellectual convictions. It is curious (and is, I think, some proof of what I say) that holding such views he was yet entirely without sympathy for the Conscientious

Objectors, whom he dubbed ' the Conscientious Cold Feet Brigade.'

It was probably due to the same dispassionate attitude that he showed as little bias in favour of any special class as he did of any special nation.　I have never met a man so devoid of class consciousness as he was.　It was not so much that he could ' get on ' with all classes, it was that for him classes simply did not exist.　A person was just a person, classified certainly and severely as to whether he were intelligent and interesting and as to whether my father had anything in common with him (' A dull chap, and we have nothing in common,' summed up a good half of his fellow-beings), but required to pass no social test.　When he was a younger man he had perhaps a touch of that common form of class feeling, the inverted type.　He would despise a man, as it seemed, partly because he had social position. Later even that contrary form of the disease disappeared. He was, I believe, one of the few entirely devoid of class feeling in any form ; for those who did possess it he had a hearty contempt ; its existence was to him the hall-mark of gross stupidity.

In religion he was a free-thinker.　Brought up as a strict Congregationalist, and retaining to the end of his life a special affection for the Congregational Church, which he believed to be broader than many others, he left college a confirmed agnostic.　His views were undoubtedly tinged with some of the materialism of the late 'seventies when he did his hard thinking.　Yet there was always something mystical in his temperament which pulled him the other way.

To the end of his life he was greatly interested in religion, would often discuss it, and would always admit in argument that all things were possible.　' Miracles may be true after all, father.'　' They may, but I should be uncommonly surprised if they were.'　He certainly retained more belief than he could intellectually justify, or indeed than he would probably have found it very easy to find words to express. The result was that a conversation with him tended to give the impression that he believed considerably less than he actually did.　I do not suppose that he himself exactly knew how much he did believe. Certain it is that he said his prayers every night and morning of his life, and that always temperamentally, if not intellectually, he was convinced of the existence of a God. During the years of the war this belief grew stronger and more definite.

He was curiously enough decidedly superstitious—it was one of the odd contradictions in his character, that a man prepared to refer everything to the unbiased judgment of the intellect should have had such a trait. But like the rest of the world, he was a mass of contradictions. His brain and his temperament might have belonged to different people. He never allowed his superstition to interfere with anything that mattered—it was always a plaything, never a master ; and he indulged in it, one imagines, half for the pleasure of it. Still it would occasionally influence decisions of a certain importance. I remember on one occasion the question of the naming of a Canadian boat came up. It was to be called ' D. A. Thomas,' but before it was quite ready for launching he was given his title. It was clear that from a purely business standpoint he would get more advertisement out of naming it after his new name than after his old one, and he discussed with me whether I should write and give an order to the effect that the name should be changed. I asked a little anxiously, ' Isn't it rather unlucky to change a ship's name ? ' That settled it. The boat was christened ' The D. A. Thomas.' I am inclined to think that he became more superstitious as he got older, or possibly allowed the instinct fuller play.

It is common enough for a man to make up his mind on political or religious questions about the time he leaves college ; common enough, too, for him to make decisions then which will stand the strain of years. He has, so far as theories go, all the necessary data before him on which to base his decisions. There are many other matters, however, less easy to classify on which his judgment at this stage of his life must still be raw, immature and tentative. D. A. Thomas formed no exception to this rule. He studied in the school of life up to his last days, and few men can have put more energy or enthusiasm into the acquiring

D

of knowledge there. That he became in his later years a past master in the management of men was due largely to the endless pains he had taken to study the ways of humanity —and to adapt his methods accordingly. As a young man he did not show this aptitude in any such marked degree. He possessed in too full a measure the pride and (despite his natural amiability) the touchy sensitiveness of youth to find the manipulation of others very easy at this stage of life. Nor does a marked intellectual sincerity, or the conviction—which he most firmly held—that most men are fools, tend to facilitate the manipulation of others until one has learnt the art of concealing one's thoughts.

His early letters, silent on political matters, contain sidelights on his views of life generally and give some insight into his character. His dislike of ' pomps and vanities ' comes out clearly (in later years he learnt to conceal it to some extent).

To Sybil Haig :

' September 26th, 1881.

' The Cardiff exhibition closes this week, and public interest is now beginning to centre in the Royal Exhibition to be held next month at Swansea. I do think this such abominable humbug, don't you ? To make oneself uncomfortable for a whole day in order to get a passing glimpse of a very ordinary individual whose fame and position are entirely due to an accident of birth, shows, I consider, a very feeble taste. It isn't loyalty, it's grovelling snobbery, and affords the Prince less enjoyment than anyone else I know, unless he is a bigger fool than he is generally accused of being. But this is hardly a subject for a letter of this kind, only I do get so riled when I hear about it.'

My mother did not share his views on Royal functions. Her reply is not extant, but may be surmised from his next letter.

' October 2nd, 1881.

' There is a good deal in what you state to be the motive that induces people to wait standing on each other's toes for hours in order to catch a glimpse of the Prince. You might get conceited if I said you were quite right, besides I hate confessing myself wrong, so will agree to think that some people are influenced by one feeling, some by the other, the rest by both. . . .'

It is not surprising shortly after this to find him confessing himself a Radical :

'2nd December, 1881.

' I had your Wednesday letter this morning, and it afforded me three pages of condensed pleasure. I was afraid your pride related to something else, Sybil, and you know what a Radical I am, though I profess to be only a moderate Liberal, so I was just a wee bit annoyed for an instant, but I should have known better.

' I am going to-morrow to look at a house or two and also to get away from here for the day, as we are going to ventilate the Colliery in the place of a furnace, and we shall have all the engineering talent of the Principality swaggering about and asserting their opinions, and chiefly on matters on which they are not competent to deal with. These gentlemen . . . who top the crest of the ever-advancing wave of science are very amusing, but one can have too much of them.'

The summary in another letter of his views on children contained some truth. As a matter of fact he was, certainly in later years, fond of children—at a distance—and decidedly popular with them, but he undoubtedly tended to avoid long personal interviews with anything under fourteen. A person's attraction did not really begin for him until he or she could carry on an intelligent conversation on subjects in which he was interested.

'October 2nd, 1881.

' I can't say I see the same fascination in children that you appear to. As the poet rather coarsely expresses it, "First puling and mukeing in their nurse's arms," then at a later stage they are always in the way and asking difficult questions and making themselves generally obnoxious, and I can't say I have experienced any fascination under twenty-three. . . .'

He never cared for games ; on the other hand, he was always a great walker. After he came down from college this was and remained his chief form of exercise—by exercise he set great store. At this period of his life he thought little of a twenty-five or thirty mile walk across country. His record in one day was forty-four miles. He used to admit that on that occasion he had felt a bit tired during the last few miles, although, so he declared, far less so than his companions, one of whom sat down on every milestone to cut off a specially painful piece of boot, and finally arrived home in his stocking soles. His love of country and of tramping across the hills crops up continually in his letters.

'August 28th, 1881.

' I went for a long walk yesterday along a ridge of mountains to get a bird's-eye view of the country, and had one of the finest I think I have ever seen of Glamorganshire. We will go and admire it together some day if we can get some conveyance up there. In the graveyard of Eglwyslan Church, which is right on top, there was the tomb of Mr. Thomas Morgan, who appears to have been very anxious that his name should be handed down to a remote posterity, though I'm not aware that he had any unusual claim to such a distinction. On the tombstone was an inscription to the effect that he had bequeathed an annuity of £5 to the Reverend John Leigh, Vicar of the Parish, and his successors for ever, conditionally upon their keeping the grave in repair and painting the stone every alternate year. Was this vanity, do you think, or might not it have been due to some morbid dread the old fellow had of appearing minus some important limb ? '

August 30.

' I believe very much in exercising and getting up early myself . . . and of course I like awfully to think you take the trouble to do anything to please me ; but I do not like you to go and do things with that object that only make you uncomfortable.'

' 28th December, 1881, Ysgyborwen.

' We have been having very foggy weather since we came back—very rheumatic.[1] How would you like to spend your honeymoon nursing me at Buxton ? . . . It is very funny, although it is so misty in the valleys the atmosphere is as

[1] He suffered from rheumatism all his life, and had six attacks of rheumatic fever.

clear as possible on the hill-tops. I never saw anything much prettier than I did yesterday in crossing the mountain from Merthyr. We couldn't see fifty feet into the mist below, which was like a sea of cotton-wool, though the mountains fifteen or twenty miles away were distinctly visible.'

He seems to have shared to the full the common youthful dislike of elders who assumed airs of superiority. He was uncommon in that he continued to remember how irritating such an attitude can be when he came to be an elder himself, and was never guilty of adopting it.

On November 15 he gives an account of his first day on the local Bench :

' I have just come back from administering justice indifferently—very. Five of us brought the combined weight of our massive intellects to bear upon the case of a wretched individual with one foot in the grave and the other generally in a police station, and sentenced him to five shillings and costs or seven days' imprisonment for being helplessly drunk on the wayside. It is the first time I have sat, and the Stipendiary, who is a very prosy man, patronised me at some length and in a most abominable manner, evidently ignorant of the fact that my discretion was so far matured that I was about to do the most important and irrevocable act in life. I think the man who habitually patronises youth without knowing anything of the merits or demerits of the individual may be set down a fool, unless there is very overwhelming evidence to the contrary.'

' 18th September, 1881.

' I came to Ysgyborwen last night because Moreton and Mary are away, and I was afraid that mother might feel lonely. Well, no, not altogether for that reason, Sybil, but I can trust you to put the best construction on what I do, can't I ? When I reached home I found an uncle preparing to occupy my bedroom [1] and to make me regret generally that I had not stayed away. He is a man that delighteth in long faces and the turning up of eyes, and whose soul yearneth after the platitudes of long prayers. The odour of sanctity would have hung about the resting-places of the ungodly for many days, and the remembrance of the

[1] Probably one of his mother's brothers or cousins.

uncleanliness of the righteous would have been present after many months, so I took prompt measures for his expulsion. He revenged himself on me this morning at breakfast by exposing my ignorance of the various styles of the different luminaries in the Nonconformist churches, and I have hardly recovered it yet.'

The following short extracts have been selected as illustrating something of his point of view and character. They are set down in order of date.

'August, 1881.

'I don't know how he is getting on, except that the Bishop of ——— persuaded him to enter the Church, and so overthrew by a few hours' persuasion a conviction that it had taken me several years to plant, as I had fondly hoped, firmly in his breast. . . .

'I am pretty good at listening, and don't expose my weaknesses to any great extent when so occupied, but if I have to talk I can never refrain from enlarging on my superiority to my fellow-beings, and converting what were really disastrous feats into brilliant victories in which I figure largely as the hero. This no doubt affords you considerable amusement, in fact you told me as much, but I warn you it will become very monotonous if the habit gets confirmed and in consequence of your encouragement. . . .

'The vicar of the place came to see me to-day. I felt very much ashamed of myself that I hadn't been to see him first, as he is not as old an inhabitant as myself, and more particularly because I knew him and his wife before. He inaugurated his settling in the district by getting helplessly drunk at the laying of the foundation-stone of a church. This was a fatal thing to do, and I'm afraid in such a hot-bed of Nonconformity will prove irretrievable, for [?] he is a very good sort of fellow sometimes and means well. I needn't tell you he came for a subscription. . . .'

'September 13th, 1881.

'I don't see that you told me much after all, except that it was hard and uncomfortable to be reserved, but I'll tell you what, it's very much more so to find that you have been too communicative and have let out secrets that were told you in confidence. But when once you have shared a secret with one there is not half the longing to tell anyone else, so you may expect to be bored pretty frequently with my uninteresting confidences.'

'Ysgyborwen, Aberdare. October 4th, 1881.

' Do you think it such a very grave offence to care more for anyone than you are cared for in return ?   I should think love was in one respect like mercy, " it blesses him that gives and him that takes," and I think that generally one's respect and sympathy would go with the man that handed forth the gold and not with him who tendered silver in exchange.'

' Glamorgan Club, Cardiff. 6th November, 1881.

' Have you read Tennyson's new poem : " Made us, foreknew us, foredoomed us and does what he will with his own " ?   Do you believe in that sentiment ? '

' Clydach Vale. 18th November, 1881.

' About keeping a kitchenmaid . . . you do as you please.   You remember you are to be the Home Secretary, and though we can discuss domestic affairs in our Cabinet Councils you will have the carrying of them out, and as you will know much more about them than I do, your opinion will carry the greater weight.   Besides, if things are a little bit uncomfortable I am more used to discomfort than you are, so you'll be the greater sufferer.   I think as a general principle one shouldn't keep more people about them than is necessary.   If they are not fully employed they keep each other from working by talking and so on, and it only gives them time to brood over their imaginary wrongs and do everything under a sort of protest because it is somebody else's duty.   This is my experience.'

CHAPTER IV

Ambitions, Equipment and First Start

Amongst the many factors which help to determine a man's career, his political views are by no means the most important. To attempt any forecast of a young man's future it is more essential to know how far he is ambitious, in what direction his ambition points, and wherein lies his apparent equipment for achieving his aim.

So far as D. A. Thomas was concerned there can never have been any doubt on the first score, from the time when as a small schoolboy he informed his uncle David, ' When I grow up I shall be a Minister too, but I shall have a much finer Church than this : *I* shall have a Church with marble pillars '—he was keenly, engrossingly ambitious. He found difficulty all his life in understanding even the point of view of the man without ambition ; he could not comprehend life without it. I need scarcely say that he had usually a considerable contempt for the ambitionless—certainly it would never have occurred to him to look on ambition as anything but a most necessary virtue. In his secret heart he believed he had powers beyond the ordinary and he meant to use them. One sentence in a letter to my mother is pregnant with meaning :

' 30th August, 1881.

' It wouldn't be very difficult to acquaint you with all my doings, but when you want to know all I think of doing you don't know what you ask. . . . Why, the briefest summary would swamp a University Library.'

The main direction of his ambitions is not far to seek. From his college days his eyes had turned towards the political field. That political men and matters were very

40

much present in his mind may be gathered even from these early letters, wherein may be found various passing references to such affairs, and especially to his political hero Mr. Gladstone.   He had originally wished to become a barrister and did indeed begin to read for the law, but his father's death, which occurred in 1879, altered his plans.   He decided to go into the family business and give up reading for the Bar.

This change, however, in no way ruled out the possibility of a political career.   When he came down from college engrossed as he was in family matters and in learning his own trade, he nevertheless set to work immediately to gain experience in public affairs, starting at the bottom of the ladder by standing for the Ystradyfodwg Local Board of Health (now the Rhondda Valley Urban District Council), to which he was elected top of the poll from among upwards of twenty candidates in 1881.   He was also made a magistrate about this time and became a Freemason.

To Sybil Haig:

'22nd October, 1881.

'I have just returned from being initiated into the mysteries of the Grand Order of Foresters.   The torrent of impromptu eloquence which burst from my overflowing lips (nothing nasty) on those several occasions in response to congratulations expressed in a tongue [Welsh] that I must confess I don't thoroughly understand, has considerably exhausted me, and to make matters worse I am now not to divulge any of the impressive ceremony I have just undergone.

'My nominee for the School Board has headed the list of fifteen with fourteen hundred votes more than the second man.   By the way, I ought to tell you that he nominated me for the Local Board when I headed the poll.'

'February 4th, 1882.

'I was too late to oppose the old fellow at the Board : the meeting being held at 12 instead of 3 as usual ; however, he lost his motion so it didn't matter, though he deserved to be very much sat on, and the Board lost the pleasure of hearing a very eloquent impromptu speech in which I should have entered at some length into the enormity of the offence Mr. —— was committing in abusing the trust confided in him by the ratepayers by making use of the position in which they had placed him to justify his own private and sordid ends, etc. etc. etc.'

To Sybil Haig :

' 27th September, 1881.

' I must be at Swansea on the 21st of October to qualify myself for a beak.   If I were not there it would look as if I didn't sufficiently appreciate the proud title : and when one is young one has to consider a little what construction other people put on one's doings, etc.'

For a short while he attended the sittings of the Local Bench, but never continued the practice after he ceased to live in Glamorganshire.

For a political career he possessed certain assets.   He was not at this time a rich man, but he was sufficiently well off to be able to pay his own election expenses and devote himself to a political career without having to consider the £ s. d. aspect.   That he possessed in a marked degree some part of the equipment necessary to a statesman he proved in the last years of his life, but in the equipment necessary to become a successful politician he was in certain respects deficient.

In the first place he lacked entirely the instincts of a courtier.   The people whom a man meets in the course of his active life may be divided into three main groups : those who are in a superior position to himself, those who are on an equality with himself, those who are in a subordinate position to himself, and to each of these three groups the average man shows himself a totally different being. If the simile be permissible, a human being may be compared in this respect to a child's picture puzzle block : the picture to be perceived from above bears no resemblance to that underneath, nor have either of these any relation to those which may be seen at the sides of the brick.

Now the picture which D. A. Thomas presented to his subordinates was an exceedingly pleasant one, scrupulously just, friendly, considerate, extraordinarily careful not to trespass on their rights, ready to assume that the fact of fate having at the moment placed him at the top did not necessarily pre-suppose that he was in any way their superior in intellect or in any other quality. He treated them in fact as his own very sensitive pride would have demanded in a like relationship. To his equals the picture was also pleasant, though it possessed—at all events in his younger days—a certain strength and pungency. If he gave loyalty in full measure he did not easily forgive less than perfect loyalty in return; usually friendly and even conciliatory, he was nevertheless occasionally a little inclined to indulge in a fight out of pure devilment for the fighting's sake. To his superiors the picture was distinctly less attractive. His somewhat thorny pride made him unconciliatory and contradictious. Moreover, he refused to assume that any man was his superior, whatever their relative official positions at the moment, unless he honestly considered him to be so in intellect and general capacity. The number of men in politics whom he honestly believed to be his superiors in intellect were notably few. (I can at the moment only call to mind four.) There were doubtless a considerable number whom he believed to be about equal in capacity to himself. . . . True, he retained the faculty for occasional hero-worship well on into middle life : some traces of it indeed right to the end ; but even where he gave his unstinted admiration, his extreme shyness (which lasted well on into the thirties) led him to make the worst of himself, while his horror of putting himself forward was apt to lead to his disappearing altogether into the background. With this he had a schoolboy love of ragging for ragging's sake and a desire to pull the legs of the pompous great.

Nor were these his only disadvantages. Social relationships no longer matter so much as they did in political circles, but they still matter. Political functions give opportunities for the great ones of the day to get to know something of the promising young men of the party, As a young man my father utterly despised all social routine. It was for him an aspect of the unpleasant detail of life which every sensible man would naturally avoid. Many years had to pass before he could bring himself to realise that details so paltry may make or mar a man's career. Had he chanced to marry a woman wise in her generation as are the children of this world she might (had they succeeded in living happily together, which is doubtful) have done much to counterbalance this particular disability. He did not. His wife was utterly unversed in the art of political climbing, nor did she ever, in all her loyal desire to help him, learn even the rudiments of it. She was an asset in that she was popular wherever she went, and that she never made an enemy, but she was not herself sufficiently enthusiastic about political functions to succeed in insisting on his accompanying her to them. He was never, it must be admitted, a very amenable husband in such matters, and her own natural instinct was to surround herself with her family and friends quite regardless of their possible political value, or lack of value. Nor for all her strongly hospitable bent was she altogether suited for the part of a political hostess. She lacked many of the necessary attributes; she was too forgetful and absent-minded, too prone to ignore, or indeed to be unaware of, certain small and perhaps rather petty social conventions which she herself considered foolish or absurd.

I well remember a business dinner party in a foreign city to which my mother, placidly unaware of the fact that we were in a place where old prejudices still held and Jews and Christians never mixed socially, had asked about half of each. She did not so much as notice that directly dinner was over the diners separated automatically into two halves which ignored each other from opposite ends of the room.

A further serious drawback lay in the fact that D. A. Thomas had not the gift of eloquent speech. Although in later years he became a fair speaker, amusing, forceful, and interesting, he could never rise to great emotional heights ; he had no touch of the Welsh ' huyl.' He was too reserved and easily conscious of absurdity, too self-controlled. Possibly a mathematical degree is not the best form of training for a man who contemplates fine emotional flights. As a young man his extreme shyness was a great drawback to him in his speeches.

To Sybil Haig :

'November 20th, 1181.

' It was my pleasing duty on Thursday night to propose a vote of thanks to a local boss for presiding : instead of this I proposed a vote of health, got extremely confused and finished up with " Believe me, Yours very sincerely, D. A. Thomas." This elicited bursts of applause from a large audience, who fortunately couldn't understand a word of English.'

It would be interesting to know how far this description exaggerated. Probably less than one might suppose. He used to tell of another occasion which took place a few years later on which, being the main speaker of the evening, he braced himself for his effort by taking a double dose of whisky before going on to the platform. His object was, however, entirely defeated by the Chairman, whose opening remarks lasted for an hour, during which time the stimulating effect of the alcohol gradually but completely wore off. In the House of Commons he never got over his diffidence, with the result that he spoke there but seldom and on no occasion can be said to have made an unqualified success.

Such were his disabilities for a political career, surface matters perhaps, but taken in the aggregate of some considerable importance.

The greatest disability of all, however, was not of his making. During the twenty years of his Parliamentary career the stars in their courses seemed to fight against him at every turn. Fate dealt the cards, and during those years she dealt him a losing hand.

Side by side with the political dreams which tinted the visions of the future in these early years lay the keen practical determination to make a success of his own particular trade.

The family fortunes were then as afterwards bound up with the Cambrian Collieries, situated in the Rhondda Valley. I have taken the following short account of the original starting of these Collieries from the ' South Wales Coal Annual ' for 1907.

' In 1870 John Osborne Riches and his brother Osborne Henry Riches placed before Samuel Thomas a proposal to sink in the Rhondda Valley. John Osborne Riches was a coal exporter, who had for some years acted as sales agent for Ysgyborwen coal, and Samuel Thomas looked to him for advice on matters relating to the commercial side of his colliery. J. O. Riches was at the same time acting as the commercial head of the Ocean Coal Company, having some years before induced David Davies to join him and others in exploiting the great steam coal area which bears that Company's name, and which lies in the Rhondda Valley to the north-west of the Cambrian property. Samuel Thomas, then a wealthy man, and possessing a knowledge gained during thirty years of close practical experience of Welsh Coal-mining, agreed to the proposal ; the leases were settled, and the winning of the coal at once proceeded with. Two pits were sunk, and in 1875 the top seams of the steam measures were reached. Thus the firm of Thomas, Riches & Co. came into existence, with Samuel Thomas, John Osborne Riches, and Osborne Henry Riches, as partners. At the collieries Samuel Thomas maintained control ; at the Port of Cardiff O. H. Riches represented the firm, and commenced to establish markets for " Cambrian Navigation Steam Coal." '

Such a venture was a bold one for an old man of seventy to enter upon, for it involved a large part of his fortune. It prospered, however, almost from the start. Perhaps the coal strike of 1873, during which Samuel Thomas stood apart from all the other coal owners, paid the increased wages demanded by the miners, kept his pits working, and gained all the Admiralty orders, helped to solidify the position of the new Colliery.[1] Anyhow, by the time of Samuel Thomas' death in 1879 the success of the Cambrian Collieries was assured. More than that he already derived the greater part of his fortune from it. He had had a quarrel with his lawyer shortly before his death, over the price which the latter proposed to charge him for drawing up his will, with the result that he died intestate. But by a settlement drawn up during his lifetime he had already made over the Cambrian Collieries to his two elder sons, Jack and David. This course had been adopted at a time when it seemed that this new property was a doubtful speculative concern which would need careful handling by experts if it were to yield any fruits. During the intervening years since this docu-

---

[1] Compare this with D. A. Thomas's action in 1898.

ment had been drawn up the position had entirely altered. It is possible that the old man scarcely realised how much it had changed.   At all events the effect of his will was that the two elder brothers found themselves rich, whilst their mother, younger brother and sisters were merely comfortably provided for.   Neither of the brothers felt this to be a fair arrangement.   They therefore tore up the settlement and shared out the whole estate between all the members of the family.

The question of management also naturally arose.   It was agreed that a new deed of partnership should be drawn up, in which John and David should take their father's place and manage the Collieries in conjunction with J. O. and O. H. Riches, the firm still to be known as Thomas, Riches & Co.   This new deed proved by no means easy to draw up.   The brothers had been willing enough to forego money unasked.   But this was a matter of bargaining, and when it came to a bargain David at least was not in the habit of coming off loser.   Moreover the terms of the new deed not only settled questions of income, they settled the more important matters of the division of power.

David's letters at this time were eloquent of the amount of thought and energy he was putting into the matter.

To Sybil Haig :

' 12th February, 1882.

' . . . Everything is going on satisfactorily except the partnership deeds which don't seem to meet with the approval of the other partners, but between ourselves, Sybil, I intend having a bit of my own way this time if possible, and I haven't yet exhausted the resources of civilisation by any means.'

' Ysgyborwen, Aberdare, 28th April, 1882.

' Nothing further has been definitely settled about the partnership so far, though I have made my proposal, which I consider a fair one, and I intend to stick to it ; but the other partners have not yet said whether they will agree to it or not, though I think very likely they will.   It gives X more than he deserves a good deal, and more than I should have suggested spontaneously, but I modified my original proposal to meet the mater's views.'

' I don't think I can be accused of having been too hasty in settling the partnership business, for I have spent nearly three years in trying to do so, but at the same time . . . I quite appreciate the value and good sense contained in your advice, and I had postponed proceeding further in the matter before I received it : for in the first place I don't want to have anything to think about except yourself . . . when we are away together. Not that anything would be likely to distract my attention, but it might just annoy a bit at times, and in the second place perhaps if the other partners think the matter over calmly for six weeks or so they will see the unreasonableness of their action.'

The deed was finally signed on August 31, 1882.

CHAPTER V

The Chief Events of His Life

I PROPOSE in this chapter to give some account of my father's early married years and a short outline of his life from that period to the time of his acceptance of office in the Lloyd George Ministry in 1916. I have asked others more competent than myself to fill in the details, but I do not think it would be possible to understand the sequence of events without some short summary of them, such as I propose to give here, which will, I hope, show how the different periods and various activities of his life fitted the one into the other, or grew the one out of the other.

His marriage took place on June 27, 1882. The honeymoon was spent in Scotland, a considerable part of it being occupied in staying with various branches of the Haig clan. The newly married couple then returned to a furnished house in Cardiff, which they had rented for six months, until they should have time to make further plans.

Up to this time it had been my father's intention to take his share in the management of the Cambrian Collieries. He proposed to settle down in the Cardiff office. He was full of plans for the better and more efficient working both of the collieries and of the Cardiff office arrangements. This, however, was just where the trouble came in. He and his new plans were not wanted by the other partners. They preferred to go on in the old ruts and disliked and distrusted the youth, energy and initiative of the new partner. D. A. Thomas fought for his place and his schemes down at Cardiff for three months, but it must have been clear from the first that he had no real chance. It was a three to one fight, since his elder brother John could always be trusted to take the conservative side. It was bitter to him to give up.

My mother has told me that he came home almost crying on one occasion when he had utterly failed to move any of them to see his point of view. It would have been quite impossible, however, for him to stay there and carry on the business on the old lines without attempting improvements, and indeed it is probable that Harry Riches did not want him there on any terms. At the end of six months he made up his mind to give up the struggle and decided to go on to the London Stock Exchange.

In the meanwhile his wife living in the furnished house in the middle of Cardiff had been as miserable as a newly and happily married woman could well be. The house was hideous ; the furniture was hideous ; she knew no one, and, country bred as she was, had never before lived in any town save London. She welcomed the decision to leave Cardiff with joy.

In December 1882 a house was taken in Prince's Square. There they lived for some nine months. There I was born. My father was disappointed : he wanted a boy. Doubtless at the time he hoped for more children and so attached less importance to the mistake in sex than he might otherwise have done, but no more came.

It would, of course, be untrue to say that whether girl or boy he took a very vivid or competent interest in babies. I was a fair blue-eyed baby, but when at the age of a few weeks a dark cousin was substituted for me and presented to him as his daughter he noticed nothing unusual. His brother, who was standing by, knew more about it. ‘ Why surely,’ he said, ‘ that's George Boyd's brat ; it's got black eyes.’

In the summer of 1883 they decided to move out of town to some place within easy daily reach. They took Ovendon near Sevenoaks in Kent, the dower-house on the Stanhope estate ; a pretty old-fashioned house in beautiful country and—a matter of importance to my mother if not to himself —situated in an agreeable neighbourhood. There they lived for four years, a pleasant sociable life, seeing a great deal of their neighbours. My father was so amenable in those days that he actually went to church every Sunday evening during the whole four years ; it was the only period of his married life when he kept the somewhat equivocally made promise of his engagement. He did this mainly to please his wife no doubt, but partly also because he disliked to offend Mr. Hammond, the charming old Rector of Sunridge, their parish church.

Every winter they used to give a big fancy-dress ball, the only form of entertainment my father really enjoyed. He loved dressing up for it. On one occasion in those early days he went as 'Three Acres and a Cow.' His great hobby at Ovendon was the keeping of bees. He had at one time as many as three hundred hives, and devoted all his spare time and energy to studying their habits and looking after them. He even went so far as to keep a hive of bees in his dressing-room. During August he used himself to load up a wagon with hives and drive it over to the heather-covered common four miles away where the hives were unloaded and left for four or five weeks so that the bees might gather heather honey for the combs.[1]

He used to sell the honey and hoped to make a commercial success of his hobby. But he never did. The bees finally got the bee disease, and the whole apiary became so affected that when he left Ovendon he decided to give it up, although he continued to keep two or three hives.

Meanwhile, in the working world his schemes were not prospering well. He used to spend a great deal of his time reading at the British Museum. After some time he got into touch with a Mr. Nicholas, a stockbroker, and arranged with him that he should go into his office and learn the business. As a partner in a private firm it was not possible for him to become a Member of the Stock Exchange himself. He had hoped to get over this difficulty by getting Thomas, Riches & Company made into a limited liability company, but he could not succeed in persuading the other partners to take this step.

In 1887, however, all his plans were changed. Mr. O. H. Riches died in this year : this necessitated some re-arrange-

---

[1] This scheme apparently had its dangers. On one occasion a few bees escaped from one of the hives, and stung the horse, which plunged, ran away, and finally upset the wagon. Chaos ensued. Both men and the horse were badly stung and they had to wait till evening when the bees had quieted down before loading up again and continuing their journey.

ment of the Cambrian Colliery concerns, and D. A. Thomas was offered the sales agency of the colliery, an offer which both pleased and flattered him. He accepted it, gave up all further thoughts of the Stock Exchange, and went back to Cardiff.

In December 1887 he gave up Ovendon and took Llanwern, a house in south Monmouthshire within easy reach of Cardiff. There he lived for the rest of his life. Llanwern, a large square red-bricked house, built in the reign of William and Mary, lies close to the ' flats ' which border the Welsh side of the Bristol Channel for a width of three or four miles. It stands on the first piece of rising ground on the edge of these flats in a beautifully wooded park full of elm, beech and lime. Between the trees one may catch a glimpse of the Bristol Channel four miles away and of the Somersetshire hills beyond. To foreign eyes the house would not perhaps be beautiful ; ' More like a factory than a house,' as one French governess complained. To English eyes the mellow brick, the four-square solidity of the place are attractive. It seems to suggest an atmosphere of peace and strength and comfort, an atmosphere which has grown with the centuries. Most people have felt conscious of the atmosphere that hangs about an old house, of rest or unrest, happiness or anxiety or horror. The atmosphere of Llanwern suggests solid hopeful peace. It is the kind of house which one always sees in one's mind's eye standing in sunshine. The most noticeable feature is a huge magnolia which grows on the south-east side of the house and covers a good half of it, reaching right to the roof and flowering profusely all through August and September. The surrounding country, flat and intersected with reeds towards the south, wooded and hilly towards the north, merging gradually into the bigger bracken and blaeberry covered hills of north Monmouthshire and the more famous Breconshire Mountains, is everywhere rich and fertile. The trees grow big, the grasses grow high, wild flowers abound. May and June see a more luxuriant growth of grass and leaf and flower there, it always seems to me, than they do in any other part of the kingdom. The climate is very similar to that of Devonshire. Few places could have suited my

LLANWERN FROM THE SOUTH

father better.   He took it at first on a yearly tenancy, then leased it for a longer term, and finally in 1903 he bought both the house and surrounding property.

It was in the autumn of 1887, just after they had decided to leave Ovendon and take a house near Cardiff so that he might be near his business, that my father received the invitation to stand for Merthyr Borough at the bye-election which was caused by the retirement of Mr. James.

He had no association behind him at that election, nor was he the candidate whom the authorities desired to put up, but he was returned unopposed.

Neither at that nor at any subsequent election did he ' canvass ' in the strict sense of the term, that is to say, he never would ask or allow his agent to ask for promises to vote.   He considered it an unjustifiable thing to ask a man to pledge himself, as it put him in the awkward position of either being rude (which, by the way, a Welshman seldom is) or of perjuring himself.   Moreover, as he pointed out, election promises are really no guide as to results.   This point of view was borne out by a curious little episode which happened after one of his elections.   He had been returned top of the poll with his usual huge majority whilst the Conservative candidate had come out bottom of the list with a paltry couple of thousand votes ; the result had just been announced when the Conservative agent came up to him.   ' I congratulate you, Mr. Thomas,' he said, ' but I think you ought to know that you have 6,000 damned liars amongst your constituents.'

It would seem that the fact of not canvassing made very little difference to his results, for he was always elected by huge majorities.

Merthyr Tydfil was a double member constituency, and at each of his four contested elections there (1892, 1895, 1900 and 1906) he headed the poll.[1]

---

[1] The elections were as follows :

1892.

D. A. Thomas. (Gladstonian Lib.)	.	.	.	11,948
W. Pritchard Morgan. (Do.)		.	.	11,756
B. Francis Williams. (Cons.)	.	.	.	2,304

Majority over Cons., 9,644.

[Continued on page 54.

A political career had always attracted him above all others : it was the one he felt himself best fitted for. During the nineties (living at Llanwern during the recess) he concentrated chiefly on politics, but he by no means neglected business—he was a partner not only in the Cambrian Collieries but in the Sales Agency of Thomas & Davey, of which he was the moving spirit, and he was very anxious to make a success of his new job. He spent much of his time thinking out possible improvements and economies, looking into figures, setting up new costing systems. At this time he was not by any means a rich man, nor did he give serious thought to the possibility of making much money himself. His main energies were engrossed in politics and he was young and still full of hope. He kept up the twin interests of business and politics side by side : but there is no doubt as to which he really gave the greater attention.

Not long after the General Election of 1900 (in June 1901) he decided to relinquish all his directorates and devote himself entirely to politics. During the years 1900 to 1906 a very violent reaction of opinion was taking place throughout the country, and it was fairly clear to the weatherwise that the Liberal Party, which, with the exception of a short and precarious tenure of office from 1893 to 1895, had been out of power upwards of twenty years, was coming into its own again. In 1901 he had been a Member of the House for fourteen years : he was a man of forty-five years of age, and it was certain that if his parliamentary career was to come to anything it must do so within the next few years.

From 1901 to 1906 he devoted himself then to politics

	1895.	
D. A. Thomas. (Liberal.)		9,250
W. Pritchard Morgan. (R.) . . .		8,554
H. C. Lewis. (C.)		6,525
Allen Upward. (Lab.)		659
	1900.	
D. A. Thomas. (L.)		8,598
J. Keir Hardie. (Ind. Lab.) . . .		5,745
W. Pritchard Morgan. (L.) . . .		4,004
	1906.	
D. A. Thomas. (L.)		13,971
J. Keir Hardie. (Lab.)		10,187
Hy. Radcliffe. (L.)		7,776

alone.   In January 1906 came the election which returned
his party to power by an enormous majority at a time when
intrigues were many.   He had been throughout (and he
remained to the end) a loyal supporter of Campbell-Bannerman, the new Prime Minister, for whom he had a strong
and genuine regard.   Many of the men who had intrigued
against the new Prime Minister were given office by that
canny Scotsman.   D. A. was passed over.   C.-B. told my
father that he would not give him office because his front
bench must consist of Parliamentary debaters of first rank,
and there was, my father felt, some justice in this remark ;
at the same time he did not believe it to be an entirely
genuine excuse.   The fact was that he had enemies and that
at Westminster he had, largely through their offices but
partly owing to his own independence, gained the reputation of being a difficult man to work with.   During his
twenty-one years of parliamentary life he was never so
much as made chairman of a committee.

The years following the 1906 election must have been
difficult for him.   Vaguely one realised at the time that
there was something wrong, that for a while he drifted
rudderless with his purpose in life uncertain.   But he
did not show very much.   My mother always used to
say that the only way she could ever tell he was feeling
depressed was that he whistled more aggressively than ever
and was more obviously cheerful.   His joys he shared but
his troubles he just ignored.   He had a horror of crying
over spilt milk.   I can remember that when one went to
him with some trouble, if there was a way out he would take
infinite pains to help one to achieve it, but if there was no
way out he would seem puzzled that one had troubled to
mention the matter at all.   One felt that though he hesitated to judge adversely he found it difficult not to despise
one for mentioning it.

It was typical of him that he wasted no time in regretting
his political failure.   In 1906 he just went back on to the
Cambrian Board and immersed himself in business.   But
this time there was a big difference.   Never before had he
really devoted his whole attention to business ; never before
had he looked upon his success there as his test of success or

failure in life—now he did. He had always held the view that the capacity to make money was no test of brains. 'My dear fellow, I look upon you,' he once remarked to a fellow docksman in a moment of frankness (and he had moments of devastating frankness), 'as a walking illustration of the fact that money can be made without brains.' But the path which he would have chosen was apparently barred to him; if money-making was to be his test of success, then money-making it should be, and on a scale to make it worth while. For the one thing that was absolutely necessary to him was success—he could not do without that. By 1907 he had re-orientated his life and was immersed in new schemes of amalgamation of every kind. . . .

He remained in Parliament still, half hoping against hope I suppose, until the second election of 1910—but from 1906 he had really accepted the inevitable and turned his chief attention elsewhere. He became more and more engrossed in business, and towards 1911 became interested in the possibilities of Anglo-American combinations—schemes which attracted him the more since he had a natural affinity for the American temperament and a high regard for the American business man.

Apart from these possibilities of linking up British and American coal and shipping he spent both time and money on schemes for developing the far North-west of Canada. The chances of being successful were, as he was perfectly well aware, ten to one against, and in any case the development could not possibly have come in his lifetime. ' I choose to spend my money in that way, and it is justifiable,' he would explain, ' because I can afford the loss. If I were not a rich man it wouldn't be justifiable.' It was the romance of the thing that attracted him of course, and its potential usefulness in opening up a new country. He used to plan to go and visit the Peace River district in Northern Alberta.

His schemes were growing apace in every direction when war broke out and shattered half of them. It was about this time that he began to come in close contact with Mr. Seymour Berry, who from 1915 onwards acted for him in many of his undertakings. He had for some time been on the look-out for younger men of enterprise and energy. ' You must always have a good man to swing a deal on,' he would say—during the last two or three years of his life he used Mr. Berry as his right-hand man on many occasions.

During the early years of the war he was not asked to help in any special way, though he was ready and anxious to do everything that he could, and did serve on one or two committees. In the main, however, he continued to concern himself with private affairs.

In the summer of 1915 he was asked by Mr. Lloyd George, then Minister of Munitions, to go to America and Canada on that Ministry's business, and was away some five months. On his return he received his peerage. He was not, however, asked for any further service until December, 1916, when Mr. Lloyd George on assuming office offered him the post of President of the Local Government Board, which he accepted.

CHAPTER VI

POLITICAL LIFE

By Llewelyn Williams, K.C.

PERHAPS the most decisive General Election ever held in Wales was the Home Rule election of 1886. Joseph Chamberlain, at a time when Gladstone was still a stern and unbending opponent of Welsh Disestablishment, had avowed his sympathy with Welsh aspirations, and in the ' Unauthorised Programme ' of 1885 he had unfolded a policy of Land Reform such as Welsh farmers, groaning under heavy rents and ill conditions of tenure, craved for. He had parted company with his old leaders over Irish Home Rule. He carried with him nearly every Welsh political leader.

Nevertheless the election of 1886 was a triumph for Liberalism, pure and undefiled. In all, Liberals only lost, on balance, three seats in the whole of Wales. It showed that Wales, with sure instinct, would have no alliance with Toryism, however limited and temporary.

Charles Henry James and Henry Richard were returned unopposed for Merthyr Tydvil. James intimated that he was willing to resign the seat whenever his friends had found a suitable successor. By the beginning of 1888 the successor had been found in the person of David Alfred Thomas, fresh from the University, whose boundless energy could not find sufficient vent even in the conduct of a great and exacting business. He had since January 1888 been ' nursing ' the constituency, and his outstanding personality and the popularity of his mother made his selection a certainty even against a tame Government nominee. In

March 1888 Charles Henry James applied for the Chiltern Hundreds. On March 7 D. A. Thomas was invited to stand in the Liberal interest. At first there was some talk of a Labour candidate taking the field. But David Davies of Cwmaman, whose name was mentioned, found that he could not get sufficient support, and withdrew from the candidature. On March 14 D. A. Thomas was returned unopposed as the colleague of the illustrious Henry Richard in the representation of Merthyr Tydvil. He was the first of the Young Wales men to join Tom Ellis in Parliament.

A few days later Sir Horace Davey, the late Solicitor-General, was forced to retire from the candidature of the Gower Division; and David Randell took his seat as the third of the new group of politicians in St. Stephen's. In 1889 Mr. (now Judge) Lloyd Morgan was returned for West Carmarthenshire; in February 1890 Mr. (afterwards Sir) Samuel Evans for Mid Glamorgan; and in March 1890 Mr. Lloyd George for the Carnarvon Boroughs. These events showed that Wales had taken great strides in realising her distinctive nationhood. No longer would she be content to be represented by drowsy squires or alien plutocrats. She began to insist that her interests should be served, if needs must, by russet-coated captains, who like Cromwell's officers, ' know what they fight for, and love what they know.'

Long before D. A. Thomas was born the question of the Anglican Established Church in Wales had been a matter of keen controversy. In the thirties Roger Edwards of Mold had incurred the wrath of the great John Elias at a ' Sassiwn ' at Bala for daring to introduce such a political matter as Disestablishment into the deliberations of the Calvinistic Methodists. Since then Gwilym Hiraethog, probably the greatest genius that Wales produced in the 19th century, had been using all his gifts of humour and satire and passion to rouse public opinion; the three brothers of Llanbrynmair, S. R., J. R. and G. R., and their nephew ' Y Gohebydd'; Henry Richard; Thomas Gee, and a host of others had been trying to further the agitation. The election of 1868 had been fought on the principle of maintaining an alien

Established Church in Ireland.   Seventy tenant farmers in
Cardiganshire and Carmarthenshire alone had been evicted
for voting against their landlords' behests, with the result
that a Ballot Act became imperative.   Watkin Williams,
the son of a North Wales clergyman, moved a resolution
in 1870 in the House of Commons in favour of Welsh Disestablishment and Disendowment.   But the result of the
election of 1874 was a rebuff to the Liberationists : and
though the election of 1880 definitely proved that Wales
was predominantly Liberal, nothing was done to meet the
demand of Wales for religious equality.   Mr. Watkin
Williams became a Judge of High Court ; Mr. Osborne
Morgan, Judge Advocate General ; and Mr. Gladstone
adopted Sir Robert Walpole's motto, *Quieta non movere*.
Mr. Dillwyn, the M.P. for Swansea, gave notice of motion
in 1883 : but he was persuaded not to proceed with it.
Various conferences and public meetings were held all over
Wales to support the Welsh demand.   Certain members of
the Liberal Government were sympathetic ; but the Government was able to resist all the sporadic efforts of Welsh
Liberationists, though they included in their midst every
illustrious name of the period.   Mr. Dillwyn's long deferred
motion came on in March 1886, when he was supported
by Henry Richard, Stuart Rendel, and Mabon.   But the
Government would do nothing, and the resolution was
defeated by a majority of twelve.

But things were happening in Wales.   The people took
up the fight.   The Tithe War broke out in Llanarmon in
Denbighshire.   It spread throughout Wales, and in time
the Tithe battles of Penbryn in the south of Cardigan
became as famous as the early skirmishes in Llanarmon.
This is not the time or place to write the history of the fight
for Disestablishment in Wales.   Suffice it to say that it was
the Tithe War which brought the question within the
realm of practical politics.   In January 1887 Mr. Dillwyn
moved his resolution a second time.   It was defeated by a
majority of over a hundred.   But this gave Mr. Chamberlain
his chance.   Some of the Welsh members had shown signs
of unrest.   He appealed to them to join him.   ' Some of the
best friends of the Dissenters, and of the most earnest sup-

porters of Disestablishment,' he said with truth and force, ' are to be found in the ranks of the Liberal Unionists.' But the Welsh members repudiated his implicit offer to help. Mr. Chamberlain drifted further and further apart from his old Radical friends, as was indeed the inevitable consequence, however little he may have desired it. Mr. Gladstone would not commit himself for years after to Welsh Disestablishment : but the Tithe War, as it had brought, so it kept, the question to the front. Mr. (afterwards Sir) John Bridge was sent down to inquire into the Tithe Riots in North Wales, with Professor Rhys as Secretary to the Commission. His report was published in September 1887. But it only served to add fuel to the flame.

When D. A. Thomas entered Parliament in March 1888, the agitation was at its height. Henry Richard, his colleague in the representation of Merthyr Tydvil, was regarded as the *doyen* of Welsh Disestablishers. The young member therefore entered Parliament when, not so much religious equality, but the question of tithes, was the burning topic of the hour. It was no wonder that in after years he was to show far greater concern about the application of tithes than about the abstract right of Wales to free herself from the incubus of an Establishment.

The election of 1892 brought the Welsh question to the forefront. It had already been included in the Newcastle Programme, though Mr. Gladstone refused to be bound by the decision of the National Liberal Federation. In September 1892 Mr. Gladstone acknowledged in a speech at Carnarvon that religious equality would be a national benefit, and that Wales had made out her claim on the Liberal party. But when the Queen's Speech was read in February 1893 the hopes of Wales were dashed to the ground. No Disestablishment Bill was promised ; but at the tag end of the gracious Speech from the Throne there was a reference to a Suspensory Bill, which would deprive all clergymen appointed to benefices after its passage into law from all claims to compensation. The indignation felt in Wales found an echo in the Welsh Parliamentary Party. Mr. Lloyd George proposed, and D. A. Thomas seconded, that the Welsh Party should express their disappointment to

Mr. Gladstone, and demand that the Government's plans should be altered. This was done to a small extent. Gladstone stated that Mr. Asquith would proceed forthwith to introduce the Suspensory Bill, and that was the utmost limit of concession accorded to the Welsh members.

The more the facts are considered the worse appears the conduct of the Government towards Wales. The election of 1892 was fought in Wales mainly, if not wholly, on the question of Disestablishment. Wales had shown her belief in Irish autonomy in 1886 and in every bye-election for six years. She had not cooled in her ardour in 1892, but the foremost issue, so far as Wales was concerned, was Disestablishment. The Liberal leaders well knew this to be the fact. They knew that every Liberal candidate had put it in the forefront of his election address. Nothing had ever been said about a Suspensory Bill, and the last phase of the Welsh Church Act shows that such a Bill was unnecessary. It was no wonder that the Welsh members and the Welsh people were wroth. When one considers the character and ability of the 31 Welsh Liberal members, one wonders how any Government dared to treat them so contemptuously.

The Chairman of the Welsh Party was Mr. (afterwards Lord) Rendel. He was an intimate personal friend of Mr. Gladstone, a man of great intellectual gifts, one who thoroughly understood Wales and Welshmen, and a firm and loyal friend of Welsh aspirations. T. E. Ellis had been appointed second Whip in 1892, a post for which he was not conspicuously fitted. But he was a great Welshman, who touched the national life at every point. He took a keen interest in all things Welsh—Welsh history, literature, religion, education, even sport. A more single-hearted patriot never represented Wales in Parliament, and he would have sacrificed his political career sooner than prove untrue to the land he loved. Mr. Samuel Evans was in those days regarded as the ablest Parliamentarian in the Welsh group. As a debater in Committee he had no superior, and if he did not shine as brightly when discussing great issues in second or third reading debates, his nimble wit, his infinite resource, and his supreme self-confidence made him a formidable opponent and a trenchant advocate. Sir George Osborne Morgan, the member for East Denbigh, had had a brilliant career at Oxford, and he had speedily attained to a leading junior practice at the Chancery Bar. He distinguished himself in the 1868 Parliament, and in the later seventies he was mentioned for the highest posts in the next Government. His misfortune was that he was enticed to accept in 1880 the ridiculous office of Judge Advocate General, an error of judgment and perhaps of character from which he never recovered. Sir Edward Reed was member for Cardiff, a fine platform speaker, an old parliamentary hand, and one who never forgot or forgave the Government for passing him over in 1892. Mr. Lloyd George, fearless, ambitious, aggressive, master of all the arts and possessor of most of the gifts of real oratory and beginning to develop the talents of a political tactician, if not a strategist, was emerging into national importance. With them was D. A. Thomas, who possessed more constructive ability than any of them, young, wealthy, ardently ambitious, a convinced Radical of the genuine kind. There were besides men like Mr. Alfred Thomas (afterwards Lord Pontypridd), Major Jones, who spoke more in the Ercles vein than any, Mr. Herbert Roberts (now Lord Clwyd), Mr. Herbert Lewis, Mr. Lloyd Morgan and Mr. Bryn Roberts, most courageous and independent of men. Such men could and should have won for Wales all that she wanted : or, at all events, should have forced a friendly Government to agree to their reasonable demands. The secret of their failure—for fail they did—was that they could not work together. Each was a man of strong and dominant personality. None had the excess of experience, success and age which would entitle him to the leadership. And so Wales, after ploughing the sands for a quarter of a century, found that when at last the rare and refreshing fruits of Disendowment fell to her lot in 1920, they were but Dead Sea apples that turned to ashes in her mouth.

The unrest in Wales grew in strength and violence during 1893. Grave suspicions were entertained, and not without some foundation, as to the genuineness of Mr. Gladstone's conversion to Welsh Disestablishment. Fiery protests came from the North Wales and the South Wales Liberal Federations. The annual meeting of the latter was held at Aberdare, in D. A. Thomas's constituency, in August, and the young member was unanimously and enthusiastically elected President—a position which he occupied till the final dissolution of the body. A policy of independence was declared if Welsh Disestablishment was not accorded first place in the Sessional Programme of 1894. This was followed by a meeting of Welsh members in September. Mr. Gladstone had been more than usually ambiguous during the recess in his references to the Welsh question. Mr. David Randell proposed and Major Jones seconded that no reply should be made to the Prime Minister but that an independent party should be started forthwith. D. A. Thomas, Frank Edwards, W. Williams, W. Pritchard Morgan, and Sir Edward Reed voted for the resolution. It was the plain, straightforward, and honest course. But the resolution was defeated by a majority of seven. Failing to carry this, D. A. Thomas then moved that the members regretted that no assurance had been given by the Government, and that if such assurance was not forthcoming by the next session they would have to take an independent line. This was supported by Tom Ellis (though a Government Whip), Major Jones, F. Edwards, Herbert Lewis, and Lloyd George. This was lost by a majority of thirteen. Ultimately a resolution moved by Mr. Lloyd George and seconded by Tom Ellis that they had confidence in the Government— but that they would have to reconsider their relation to it, and take their own course if the Disestablishment Bill did not occupy the place that it in their opinion should, was carried. A truly characteristic proceeding of what is called in sardonic mockery ' the Welsh Parliamentary Party,' which helps to explain and justify the utter contempt which D. A. Thomas came to feel for it.

It will be seen from this account that the two Welsh members who steered a consistent course were D. A. Thomas and Mr. Frank Edwards. On March 1, 1894, Mr. Gladstone made his last appearance in the House which he had adorned for sixty years. Welsh Disestablishment had been mentioned in the Queen's Speech, but fears were expressed that the Government had so overloaded their programme that there was little or no chance of the Welsh measure being passed through the House of Commons. On the eve of the introduction of the Bill by Mr. Asquith on April 26, four Welsh members came out 'in revolt,' D. A. Thomas, Lloyd George, Herbert Lewis, and Frank Edwards. The other five who had spoken such ' prave 'orts ' in the previous autumn turned tail and fled. Nay more, they appeared in the Press as critics and condemners of the revolting four. The justification of the Welsh Revolt was given a month later by Mr. Lloyd George at Holywell :

' We saw that whatever the good intentions of the Government might be, it was a matter of physical impossibility for them to carry that Bill if they stuck to the programme they had mapped out. So we struck for Wales.'

The four members shook the dust of St. Stephen's from off their feet, refused to accept the Government Whip, and went on a ' revolting tour ' through Wales. Their first meeting was held at Carnarvon, and their last at Holywell. At first the Government was disposed to bluster. Mr. Fowler talked of holding a pistol at the Government's head. But Wales was roused to the core. The meetings in North Wales were enthusiastic, and other meetings were arranged to take place at Merthyr Tydvil, Cardiff, Swansea, and other popular centres in South Wales. But the Revolt came to a sudden and unexpected end. Lord Rosebery in a speech at Birmingham asserted that when the Government went to the country they would meet it with a measure of Welsh Disestablishment passed through the House of Commons. The Welsh Party met in jubilant mood on May 25. They expressed satisfaction at the efforts of the Government and stated that in the interests of Wales, and particularly of Welsh Disestablishment, they should give the Government an honourable and consistent support. All parties were satisfied. The four felt that the Revolt had been justified : the rest asserted that their own touching loyalty was rewarded ; while still others were of opinion that the quiet and persistent loyalty of Tom Ellis, who was now Chief Liberal Whip, had been the main cause of the

F

Government's change of front. Perhaps there was a measure of truth in all three claims.

The co-operation between D. A. Thomas and Mr. Lloyd George during the Welsh Revolt was not destined to last. Mr. George's numerous biographers are fond of describing him as the ' leader ' of that dramatic episode. In one sense he was undoubtedly the foremost of the little group : for he excelled his comrades in gifts of speech and power of popular appeal. But it must be remembered that at that time Mr. Lloyd George was comparatively an unknown man. D. A. Thomas, on the other hand, was older and more experienced. As President of the South Wales Liberal Federation he was at the head of a strong and active organisation. He had been returned for the most populous constituency in Wales in 1892 by the record majority of 11,948. His large and increasing business interests made him a familiar figure in the famous valley from which he afterwards took his title, as well as in the city of Cardiff which he afterwards represented in Parliament. It is certain that in those days the name of D. A. Thomas counted for more in South Wales, which contains three-fourths of the people of the Principality, than that of the future Prime Minister.

The two masterful men were to drift apart for many years, only to be brought together again by the stress and crisis of the Great War. The rift began almost immediately after the Revolt. The South Wales Liberal Federation, at the instigation of the President, decided to send a deputation to Mr. Asquith to demand that the tithes should be paid into a central treasury and should be used for national and not for local purposes. This was fiercely opposed by Mr. Gee in the *Baner*, and by the North Wales members generally.

In January 1895 the National Liberal Federation held its Annual Meeting at Cardiff. Mr. Lloyd George, whose personal friendship with Tom Ellis, the Chief Whip, had not been impaired by the events of 1894, made his peace with the Government. D. A. Thomas was not so amenable. He did, however, attend the Federation meetings at Cardiff, and appeared on the platform with Lord Rosebery. In the course of his speech the Prime Minister definitely promised that Welsh Disestablishment would be the first measure of the coming session. But though this was a confession of surrender to the Welsh revolters, the adroit orator turned round dramatically to D. A. Thomas and with a magnificent gesture exclaimed : ' I am glad to see my friend Mr. D. A. Thomas on the platform. I enfold the returning prodigal in my arms.' No one enjoyed the jest or more admired the diplomacy of the great man than D. A. Thomas himself.

The Bill was introduced on February 25, 1895. On April 1 it passed its second reading by a majority of forty-five. When the Bill is compared with the miserable simulacrum which found its way last year on to the Statute Book, it will be found surprisingly good. But in those days the Welsh people made a real study of the question ; they had made many sacrifices for it ; some of them had suffered socially and financially for their adhesion to the principles of religious equality. They were far from being satisfied with the measure. A National Convention was held at Aberystwyth at the end of April to consider it, and in the light of recent events it is interesting to note in what directions it was sought to amend and strengthen the Bill. First, it was demanded that a National Council should be created to administer the funds, instead of the three Commissioners proposed by the Bill ; that lay tithes should be appropriated as well as clerical tithes ; that the tithes paid to English colleges should be applied to Welsh education ; that an equivalent sum to that expended out of public funds on parsonages should be refunded ; that the Church fabrics should be transferred to the parish councils, but that the Anglican Church should retain their use, provided they became responsible for their repair ; and that the disestablished clergy should only be entitled to two-thirds of the emoluments of the benefice during their lives.

When therefore the Bill entered the Committee stage on May 3, two at least of the Welsh members were prepared to fight. Mr. Lloyd George fathered the proposal to create a National Council, D. A. Thomas fought for a national allocation of tithes. When Mr. George moved his amendment, Mr. Asquith, who was in charge of the Bill, pleaded that he was taken by surprise and wanted time to consider the matter. The Tories, who saw a chance to defeat the Government on a vital measure, insisted on a division. Mr. George, ever wary, voted against his own amendment, which was, however, ultimately accepted by Mr. Asquith.

D. A. Thomas was not to be cajoled or frightened out of his proposal. The Welsh members, who have ever been a timid folk, had become so frightened that he could not get one of them to second his amendment. Sir Richard Temple, a fine old crusted Tory who probably hated the Welsh Bill more than any Liberal measure, seconded the amendment. All sorts of pressure was brought to bear on the intrepid Free Lance, but without avail ; the Government only escaped defeat by a majority of seven. Soon after, on August 11, the Government was defeated on the ' Cordite Vote.' Lord Rosebery resigned, and the Liberal party went into the cold shades of opposition for over ten years.

The action of the two Welsh members was bitterly assailed at the time and for years after. But it must be remembered that both of them wished to create an Independent Welsh Parliamentary Party. Both of them were disgusted with the invertebrate policy pursued by their colleagues.

Mr. Lloyd George used to say that his ambition was to become an influential independent member, and he had no hope ever of attaining office. D. A. Thomas was even more pronounced in his independent views than his colleague. He lacked the adroit suppleness of Mr. George. He could not suffer fools gladly. He foresaw only too clearly how degenerate a small party would become, if it was dependent on a Government which had honours and offices at its disposal. During the whole of his career in the House of Commons, D. A. Thomas clung to the same ideal. During his latter years he refused to attend the meetings of the Welsh Party, and though he continued to receive the Government Whip, it was more a matter of convenience than of allegiance. D. A. Thomas may well be termed the last of the eminent series of independent members.

THE MEMBER FOR MERTHYR

CHAPTER VII

POLITICAL LIFE (*continued*)

By Llewelyn Williams, K.C.

PROBABLY no subject has been the victim of so much misapprehension and misstatement as the story of the Cymru Fydd movement which convulsed Welsh politics from 1894 to 1897. It was not to be expected that aliens like Mr. Du Parck and Mr. Harold Spender could have mastered the intricacies of Welsh politics, but one might have supposed that Mr. Beriah Evans, the first and only paid organiser of that promising but unfortunate movement, would have been able to supply a fairly adequate and accurate account. Mr. Du Parck and Mr. Spender have told the story as, I suppose, it is reflected in the memory of Mr. Lloyd George : Mr. Beriah Evans has told it with the inaccuracy of a brilliant journalist. This is Mr. Spender's romantic narrative [1] :

' Mr. Lloyd George aspired to bring into Welsh politics some of the strength and hope of this new national rebirth. His definite aim, in the long series of great orations which he delivered on this subject between 1889 and 1896, was to bring patriotism to the help of Welsh politics in place of party. . . . A simple aim, it would seem. But no sooner did he set finger on the various political Arks that had been set up for worship in the different competing capitals of Wales [What does this mean ?], than he found himself faced with the fiercest hostility. Among his bitterest opponents was one of his own followers, Mr. D. A. Thomas (afterwards Lord Rhondda). Mr. Thomas set himself up as the champion of the South Wales Federation ; and he succeeded in maintaining the cause of local independence.

[1] *The Prime Minister*, pp. 108–109.

So tense and prolonged was the struggle that Mr. Lloyd George was content to achieve his purposes in another way, by way of a Welsh National Council.'

If this confused and jangling paragraph has any meaning at all, it must be taken to suggest that Mr. Lloyd George came out as a champion of Welsh Nationalism against the parochialism of D. A. Thomas. Not dissimilar is the view taken by Mr. Du Parck, the official biographer of Mr. Lloyd George.[1] Mr. Beriah Evans has none of the excuses which may be suggested for the Prime Minister's friendly biographers. He ascribes the Cymru Fydd movement to the patriotic enthusiasm of Mr. Lloyd George,[2] and goes on to say that 'Cymru Fydd Societies were established all over the Principality, Mr. Lloyd George and his colleagues acting as missioners of the new evangel, seeking converts, and incorporating associations everywhere.'

The real story of the Cymru Fydd movement is far different. Its origin had nothing to do with Mr. Lloyd George. Though naturally it did not eschew politics, its aim and purpose was not exclusively political. The first Society was formed in London in 1886, and a year or two later another was founded in Manchester. The first Society in Wales was established in Barry, near Cardiff, in 1891. In 1894 the movement spread throughout South Wales. A Society was formed in Cardiff in June of that year, and before the end of the year between thirty and forty Societies were formed in the populous centres of Glamorganshire, Monmouthshire and Carmarthenshire. The present writer constituted himself the honorary secretary of the South Wales branch of the movement, and on August 15 he published a pamphlet—dedicated by permission to Mr. Gladstone—explaining the aims and objects of the movement. Cymru Fydd, it was said, was 'Liberalism in Welsh costume.' It was not intended that it should supplant, but supplement, the work of the South Wales and the North Wales Liberal Federations. These were purely

---

[1] *Life of the Rt. Hon. D. Lloyd George*, vol. i. pp. 138–139.
[2] *Life Romance of Lloyd George*, pp. 68, 69, 70.

political bodies, which took no concern in Welsh literature, art, or local politics. The idea of the promoters of Cymru Fydd was similar to that of Thomas Davis, the finest and sanest of Irish patriots. ' Nationality,' said the Welsh-Irishman, ' is the summary name for many things. It seeks a literature made by Irishmen, and coloured by our scenery, manners, and character. It desires to see art applied to express Irish thoughts and beliefs. It would make our music sound in every parish at twilight, and our poetry and history sit at every hearth.' The tragedy of Irish history is rooted in the fact that for generations Irishmen devoted themselves exclusively to the political side of Irish Nationalism, and forgot the ideals of Thomas Davis and the Young Ireland of 1848. What horrors might that distressful country not have escaped if Thomas Davis' idea of making Nationalism commensurate with the whole national life had been steadfastly pursued ! It would have saved the Irish language from the perils which still encompass it ; it would have inevitably attracted the best and wisest men from every province ; it would have made unnecessary the old Fenianism and the modern Sinn Fein ; and it would have rescued the most brilliant nation in Europe from the terrors of extremism and reprisals.

It was the conviction of the promoters of Cymru Fydd that Wales was in danger of incurring a like fate. As has been pointed out, the people were engrossed in the fight for Disestablishment : exactly as Ireland concentrated on the demand for Home Rule. Political education and propaganda were at a standstill ; no active work was done by any Liberal organisation. The Liberal Federations met once or twice a year, passed resolutions, formulated policies, and that was all. The intentions of the promoters of Cymru Fydd were to supplement the useful and necessary work of the Federations by active work in every locality in Wales. Local elections were to be fought by Welsh Nationalists. Education was to be democratised and brought into consonance with the needs of the people and with the traditions of the country. Lectures were to be delivered on Welsh history and literature. The Welsh language was to be rescued from its position of servitude, and restored to its

ancient status of being the companion of the learned and
the instructress of the young. Such were the generous
dreams of Young Wales, and Cymru Fydd was the
organisation designed by them to carry out their ideals
into practice.

It was essential that the President of the South Wales
Liberal Federation should be convinced that the new movement was not in any sense inimical to the existing organisations. The present writer had several conferences with
D. A. Thomas, with the result that it was arranged that the
Federation President should take the Chair at the meeting
which had been convened for August 15 at Neath to establish a Cymru Fydd League for South Wales. Unfortunately
D. A. Thomas was at the last moment unable to attend.
The Eight Hours Bill was before the House, and as ill-luck
would have it, on that very day an important amendment
by the senior Member for Merthyr came on for discussion.
He telegraphed to express his great regret at his inability
to be present, with his best wishes for the success of the new
movement, and his place in the Chair was filled by Mr.
Alfred Thomas, now Lord Pontypridd. From this accident
flowed much tribulation in the future, and it may truly be
said that D. A. Thomas' political career was untowardly
affected and the whole course of Welsh politics changed
for the worse. Had he been able to be present, he would
have been recognised as the head of the Cymru Fydd movement, he would in all probability have been appointed its
President, the unhappy controversy between the old and
the new organisations would have been avoided, and Wales
would have been saved from the political sterility of the
loud-sounding Welsh National Liberal Federation.

Meanwhile some Cymru Fydd Societies had been formed
in North Wales, and Mr. R. A. Griffith, then of Bangor, now
the stipendiary magistrate at Merthyr, was the provisional
secretary. It was arranged that a joint meeting of the
North and South Wales Leagues should be held at Lan-
drindod on August 23, in order to frame a constitution for
a National Cymru Fydd League. The date was fixed a day
before the joint meeting of the North and South Wales
Federations to discuss the moot question of Disestablish-

ment at the same place. Again, unfortunately, D. A. Thomas was unable to attend the Cymru Fydd gathering : again his place was taken by Mr. Alfred Thomas ; but Mrs. D. A. Thomas was present, and took part in the protracted discussion. It was made clear that the new organisation was not designed to supplant the old. Indeed, among those present were not only the wife of the President of the South Wales Liberal Federation, but Thomas Williams, Gwaelody-garth, the Chairman of the Federation Committee, David Morgan, the eloquent miner's agent, ' Dai Abernant,' who was one of D. A. Thomas' warmest and most loyal supporters, and most of the members of the Federation's Executive. There was at the time no thought of antag-onism between the two organisations. At the end of August a branch of the Cymru Fydd League was formed at Merthyr under the chairmanship of the Rev. John Thomas, Soar. Throughout the autumn the new League continued its activities. There was hardly a populous centre in South Wales which was left unvisited. Mr. Lloyd George addressed meetings, with the provisional secretary, at Neath, Cwmavon, Swansea, and elsewhere. Sir George Osborne Morgan took part in the formation of a branch at Brymbo. Mr. Lloyd George and Mr. Herbert Lewis helped the North Wales Secretary to start a score of branches in North Wales. Over a thousand members belonged to the Swansea branch. Over 10,000 subscrip tions were received from South Wales. It was decided to appoint a paid secretary for South Wales at a salary of £200 a year. By the end of the year sufficient funds to guarantee the salary for 2½ years had been collected, and Mr. Beriah Evans, the editor of the *Genedl*, Mr. George's organ at Carnarvon, was appointed.

Still matters proceeded amicably. Mr. R. N. Hall, the secretary of the South Wales Liberal Federation, attended some of the meetings of Cymru Fydd and extended his blessings to its efforts. But it became apparent, as time went on, that there was not sufficient room for two organi-sations, both largely consisting of the same men, and supported by the same body of politicians. Accordingly a Conference was held at Cardiff on January 4, 1895,

of representatives of the South Wales Liberal Federation
and the Cymru Fydd League, with a view to effecting an
amalgamation of the two organisations. Mr. Wynford
Philipps (now Viscount St. Davids) took the Chair, and
among those present were (to quote the official report) :

‘ Mr. D. A. Thomas, M.P., Mr. Alfred Thomas, M.P.,
Mabon, M.P., Principal Edwards, Cardiff, Mr. Isaac Evans
(miners' agent), Neath, the Rev. Tydu James, Mr. D. Davies,
Glebeland, Merthyr, Miss Kate Jenkins, Llangadock, Miss
Elsie Jenkins, Cardiff, Mrs. Viriamu Jones, Alderman
Aaron Davies, Mr. Robert Bird, Cardiff, Mr. D. Morgan,
miners' agent, Councillor E. Thomas (" Cochfarf"), Mr.
William Brace (miners' agent), the Rev. Towyn Jones, the
Rev. J. Morgan Jones, Cardiff, Mr. W. Griffith, Aberyst-
wyth, Mr. Llewelyn Williams, Cardiff, Mr. R. N. Hall,
secretary of the South Wales Liberal Federation, and Mr.
Beriah Evans, organising secretary of the Cymru Fydd
League.'

Already it had been determined to amalgamate the
North Wales Liberal Federation with the League. Principal Edwards proposed the first Resolution taken from
the programme of the North Wales Conference, ‘ That in
the opinion of this Conference it is desirable that there
should be one national political organisation instead of
two.'

‘ Mr. D. A. Thomas, M.P., seconded the Motion, and
congratulated the meeting on the spirit which had already
been evinced. For purposes of organisation, quite apart
from the question of policy, it was absolutely necessary
not to have more than one body. The idea which prevailed
at the Chester Conference was that Cymru Fydd should be a
body supplementary to, and not a rival of, the Federation,
but as now the apparent objects of both were identical, all
agreed that one organisation for purposes of policy was
equally desirable. The organisation should meet beforehand to dictate the policy of the whole of Wales. As
regarded the question of organisation, difficulties of distance
and the inconvenience of railway communication would
seriously militate against effective work. It had been their

experience at executive meetings that they were not properly representative of the more remote counties for the reasons he had given.'

Mr. Llewelyn Williams explained the motives of the promoters of the Cymru Fydd League. He agreed with D. A. Thomas that one organisation for the purpose of policy was absolutely necessary. The Resolution was unanimously passed, and it was further determined that the name of the new organisation should be the Cymru Fydd National Federation. The greatest harmony prevailed at the meeting, which was representative of all sections of South Wales Liberals. It appeared as if all difficulties had been removed, and that an amalgamation of the two organisations had been secured. The pressing necessity of the hour was to secure absolute union with regard to the policy to be pursued on the Disestablishment Bill, which was about to be introduced. The Cymru Fydd delegates, in their anxiety to have Wales speaking with a united voice, surrendered their own opinions as to organisation : while the Federationists, equally concerned for the Welsh Bill, agreed to espouse the name and policy of the League. The English National Liberal Federation was to meet in Cardiff within a few weeks, Lord Rosebery, the Prime Minister, was to be present, and so it was decided to close the Welsh ranks and to speak with one voice lest the Prime Minister might prove recalcitrant.

Such being the plain facts of the story, it is idle to speak of Mr. Lloyd George as the inspirer and founder of the Cymru Fydd movement, and of D. A. Thomas as the enemy of Welsh Nationalism. Neither had anything to do with the inception of the movement. D. A. Thomas, up to January 1895, regarded it with favour ; and Mr. Lloyd George accorded to it his good wishes. What happened afterwards, and the reasons for it, cannot at present be told in detail. Perhaps Mr. Beriah Evans, in his posthumous papers, may throw some light on the lamentable events which destroyed the brightest hopes of Welsh Nationalism. Suffice it to say here that by April 1895 D. A. Thomas, who had agreed to amalgamation in January, was not only suspicious but indignant. He fought hard and he fought well against amalgamation or fusion. An excited meeting of the South Wales Liberal Federation was held at Newport in April. Mr. Lloyd George, who suddenly appeared as the champion of Cymru Fydd, attended as a delegate appointed by a South Wales constituency. He was refused permission to speak, but he harangued a crowded meeting in the streets. An indiscreet member of the Federation had publicly stated that there were thousands of ' cosmopolitans ' in South Wales who would never allow Welsh ideas to dominate. The words were used for years to discredit the Federation by Welsh Nationalists, *quorum pars parva fui.*

D. A. Thomas was able to hold his own for years, but at last, in 1897, the South Wales Liberal Federation came to an end. Perhaps the last word that can usefully be said, for the present, on this pitiful dispute has been said by Mr. Beriah Evans (' Lloyd George,' p. 72) :

' Thanks entirely to the predominant personal influence of Mr. D. A. Thomas the attack upon South Wales failed. It should, perhaps, in justice to Mr. D. A. Thomas, be here stated that he was at least as ardent a Nationalist as Mr. Lloyd George himself, and even more emphatic and persistent in his demand that the Welsh Members should form themselves into an Independent Party on Irish lines. His objection to the Cymru Fydd proposals was based on the method of organisation rather than on the principles underlying the movement. His main objection was based on the alleged fact that the geographical divisions of Wales made one central authority in more or less frequent session for the whole Principality practically unworkable. A sort of compromise was later attempted, establishing four Provincial Federations centred in one National Council, but it proved abortive. Cymru Fydd Societies continued in various localities for a time, but ultimately disappeared. The present party organisation in Wales, under the name of the " Welsh National Liberal Council," is a pitiful parody of Mr. Lloyd George's " Cymru Fydd " ideal, and is sometimes regarded as a mere machine whereby Mr. Lloyd George may, through its nominative head, Lord St. Davids, impose his will upon Welsh constituencies.'

On looking back and considering the whole matter, may it not be that, even in 1895, D. A. Thomas foresaw the danger which Mr. Beriah Evans notes in his concluding paragraph, and that he did what he could to prevent the Cymru Fydd ideal culminating in a Lloyd George dictatorship ?

The two Welsh leaders were not brought together again in political alliance until Mr. Lloyd George, as Prime Minister, in 1916 called in to the aid of his administration some of the foremost business men in the country. Until then, D. A. Thomas stood apart from the future Prime Minister. Not even the similarity of their views on the Boer War sufficed to bring them together. Like Mr. George, D. A. Thomas looked upon the war as unjust and unnecessary. Unlike Mr. George, he distrusted and disliked Chamberlain. He was a loyal follower of ' C.-B.' The famous ' methods of barbarism ' speech did not cool the ardour of his allegiance. When Lord Rosebery, Mr. Asquith, and Sir Edward Grey started the Liberal Imperialist League, and proclaimed ' war to the knife and fork ' against the elected Liberal leader, D. A. Thomas was outspoken and emphatic in his condemnation of what he wittily described as ' the New Primrose League.' But he played a lone hand. He made no fresh alliance with his old fellow-revolter, but was content to plough his lonely furrow. If war, as is sometimes said, supplies the acid test to Liberalism, D. A. Thomas emerged from the fiery ordeal of the Boer War with his Radicalism unscathed, strengthened, and purified.

D. A. Thomas never considered himself a ' follower ' of Mr. Lloyd George. He was the older man and the senior Parliamentarian of the two. Nor was he ever, in the words of Mr. Beriah Evans, Mr. George's ' bosom friend.' They had been brought together by the ' Welsh Revolt,' and the two fearless fighters grew to recognise and admire each other's qualities. But, except for this adventure, they were never really comrades-in-arms. Mr. Lloyd George refused to support his ' fellow-rebels' ' amendment to the Disestablishment Bill, and the Cymru Fydd controversy forced them definitely apart. When the next Welsh Revolt occurred, over the Education Act of 1902, the two were found in opposite camps. On January 17, 1903, Mr. Lloyd George issued a manifesto to the people of Wales urging them, through their representatives on the County Councils, to refuse to administer the Act except in a grudging and niggardly way. It would be tedious to go into much detail over the matter, but it is essential to a right judgment of D. A. Thomas's conduct to remember what the 'Welsh Revolt' policy was. Mr. George enjoined his countrymen to give 'the ecclesiastical Shylock' his pound of flesh, and no more. Mr. Du Parck has summarised the policy in a few clear sentences.

'His plan, as he now propounded it, was one which he summarised later in the phrase " no control, no cash." He advised that only the Parliamentary grant should be transmitted to the (voluntary) schools, and that no rate aid should be afforded them, unless the trustees consented to public control of the funds voted and to the abandonment of all religious tests for the teachers engaged.'

'At first sight,' says the enthusiastic panegyrist, 'Mr. Lloyd George's advice to refuse rate aid looked like flat rebellion. But he was able to justify even that part of his plan according to the letter of the law which no one had studied more carefully than himself. His scheme was as ingenious as it was daring.'

Almost every County Council in Wales accepted Mr. Lloyd George's advice. Nearly every Welsh Member followed in his wake. But D. A. Thomas assailed the plan with withering scorn and mockery. Mr. Lloyd Morgan for a time rescued Carmarthenshire; Mr. Bryn Roberts protested in Carnarvonshire. The secretary and organiser of the 'Revolt' was Mr. (now Sir) Thomas Hughes, then a solicitor at Bridgend. This gave D. A. Thomas his opportunity to dub the plan as 'the Bridgend policy,' alluding of course to the fact that the County Asylum is situated at Bridgend. That D. A. Thomas was right was attested by every event that followed. The whole of Wales was thrown into unrest and confusion until the General Election of 1906. In 1904 the Board of Education sent Mr. A. T. Lawrence, K.C. (now the Lord Chief Justice of England), as Commissioner

to inquire into the conduct of the Carmarthenshire County
Council. He found that their proceedings were altogether
illegal, and the Council had to submit. In 1906 the Barry
Urban District Council were sued in the County Court for
salaries which they had, on the plan of the ' Welsh Revolt,'
refused to pay to teachers in the Roman Catholic School.
Judgment was given against the Council, and their counsel,
Mr. (afterwards Sir) S. T. Evans, refused to advise an appeal.
Still later the Swansea Corporation, which had proceeded
most warily, was adjudged to be in the wrong by the Court
of Appeal. The Welsh Education Revolt began and ended
in a fiasco. At one time it almost looked as if Sir William
Anson, Parliamentary Secretary to the Board of Education,
would accede to the ultimate demand which was made in
order to hide the discomfiture of the ' revolters ' that a
Welsh National Council should be created to administer
Welsh elementary education. The Board of Education,
weary of strife, was willing enough ; but the opposition of
the Carmarthenshire Council, backed up by the clear-sighted
hostility of D. A. Thomas and two or three other Welsh
Members, brought the proposal to naught. An attempt
was made in Part IV of the Education Bill of 1906 to
establish by Act of Parliament the Welsh Council. No
one who heard Mr. Balfour's deadly speech, or who reads it
in Hansard, or the late Lord Cawdor's caustic criticisms
in the House of Lords of the absurd and ill-digested proposal, will have any doubt that D. A. Thomas was right in
castigating the scheme as ' the Bridgend policy.' It is,
perhaps, worth mentioning that nothing has ever been
done by Parliament to redress the grievances of Non-
conformists under the 1902 Act, that the policy of the
' Welsh Revolt ' has either been forgotten or repudiated
by its promoters since they have achieved supreme power
in the realm, and that the candid and impartial historian
must award the palm to the few public men in Wales who,
like D. A. Thomas, faced obloquy and misrepresentation
because they saw and pronounced that the ' Welsh Revolt '
was founded on illegality and unreason. Thousands of
pounds were collected to assist a chimerical scheme, and
that money is still locked in some bank safes, awaiting the

time when the Courts of Justice will be willing to apply the *cy-près* doctrine to the ' Bridgend policy.'

In the summer of 1903 Joseph Chamberlain, fresh from his reveries on the illimitable veldt, and his contact with the hard-faced millionaires of the ' Golden City,' launched a bolt from the blue, by advocating a policy of Protection, disguised as Tariff Reform. In the autumn of the same year Mr. Balfour, the Prime Minister, executed a characteristic manœuvre by excluding from his Cabinet the chief protagonists of both Free Trade and Tariff Reform. The country became embroiled in a controversy which was thought to have been settled for good and all two generations before. D. A. Thomas seized the opportunity and became one of the foremost and weightiest advocates of Free Trade. His unique position in the coal trade, his clear, logical, and well-trained mind, his business instincts, and his keen perception of realities, made him an ideal champion of a cause which he espoused probably with more conviction and enthusiasm than he had ever felt for any other public question. The last time I saw him, a few weeks before he was seized with his last illness, he said that all his experiences during the Great War had convinced him more than ever that not only our industrial prosperity but the status of Great Britain as a first-class Power was absolutely dependent on our maintaining our system of Free Trade.

But though a stalwart and unflinching Free Trader, D. A. Thomas never lost his sense of proportion. His advocacy was always sane and businesslike, for he was the last man who would develop into a crank. He was in no sense a doctrinaire, and to him certainly Free Trade was not a shibboleth but a plain business proposition. Soon after the fiscal controversy had started in 1903 Mr. Harold Cox edited a volume entitled ' British Industries under Free Trade,' and to it D. A. Thomas contributed an article on ' The Coal Trade.' It is a model of its kind. It only covers twenty-eight pages, and cannot therefore be presumed to be a complete exposition of the subject. But it is a balanced and considered judgment of an expert on a matter of national importance, and it can be still read with interest and with advantage. ' Few British industries, if any,' says the writer, ' have made greater strides during the past fifty years than has that of the production of coal, and probably no one of our leading industries has derived so much help from the adoption by this country of a Free Trade policy. But how much of the progress has been due to our fiscal system, and how much should be attributed to other stimulating causes, it is difficult, if not impossible, to determine with any approach to precision.' It is in this calm and detached spirit that the writer proceeds :

' Let me say frankly that in my opinion natural forces, such as (1) the possession of abundant supplies of raw material, and more especially easy access to cheap fuel, (2) climate, and (3) geographical position, exercise an immeasurably greater influence on the prosperity or otherwise of a country and on its foreign trade than any fiscal policy which man may vainly devise. All that Free Traders may fairly claim is that the system they advocate enables the country that adopts it to make from the economic point of view the best of its position, to emphasise any natural advantages it may possess, and to modify the effect of disadvantages. When Free Traders go beyond this and attribute the prosperity and progress which Great Britain has enjoyed during recent years entirely to our fiscal system, they unnecessarily lay themselves open to attack, and thereby weaken their case.'

Another eminent South Wales business man, the late Lord Glantawe, took the same view. He summarised the argument in an epigram : ' You can grow grapes on Snowdon, if you are prepared to pay the cost.' D. A. Thomas always emphasised that, whatever might be the case with other countries, to Great Britain Free Trade was essential because it enabled it to use to the full the natural advantages that it possessed.

But if fiscal policy was a subordinate matter, why make such a pother about it ? D. A. Thomas gave the answer, at once shrewd, penetrating, and even profound :

' The importance given to it in economic discussion arises from the fact that it is practically the only influence we can control. We can modify geographical conditions to

G

a small extent by improved communication, but we cannot change the relative position of the United States, Canada, and the Mother Country any more than we can produce coal in Ireland, Sweden, or Italy. A Protectionist tariff is an attempt to forge weapons to fight conditions imposed by nature.'

In his opinion cheap fuel was the most powerful factor in industrial progress. His remarks on the subject are well worthy of careful consideration in these latter days. Even in those days America was our most formidable competitor in the world's markets. The ' Dumping Bogey,' he confessed, had no terrors for him, so that it is fairly certain what his views on such measures as the Safeguarding of Industries would have been. But he was seriously alarmed about the competition with America, mainly because ' the average price of bituminous coal had fallen in the States to half of what it was thirty years ago.' The vital importance of cheap coal lay in the fact that ' coal enters into the production of every manufactured article. Coal is the finished article of the most important industries in the kingdom.' The British people were the carriers of the world, largely because of British coal.

' Protection would spell ruin and devastation to South Wales, Northumberland, and Durham and other coal-exporting districts, involving directly the livelihood of a million people and indirectly the welfare of as many more.'

The statistics with which he exemplified his arguments are out of date : but it would not be amiss if they were revised and the articles were re-issued in these days when the fiscal problem is once more fluttering the political dovecotes. For never was the case for Free Trade more clearly or more convincingly put. The article was clear because the writer possessed a singularly lucid mind ; it was convincing because it sprang out of the writer's genuine conviction.

One of the few mistakes that Campbell-Bannerman made in the formation of his Government in December 1905 was to ignore the great services of D. A. Thomas to Free Trade and his capacity for still greater services to Liberalism in the future by passing over his undoubted claim to responsible office under the Crown. There can be little doubt that D. A. Thomas himself was happier without the trammels of office, where, at least for a time, he would have to play a subordinate part. But what the country lost was made manifest when the testing time of the Great War gave him the opportunity of showing what unique powers of administration he possessed.

CHAPTER VIII

LLANWERN AND CARDIFF

.　　.　　.　　.　　.　　.

When from the hills of Gwent I saw the earth
Burned into two by Severn's silver flood :

Can I forget the sweet days that have been,
The villages so green I have been in ;
Llantarnam, Magor, Malpas and Llanwern,
Liswery, old Caerleon, and Alteryn ?

William H. Davies.

IF the outside of Llanwern suggested solid English comfort it must be admitted that the inside arrangements
scarcely justified that promise. My mother loves and
understands gardens and old furniture : she has never
loved housekeeping. The garden in its untidy luxuriant
way was charming—a fascinating wilderness to which year
by year a new bit would be added. The house, also untidy,
was filled to the brim with nice old china and furniture.
In parts it resembled an old curiosity shop rather than
a private dwelling : nevertheless it was very pleasant to
look at.

So far as household arrangements were concerned
Llanwern lacked only one thing—physical comfort. It was
a house full of happiness, but it was frankly not a comfortable house.

Meals seldom appeared on the table within half an hour
of the time they were ostensibly due. The bath water was
frequently cold, in winter the fires often failed to warm
the large rooms. Domestic crises of all kinds were re-
current, and after the manner of their kind usually happened at the most awkward moments. Outside my father's
study there was only one really comfortable chair in the

HIS WIFE

house : the chair he used when he sat in the drawing-room in the evenings. From April to October it was the custom, wet, fine or frost, to serve meals in the loggia outside.

My mother has never learnt the meaning of the word comfort. There is a certain Spartan puritanism about her which causes her to despise and perhaps fear its insidious softness. She has a horror of depending on material things. On one occasion she gave up drinking hot water at night because she suspected herself of developing a ' craving ' for it. My own belief is that she really prefers discomfort : she likes hard chairs and unpunctual meals and fires that won't burn and water that won't heat.

It might be supposed that with these rather obvious drawbacks Llanwern would not be much sought out by visitors : it was, on the contrary, most popular. The house was seldom empty of guests, and at Christmas, Easter, Whitsuntide and in September it was usually full, though there certainly was one lady who always used to refuse to visit us in winter for fear of being frozen, and we were perhaps more generally popular during the summer months. I have always supposed that our attraction lay partly in the cheery atmosphere of the house, partly in the fact that no one ever interfered with the visitors ; they were allowed complete freedom of action, and were seldom if ever ' entertained.' Certainly the policy of non-interference was carried farther than is at all usual, and I well remember one terrible occasion when at the age of fourteen I was left to feel responsible for a houseful of guests, my mother having placidly departed to town. It was a further source of anxiety to me on this occasion that at dinner that night there was not nearly enough fish to go round. That our guests were for the most part relations and for the rest usually old friends made it easier to treat them without ceremony.

How did my father fit into this establishment ? The lack of ceremony suited him admirably, the lack of comfort was less to his taste. He was, however, always perfectly aware of the limitations of human nature, and he well knew that it is given to no man to alter seriously his wife's conceptions of housekeeping. He was too wise to make an attempt which could only have troubled both himself and my mother : he might, and did, prize physical comfort (though he prized it less than do many men), but he prized mental and spiritual comfort much more. How to achieve physical comfort for himself without interfering in the general household arrangements, how to keep a track of comfort and order for himself in the midst of the general disorder, was a problem which it took him some years to master, but in the end he solved it pretty satisfactorily.

His breakfast, which he usually ate, and indeed preferred to eat, alone, was the one punctual meal of the day. It was served at ten minutes to nine. It was a taciturn meal with him ; he was busy considering his letters and the papers and hurriedly getting through his food. Guests were not encouraged to breakfast with him, but some people are not easily warned off, and I remember one young man of whom he later confided to my mother, ' If I'd had a revolver I believe I should have shot him.' There was another, who, watching him eat some unusually unattractive patent food (doubtless the fad of the moment), inquired by way of making conversation, ' Do you really *want* to eat that, Mr. Thomas ? ' My father regarded him gravely over his eye-glasses. ' Do you suppose I should eat it if I didn't ? ' he replied. Conversation lapsed.

At nine o'clock he would hurry off to the waiting carriage, catch the 9.13 at Llanwern, and reach Cardiff just before ten o'clock. With very slight alterations as to time that was his morning programme for thirty years. He usually caught the 5.32 back from Cardiff to Newport, and drove, or more often walked, home from that station, some four and a half miles distant. On Saturdays he caught an early afternoon train home. That, up to within a couple of years of the end, was his invariable routine when at Llanwern. If ever a man enjoyed his work he did. He never wanted to stay away from Cardiff. ' David is like a pit horse,' said one of my mother's cousins ; ' if you stopped him working he wouldn't know what to do.'

The train stopped at Newport station on its way to Cardiff, and he had a standing order at the bookstall for most of the daily papers. Between Newport and Cardiff he would glance at practically every one of them. He said that to look at dailies of every shade of politics was one of the best ways of keeping in touch with public opinion. He used to buy most of the weeklies too, and treated them in much the same fashion as the dailies, except the *Economist,* which he read through.

Once inside his office at Cardiff he seemed a different person ; not that *he* changed, it was merely the attitude towards him which did that. For himself he was just the same simple person enjoying every minute of his time with a keenness which made work with him a pleasure. It is always more interesting to see a person at work than at play, and to watch him concentrating on anything was a joy—it gave new meaning to the word. His comfortable airy room, with its panelled walls, thick carpet, huge desk, comfortable chairs, and large open fire-place in which in winter burnt a bright fire and which in summer was by his order kept filled with plants by the local florist, was an easy one to work or talk in : the same atmosphere of competent peace seemed to pervade it that did his room at Llanwern, though it was considerably tidier. He was very proud of this room, which he had had designed according to his special taste when the Cambrian Buildings were put up. It was a very pleasant room and for an office pleasing to the eye. In some things his taste was good ; so far as furniture and fittings were concerned, however, I should say it was much that of the average man.

When he arrived he began by attending to his letters, usually dictating them himself. I have spoken of the care with which he phrased his letters and the pain and grief it was to draft one for him. This was a pain shared by many, for my father was no respecter of persons and corrected with equal vigour every letter that went out under his name, however qualified the draftsman might be. There was one young man, a friend of his, whose business it was at one time to draft his letters, who could, and occasionally did, retort on him when corrected : ' Well, considering I took a first in Literature and you only took a second in Mathematics I *ought* to know best.' My father chuckled, but continued his corrections unmoved.

After he had finished his letters—and he had a way (most trying to his secretary) of answering all sorts of queer letters from unimportant people at great length, if they happened to interest him—his time was taken up in seeing people—colliery managers, general managers, company secretaries, sales-agents, men who wanted to do a deal with him, brokers, solicitors, coal exporters, labour men, political friends, press men, old colliers from the hills, business associates. There was usually a group waiting outside in the secretary's room, all anxious to catch him next. If he liked a man he was apt to get interested in his talk with him and keep him chatting there for three-quarters of an hour or more, to the furious impatience of the men next on the list, convinced that their affairs were of infinitely greater importance, and that D. A. himself really thought so. I don't doubt he had given each of them that impression—he was very Welsh, and was usually on the best and most intimate terms with every one who frequented his office.

He had a theory, which no doubt accounted for the length of some of the interviews, that if you saw a person at all you should let him talk himself out, and not let him go with a feeling that he had been dismissed before he had said all he had to say. He declared it doubled the value of the interview, and you might as well do it thoroughly if you were going to do it at all. One used to wonder sometimes how he had the patience.

There were certain people closely associated with him whom he made a point of seeing once or twice a week, if not oftener. Amongst these were several press men. He was always in close touch with the press, and his methods were very successful. ' I shouldn't wonder if that were to leak out,' he would say with a twinkle about something which he wanted to have put in the papers, and leak out it invariably did.

He had certain rules. He never kept a man waiting without a reason ; it was a form of bluff or swank which he disliked. He never stood on his dignity as to whether he should go to the other man or the other man come to him. If there was any difficulty about it he went to the other.

This was done on principle, and it was one of the first pieces of advice which he gave me when I went into business that I should always do likewise.

He was always interested in new patents, spent a considerable time in investigating them, and often took them up. Patent fuel processes, improved coal washeries, new methods of mending motor tyres, patent processes of making paint, roof tiles, new methods of using clay, by-products schemes of all sorts. . . . These are just a few instances which occur to me. Very few attained any great measure of success, but he never supposed that many would ; they were his luxury, and he looked on them as a peculiarly attractive form of gamble. For years the flat roof of the Cambrian offices was covered with a number of wire-netting cages in which patent fuel made according to a new process was weathering. My father would go up once a fortnight or so to have a look at it and see how it stood the test.

It used to interest me that as his income grew the greater part of it always went in one way or another to the financing of fresh ventures. The idea of spending much of it on himself in the ordinary sense of the word never occurred to him, nor indeed to my mother, who was naturally economical, and though she was automatically supplied with all she required, and was perfectly well aware of the small proportion her expenditure bore to the whole (for he took some trouble to explain his financial position to her), would not have dreamed of increasing it. I have sometimes wondered what would have happened if he had married an extravagant wife.

When he got back to Llanwern in the evening he would lie down on his bed and go to sleep for an hour.

After that he, like the rest of the household, might have to wait anything from twenty to forty minutes for dinner— but he usually accepted this with perfect good temper. He always accepted the inevitable gracefully.

Every servant in the house was devoted to him, from Moore the parlourmaid (he never would have a man-servant in the house, he thought they savoured of ostentation), whose first preoccupation was with his comfort and well-being, and who acted as his most faithful valet, to Black-more, the old chauffeur, whom he alone could manage, and of whom everyone else was slightly afraid. As one of his nieces remarked, ' Blackmore thinks the sun sets in Uncle David's pocket.'

He spent most of his indoor time in his own study. It was a big, pleasant, book-lined room, into which, in later years at least, no one was allowed without his tacit or expressed permission, but from which my mother and I were seldom, if ever, excluded. Once inside it the whole atmosphere seemed changed ; it was a sanctum of warmth and peace and comfort in the midst of that draughty, haphazard house. Not that it was actually tidy ; the desk and sofa were littered and piled high with masses of papers. (He always declared that he was naturally a tidy man : ' If it weren't for your mother ' ; but I am bound to admit that this characteristic showed neither in his person nor in his methods with papers. His coat tails always bulged with masses of papers. I once, at his request, sorted out the contents of one and found in it the refuse of months. Everything from important letters and papers down to prescriptions for pills. He was not quite pleased when I chaffed him about it.) His fire always burnt beautifully— he did not fancy my mother's taste in coal, and insisted on a special brand of his own for his own fire. He had really comfortable chairs. When he was at home he spent almost all his time in this room, reading and writing there late into the night, playing bridge with two other carefully selected partners for dinner, selected for their personal rather than for their bridge-playing qualities. His bridge, which he learnt late in life, was entirely his own game, and a true bridge player would scarcely have called it ' bridge.' He had never read a bridge book in his life, and knew scarcely any of the conventions. He would never play four-handed. Cut-throat auction was the only thing that amused him. He usually won ; his play was not good, but then neither was ours, and he had considerable luck and was a first-class bluffer. When he won he was full of glee : ' By Jove ! have I really won all that ? ' he would say. If by chance he started losing he would keep one up till all hours of the night in the hope his luck would turn. He preferred to play for money (though this always shocked my mother) and he usually did—2s. 6d. a hundred. When, as often happened, the other players were badly off, and he was sufficiently well acquainted with them, which he usually was, he would present them with £5 to play with at the beginning of their visit—he almost always won it all back before they left.

At other times he would get one in there to talk business, politics, theories of life of all sorts. I think there was nothing in heaven or earth that we did not discuss together. He was easy to talk to even when one was a child, because he always spoke as if he were talking to an equal and gave one's opinion full weight.

Often when we were alone in the evenings he would sit and write or read in his room and would get my mother to play to him ; he always declared that nothing helped him so much, particularly in composing a speech, as her playing. Or in summer he would walk up and down outside from gate to gate (and he always had to touch the gate each time), discoursing of the day's doings and successes, or discussing life in general.

If the physical aspects of the house left something to be desired, it was mentally and spiritually all that could be asked for. He and his wife lived happily together all their days. I should doubt if they ever had a serious quarrel in their lives.

He preferred women to men as guests, his main contention being that if women were asked my mother was responsible for entertaining them, whereas in the case of men it was almost impossible for him to escape altogether from his duties as host. I am bound to say that in later years he did escape to an almost unbelievable extent ; the men's smoking-room was no longer his library as it had been originally, so that he saw nothing of them in the evening unless he chose—and unless they were business or political associates he practically never did choose—and as latterly he neither drank nor smoked he would very often leave them in the dining-room after dinner at the same time as we did.

He also said that at home he preferred the society of women to men : ' I am talking to men all day in the office, and when I get home I like a change.' The fact of the matter was, of course, that what he needed in his moments of recreation was a good listener, a rôle vastly more often played by women than by men.

If he had an intelligent and appreciative listener he could and would talk by the hour, but his saving grace was that he differed from many men of his age in that he would never talk unless the listener was honestly interested. He recognised boredom in a moment and had the kind of sensitiveness that cannot endure the thought of boring a person. It may sound queer that he did not bore, particularly as he did frankly talk a great deal about himself, but he was in fact as entertaining a companion as one would wish to meet. He avoided the people who would have been bored, but, for anyone, there was a savour of wit about his talk that saved it ; moreover, he never set himself up on a pedestal, and if his talk was at times egotistical he was himself perfectly aware of it, and indeed the first to admit it. ' I've been boasting for the last hour. X—— always makes me talk about myself,' he would say, and X—— naturally felt pleased to think that she had so successfully performed her *métier de femme*. If she were a really innocent woman she was possibly even flattered into believing that she was singular, and alone had the peculiar effect he referred to. I have met not a few outstanding men and have found that practically every one of them, certainly when over the age of fifty, talked egotistically. I don't know why they should not, they are after all as interesting a subject of conversation as one could find, but I have sometimes felt that it would be refreshing if like my father they showed themselves aware of what they were doing.

Nor was one ever expected to keep up an attitude of open-mouthed admiration—he could stand both chaff and criticism. For this some credit was due to my mother, who had always firmly refused to take up the correct wifely ' You must be right, dear,' attitude of her generation. He was never spoilt or allowed to suppose that he was a little tin god at home. She had the Puritan horror of spoiling or praising ; she never praised unless she meant it, and not always then, and so far as in her lay she tried to judge impartially even those nearest to her. He remarked to her one morning whilst shaving (he was at the Food Ministry at the time), ' If only I had a good memory I believe I should be a very clever man.' ' Perhaps you would, darling,' replied my mother gently but slightly doubtfully. He retailed the conversation at breakfast, and I always remembered it, it was so typical of them both.

It gave me a curious shock of surprise after seeing him treated ordinarily at home (sometimes like a beloved and charming but rather spoilt schoolboy) to go for the first time into the Cardiff office and hear his very name uttered with awe, not only by his own staff but by all with whom one came in contact. It was rather more than one usually meets in an office, the respect given to honest power and outstanding personality, a respect strongly tinged with affection. It made me conscious of a power I had not before been aware of. He put on so few frills, there was never a man so free from all pomposity or false dignity, though he had a certain natural personal dignity which was rather strong. I cannot imagine that any one would ever have taken a liberty with him.

There were few things that happened during the course of his business career that he did not discuss fully and freely at home. He had in later years three main themes of conversation—business, politics and cattle. His herd of pedigree Hereford cattle, which he started in 1900, was a source of perpetual interest and pleasure to him. He gradually worked it up with the help of his bailiff Trotman, and before the end it was said to be one of the best herds in Europe.

Personally I always steered him into politics if I could, and, failing that, business. Pedigree Herefords, even when taken as illustrations of the Mendelian theory (he was greatly interested in heredity, his cattle had turned his attention to the question), were occasionally boring as a subject of conversation. But even on cattle he was a delightful conversationalist ; his own vivid personality and aliveness seemed to light up any subject he discussed.

He loved walking : we would go for long tramps across the fields or through the muddy Monmouthshire lanes, talking . . . talking . . . talking. . . .

I remember one beautiful spring Sunday the year before he died being lured out in my high-heeled indoor shoes (he hated waiting whilst one changed) on the plea that we would only go as far as the first gate in the park ; and then, of course, he wanted to go on, and we wandered along slowly (he had just been to a heart specialist and been told he must not walk fast) past the best of the Herefords and on along the top of the wood where the herons' nests were and stopped to watch and listen (he loved the heronry), and then in a field we came across the entrance to one of those green disused old sunken lanes of which one finds so many in our part of the world. In this he was immensely interested : he theorised about it. It must, he said, have led up to Pencoed Castle a mile or so away, and if so that made three disused lanes that had once led there. He reconstructed things as they must have been three hundred years ago or more, and made one see a vivid picture of life as he pictured it in those old days. He insisted on following down the brambly lane to see what village it started from ; it wound round the hill for a couple of miles or more and finally emerged, much to his satisfaction, in the very village he expected. From there we strolled home at sunset with the rooks cawing round their nests.

I remember another time we went out, this time on bicycles, to see the May in flower down on the flats, and wandered on talking hard through May-hedged lanes till we got lost (he wouldn't ask the way of course) and found ourselves at nearly dinner-time miles from home. He did so love wandering over the country-side, watching the birds, hunting for birds'-nests, listening to the rooks, and at night going out to listen to a nightingale. Above every time of the year he loved the third week in May. Wherever he was, whether at home or abroad, he would try and get back to Llanwern for the third week in May, when leaf and tree and flower were all at their luxuriant West-country best and birds'-nesting was in full swing.

His birds'-nesting, by the way, was considerately done.

One was taught most carefully never to touch the nest if one could possibly help it, to take but one egg, and that only if there were more than one (preferably several) in the nest, and to steal quickly away.

Often on Sunday he with four or five of those staying in the house would take the car and go over to Abergavenny to be set down at the foot of the Sugar Loaf Mountain, which we would climb, or over to the foot of the Breconshire Beacon, another favourite climb, or when the May was out on the road to Talgarth high up on the Black Mountains, where the country for a square mile was covered with May trees which looked like lumps of sugar ; we would picnic there and come home at sunset.

He was not in early days a very parentally inclined father. He had one or two theories about the bringing up of children, which were, I think, placidly ignored by my mother. The chief ones which I remember were that a child should learn nothing till it was ten years old (my mother, however, had instituted a governess and had me taught to read at the more usual age of five) and that it should then be sent to the local Board School for some years —I can never make up my mind whether to be glad or sorry that this part of his programme was ignored. I cannot remember that he ever punished me in his life ; his general policy was one of non-interference in what he looked upon as his wife's business. He was, however, the person to go to for holidays and late nights, for he took a less disciplinarian view of such indulgences than my mother, and could often be prevailed upon to persuade her to allow them.

I must have been about eleven or twelve when he first ' talked business ' to me ; that is poured out a stream of description of some deal he was engaged on at the time without any explanations (he hated explaining anything, it bored him). He walked up and down the room as he talked, turning his coins over in his pocket and I, seated in the big armchair, listened palpitating with pride at being treated in so grown up a fashion, but terrified of saying the wrong thing and so showing that I was only understanding about one quarter of what he was saying, which I knew very well would have instantly stopped the flood. On that occasion my mother was up in town ill, and there was no one else at home for him to talk to. He always talked business a great deal ; he would retail all that had interested him in the day's events.

Later his views on my education began to have more weight. I think it was largely due to him that at thirteen I was sent to a good high school, and when a couple of years later I decided that I wished to go to a public school it was to him I appealed. He had some doubts ; he did not know much about girls' boarding-schools, but his sisters had been to one and he thought the girls there had learnt to be ' silly.' The school which I wished to go to was, I assured him, quite different, no one was ever ' silly ' there. It was characteristic of him that he took my word for this, and a few months later I found myself at the coveted school.

There was one uncomfortable period when he tried to teach me Euclid. Teaching was certainly not his rôle. We struggled as far as the fifth proposition, when I was relieved to be able to learn at school instead of at home.

I remember on one occasion in my teens I was going through those religious heartsearchings common to many children. I asked him whether he believed the whole of the New Testament, and he replied with some slight embarrassment that that was a question I had better ask my mother. There was no need—I was answered.

He left off his church-going habits when he got to Llanwern. There was certainly some excuse, for the local clergyman was not only inaudible but inaccurate in his reading of the service ; he had a trick of leaving out words, and his ' Thou shalt murder,' ' Thou shalt steal,' were a perpetual joy to the unregenerate amongst his young hearers. My father did go very occasionally. I can remember one occasion when he was there the sermon was from the text ' The man of the world waxeth fat.' I looked round at my father to see if he appreciated the allusion, but he was already asleep.

In those early days the house was very often full of growing-up and just grown up young nieces, and nephews and cousins of my mother, and it was one of our favourite amusements to get him to act as conductor to a Welsh choir ; we were the Welsh choir ; the song chosen was usually ' Old Dog Tray,' or ' A pink trip slip for a ten cent fare,' and he, mounted on a chair, gave a rendering of an impassioned conductor which reduced his audience to impotent laughter.

At dinner he would be egged on by the same uproarious crew, who always sat next him, either to jiggle the table about, a form of amusement which would never have achieved the savour it did were it not that for some reason my mother violently disapproved of it, or to say something calculated to shock my mother, not a very difficult task. My mother, very short-sighted, raising her long-handled glasses and stretching round a large plant in the middle would look down the table : ' Da—vid.' ' Yes, Sybil dear, what have I done ? ' Artificial innocence exuded from every pore.

We used to laugh at the way he would always frankly and unashamedly take the best of anything that was going in fruit, or anything else he fancied. (He loved fruit. I have seen him in Algeria eat twelve oranges at a sitting.) I well remember the chortles of joy in the family one evening when he handed round the last banana, saying with his usual twinkle, ' Does anyone else want this banana ? ' and the new German governess replied ' *Danke sehr* ' and ate it. We used to tell him laughing that he was very selfish. He always defended himself by saying ' Only in small things,' and I think he was right. Many a man living in such a household as I have described would have made life unbearable by grumbling. He very characteristically summed up the possibilities of the situation and proceeded to arrange matters so that without attempting the impossible of interfering with the household he got what, or most of what, he wanted. It was a sort of faculty for adapting himself to circumstances.

In the early days of marriage he was abstemious, but during the 'nineties he took to smoking huge cigars, and would consume as many as fifteen a day, and he usually drank nearly a whole bottle of port at dinner. That such habits were not desirable for a man with rheumatic tendencies and a " heart" he was, of course, well aware, and in 1898,

H

whilst my mother and I were abroad, he decided to give up smoking for three months. He thought it would be easier to do this if he turned teetotaler, and in order to facilitate the break he retired to bed for three days. He never smoked again, and except on the night after the *Lusitania* went down never touched alcohol of any sort. It was very like him to give the whole thing up—he would probably have found it almost impossible to continue in moderation. It was always all or nothing.

In every other way his own tastes were simple. On one occasion a big lunch took place, and after most of the guests (including my father) had left, a well-known Labour leader lingered on smoking and talking to a couple of friends. ' Queer thing fate,' he said ; ' there's Rhondda with the income of a duke and the tastes of a peasant, and me with the income of a peasant and the tastes of a duke.' The story was carried back to my father, who much appreciated it.

[See also Appendix B and Appendix C.]

CHAPTER IX

THE SOUTH WALES COAL INDUSTRY

By David Evans

THE story of the business life of D. A. Thomas, or ' D. A.' as he was soon to be familiarly known to gentle and simple throughout Wales and beyond, is during the quarter of a century that followed his return to Cardiff, to all intents and purposes the history of the South Wales coalfield. During the first half of this period he was not, as he afterwards became, important on account of the great interests he controlled : the Cambrian Collieries, standing outside the Association, represented a relatively small area and output ; the obvious Big Man was the Chairman of the Association, Sir W. T. Lewis, with whom, during this time, D. A., his kinsman by blood, but divided from him by his whole outlook and composition, was perpetually at war. If, however, D. A. stood out more and more as the man who counted, the reason lay in his own personality : in the fact that he was not only an individualist but an individual. Just as he was an individualist in no narrow sense, but one who conceived wide social aims and had a view of the coal-mining industry that transcended the limits of his own pits, so, as an individual, while ambitious and full of the desire which animates everyone endowed with a high degree of will and of intellectual as well as physical vitality to impress that will and express that vitality in terms of power, he was never isolated from or forgetful of the personalities of other people. His feuds were conducted in a large and generous spirit : his combativeness was seldom directed to purely personal ends. He got across his fellow coal-owners largely because he took a wider view of the

99

economics and politics of coal than they did ; partly for this reason, partly because they realised his essential fair-mindedness, he enjoyed the respect of the miners, even at periods when that respect expressed itself in a recognition that he was the real man they had to fight.

This is why the record of his career as a coal-owner is something bigger and more complicated than the record of the application of a first-class mind to business ; it resumes the industrial development of the period : illustrates the movement of capitalism towards combination as well as the struggles between capital and labour that marked the transition. To Labour in South Wales D. A. stood for capitalism as no other man did. At the same time, the expansion of his business activities reveal capitalism as a growing force, reaching out to new forms. One of the great Captains of Industry, he brought to business management something of the spirit of the artist, to whom his material is a medium for the expression of ideas : but always, doubled with this side of him, there was the other, the naïvely human, which regarded the whole affair as a great game, and caused him to be viewed by his fellow owners as something of an *enfant terrible.* His alert, comprehensive, and forward-looking mind, and the irresistible vitality with which he threw himself into disputes, whether by word or pen (he was an indefatigable controversialist, and the local press was enlivened by a constant stream of letters from him) inevitably brought him into collision with men of conservative, not to say reactionary ideas and a stiff conception of their own dignity, like Sir W. T. Lewis. Sir W. T. Lewis in the 'nineties was certainly the Goliath of the coalfields. But although, for instance in the 1898 strike, the apparent victory was with him and the ideas he represented, D. A. was the David in whose sling was the stone of the future.

The South Wales coalfield in the 'nineties was a scene of more or less constant unrest, breaking out periodically into eruption in the form of strikes. Economically, conditions were most unsatisfactory, both from the standpoint of owners and of men.

In other industries both profits and wages had advanced.

In South Wales the unequalled steam coals had, for decades, been sold to the foreign market at very low prices. Colliery profits averaged only a few pence per ton. Capital and labour were in fact working on the margin of starvation. The workmen blamed the sliding scale of 1892. D. A., as the outcome of much thought devoted to the whole question, agreed in so far as he condemned that instrument for the regulation of wages, on the ground that it placed too great an influence on the movements of coal prices in the hands of the speculators on the Cardiff Coal Exchange.

Since 1894 the changes in the general wage rate under the operation of the sliding scale had been, almost without exception, in a downward direction. There had been only two increases and those in each case of only 1¼ per cent. ; in the spring of 1889 the general wage rate was only 12¼ per cent. above the standard of 1879, whereas in 1891 the wage had averaged 55·83 per cent. The variations in the successive years had been as follows : 1893, 15 per cent. ; 1894, 25 per cent. ; 1895, 16·77 per cent. ; 1896, 11·94 per cent. ; and 1897, 10·94 per cent.

In the course of an experience of seven or eight years as Sales Agent for the Cambrian Collieries, D. A. had, and took advantage of, opportunities to grasp the economics of coal on the distributive as well as on the productive side. He came to the conclusion that the existing organisation of the industry was fair neither to the capital nor to the labour engaged in it. The complete separation between the commercial (marketing) and industrial (coal-getting) sides, with unrestricted competition between individuals on both, represented an organisation wasteful in itself and one that put too great a power over prices in the hands of speculative middlemen. The foreign consumer was profiting at the expense of the producer.

In 1896 he embodied the results of his thinking on and actual experience in the problem in a pamphlet called 'Some Notes on the Present State of the Coal Trade in the United Kingdom with Special Reference to that of South Wales and Monmouthshire, together with a Proposal for the Prevention of Undue Competition and for Maintaining Prices at a Remunerative Level.'

These ' Notes ' were not merely analytic. He believed that the existing evils of the competitive system could and should be minimised by combined action on the part of the colliery owners to adjust, within certain well-defined limits, the production of coal to the fluctuating conditions of trade, and maintain prices at a remunerative level. To that end he proposed a scheme which is described, in outline, as follows in the ' Notes ' :

' The South Wales and Monmouthshire steam coal owners, having ascertained their present output and the proportion of percentage of each Company's output to the total production embraced in the combination, shall agree for some fixed period (say twelve months) that each undertaking is entitled to produce, month by month, an agreed percentage of the total production of the month, whatever it may prove to be ; and they shall further enter into a binding agreement that any Company exceeding its percentage quantity shall contribute a fixed amount on every ton of such excess as liquidated damages towards indemnifying those who produced short of their percentage quantities.'

The ' Notes,' published in 1896, produced a very considerable effect on opinion in the coalfield. In the immediately subsequent years he strove to get his scheme, or any modification of it that retained its essential features, adopted. In this, however, he was ahead of his times. There were very few owners who were prepared or competent to consider the industry as a whole, or able to see that their own interest was bound up with such a view. As it was, he had to endure the experience, profoundly irritating to a man of his intellect, of witnessing sham acceptance of his ideas by people who never intended to carry them out, and used their failure to precipitate catastrophe.

What happened was this.

By the summer of 1897 dissatisfaction with the working of the 1892 Sliding Scale was general all over the field : the men were preparing to denounce it. The Coal Owners' Association was therefore faced with a grave situation. D. A. was not a member of the Association ; but his views were widely known and could not be simply disregarded. At a meeting of the Association a scheme really, though not avowedly based on his ' Notes,' was proposed by Sir William Thomas Lewis (afterwards Lord Merthyr), the Chairman of the Sliding Scale Joint Committee, and unanimously adopted. Although in D. A.'s view it was most desirable that the men should be parties to any scheme of output regulation, the Associated Owners Committee expressed ' their inability to entertain any alliance with the workmen beyond that embraced in the present Sliding Scale Agreement.' Moreover they added a rider, showing where they really stood, to the effect that ' no scheme dependent upon the regulation of prices could be relied upon.' Further, Sir W. T. Lewis laid down the condition that at least 95 per cent. of the colliery owners in South Wales and Monmouthshire ought to be embraced in the compact, and that an arrangement should be made with the workmen's representative on the Sliding Scale Committee that the Sliding Scale Agreement then in force should not be terminated for at least two years from January 1, 1898.

All the colliery owners in the coalfield were asked to join in this scheme. The Cambrian Collieries, although outside the Association, were prepared to do all in their power to secure that, such as it was, it had every chance of success. In their reply to a questionnaire issued by the Association, the Directors expressed approval of and readiness to join the proposed new Association. Further, they intimated that ' provided the twenty largest companies and firms producing steam coal were embraced in the scheme we think its success would be ensured.'

In fact, over 80 per cent. of the coal-owners gave their conditional approval to the scheme. Sir W. T. Lewis then disclosed his real attitude to the plan for which he nominally stood sponsor. He at once declared the adherence of 95 per cent. was indispensable. The scheme was therefore abandoned. Plainly, it had never been meant to be taken seriously.

D. A. had supported Sir W. T. Lewis's plan, though less comprehensive and elastic than his own. He had urged that it was unnecessary to include the house coal or anthracite collieries in any arrangement for the controlling of the output of steam coal, and deplored as destructive the insistence on a 95 per cent. proportion, of which he perfectly understood the object.

' I know of only one large steam coal Company which at the time of its abandonment had not accepted the principle of the scheme, but many, I believe, attached impossible conditions to their adhesion, and as Prince Bismarck once said, acceptance of principle is often only a polite form of rejection.'

The effect of abandonment was immediate. The miners, considering that there was no hope of voluntary action on the part of the coal-owners for the regulation of output, and, therefore, for the maintenance of wages, took the matter into their own hands. On October 1, 1897, they served a six months' notice for the termination of the Sliding Scale. Three months drifted by, during which the Sliding Scale Committee made no serious effort to deal with the question of the arrangement of a new scale. On January 11, 1898, the miners, at a general conference, instructed their representatives to ' open negotiations with a view to improving the Sliding Scale Agreement in as many ways as circumstances might warrant between this and the end of March, but especially to endeavour to secure for the dovetailing of a scheme for the control of the output of coal with a minimum which will retain wages upon a fair and equitable basis.' It was, however, not until February that negotiations were formally opened, in the form of meetings of the Sliding Scale Committee.

Then on Saturday, February 26, the Associated Coal Owners suddenly decided to serve a month's notice for the termination of all individual contracts simultaneously with the expiration of the workmen's notice terminating the 1892 Sliding Scale.

This action was severely condemned by D. A. On March 1, in an interview, he described it as ' a silly piece of bluff, too weak to deceive the meanest intelligence.'

' Nobody imagines for one moment that, in the event of no agreement being come to for the continuance of the Scale, the employers in the present condition of trade would dream

of asking any concession from the men.   Then why should
the employers give notice to terminate contracts ?   The
point is as to what conditions the workmen would demand ;
and it is they whom one would suppose would desire to
terminate contracts in order to be ready at the end of the
month to make their demands.   By giving notice the
employers are simply putting the workmen in a position
to legally make their demands.   They themselves had no
intention whatever to ask any concession from the workmen.'

His sympathies at this stage were with the men.   Nor
had he any apprehensions of a stoppage.   A few days later
he put this point expressly :

'I do not think for a moment that there is the slightest
danger of an actual stoppage.   Neither the employer nor
the workmen desire to push things to extremes. . . . From
the workmen's point of view the position is decidedly
hopeful.   They occupy an exceedingly strong position.   In
fact, I don't remember an occasion when they occupied a
stronger one in regard to their relations with the employers.
The men have put forward most reasonable proposals, and
80 per cent. of the employers have expressed their readiness
to adopt a scheme for the control of production.   Moreover,
a cessation of work is the very last thing the employers
desire, for prices are rising and trade expanding ; but even
if, at the end of the month, a settlement had not been arrived
at, it does not at all mean that there will be a stoppage.   It
simply means that work will go on as it did before the Scale
came into operation ; and in that event it seems to me that
the adoption of the control scheme—in other words the
acceptance of the proposals of the workmen—is the simplest
and most effective way of surmounting the crisis.'

On the facts as they were known to him, this judgment was
reasonable.   But he did not know what had been taking
place at the secret conferences of the Sliding Scale Committee.   Without any previous warning of serious differences
between the workmen's and the owners' representatives on
that Committee, the coalfield was staggered on March 2
by the announcement that the coal-owners had taken the
extreme step of suspending the negotiations.   They did
this because they alleged that the scheme for the control

of output, which the workmen demanded to have included in the new Sliding Scale Agreement, had already been put before the Associated Owners, and had failed to obtain the assent of a sufficient number to make it effective.

D. A., however, his mind focussed upon the general good of the industry, and unaware of what had been happening in the owners' councils, to which he was not privy, encouraged the miners to insist on their demand. Trade conditions, he argued, were more favourable for control than they had been six months earlier, when 80 per cent. of the coal-owners had accepted the scheme submitted by Sir W. T. Lewis. He therefore urged the rank and file of the miners ' to express confidence in the attitude taken up by their representatives and instruct them to insist upon the adoption of the control of output, without which no renewal of the Sliding Scale should be agreed to. They might, however,' he added, ' accept some definite promise in the shape of a guarantee that the scheme should come into operation at the end of the year, and then they might give representatives plenary powers to make the best arrangements they could for the renewal of the Scale with that reservation.'

When reminded, a few days later, that the miners were unprepared financially for any stoppage, he was again not only hopeful but confident that such a calamity would be averted.

' I do not for a moment anticipate a stoppage, or, at all events, not more than a few days, and their position financially is no worse than it has been on previous occasions, while, with the summer coming on, it would soon be much easier to get work at harvesting and so on. I hope the workmen will not allow themselves to be frightened by any threats, however loudly expressed. If, with all the conditions in their favour, they do not insist on their rights, then let them for ever be silent, and silently accept their position of bondage. Mere denunciations of the Scale are empty talk and will not improve their position or that of their families.'

The effect, however, of the action of the employers in suspending negotiations was to intimidate the weaker among the miners' leaders, and to disclose long-suspected differences of opinion between them on the question of the expediency of making output regulation an essential condition of agreement over a new sliding scale.   The rank and file of the workmen adhered firmly to their demand ; but among the leaders a fatal weakness soon disclosed itself. In fact, within three weeks of the owners' ultimatum, Mabon (Mr. W. Abraham), to D. A.'s disgust, formally abandoned some of the more important of the demands which up to that moment had been included in the miners' programme. This policy of surrender overwhelmed Mabon with unpopularity, and a fortnight later he was unseated by a vote of a delegate conference from his position as leader.

D. A. throughout this period supported the miners in all their demands.   On the question of the minimum wage he gave expression to the following views :

' I have always advocated the minimum wage irrespective of the selling price because I believe that the men are entitled to have some voice in the matter.   It is impracticable for them to have any voice in the actual selling price, but at the same time they are entitled to say that their wages must not go below a certain figure because of the internecine competition amongst the owners.   Then, I would say that this minimum wage would be very much better secured directly by the control of the scheme.'

He viewed, however, wlth grave disgust the process of disintegration that went on, in the days that followed, among the miners.   Their leaders, in conference with the Sliding Scale Committee, allowed the demand for output control to be whittled down.   This further weakened their hold on the rank and file, with the result that although the owners agreed to a postponement of their notices from April 1 to April 9, there was a bad break-away, and on April 1, notwithstanding the fact that the notices had been extended, stoppages took place at the Associated Collieries in all parts of the coalfield.

D. A. condemned this disruption as much as he deplored it.   While he thought that the action of the owners in tendering notices to terminate all contracts at the end of

March had been provocative, he still counselled the miners to observe loyally the arrangement under which the owners had agreed to prolong the notices to April 9.

' By doing what you have done,' he wrote, ' you have thrown away the golden opportunity of securing a permanent and not merely a temporary advantage in your position, and have missed a chance of compelling dissentient employers to accept the control scheme put forward in the name of Sir William Thomas Lewis and accepted in principle and under conditions by four-fifths of the employers.'

His advice to the men was that if they had lost faith in some leaders they should choose others in whom they had confidence and act with unity and determination. He wrote :

' Do not give heed to that particular class of orator who is always waiting to see from which quarter the popular breeze is blowing. Men are apt in these crises to act like a flock of sheep, and the idea of leadership of the particular class to which I refer is to occupy the position of the sheep's tail—to wag merrily when the sheep is pleased and to follow whithersoever the sheep carries them. But even in the sheep the seat of wisdom is not usually supposed to reside in the tail, nor however actively the tail may wag does this appendage really direct the course of the sheep.'

It is difficult to say whose conduct during the weeks preceding the strike D. A. deprecated most ; that of the miners, in failing to take advantage of what he regarded as the very favourable strategic position which they held—in his judgment strong enough, had they shown unity, discipline and determination, to secure the adoption of a scheme for the regulation of output—or what he considered the autocratic, if not vindictive, actions of the Associated Owners under the leadership of Sir W. T. Lewis. In his view, the Associated Owners had forced the crisis by their delay in entering into negotiations for a renewal of the Sliding Scale, by the notices they had served on their workmen on March 1, terminating contracts at the end of that month, and by their refusal to authorise an audit of the average selling price of coal for the last few months of the Scale period.

Even worse in his eyes was their insincerity over the control scheme. In the last few days of March 1898 Sir W. T. Lewis admitted that he had never considered that a scheme for the regulation of output was practicable, and that the proposals which bore his name, which had been unanimously adopted by the Association and endorsed by 80 per cent. of the owners, were never really intended to form a permanent, or even a temporary feature of the organisation of the South Wales coal trade. D. A. characterised such action as 'heartless hypocrisy.' Moreover, he accused Sir William of a large measure of personal responsibility for the strike. Ten days before the stoppage began he wrote :

'I still see no reason whatever for trouble, but Sir William Thomas Lewis seems to be making in that direction. Last May, when the Compensation Bill was before the House of Commons, Sir William Thomas Lewis, who lobbied against it for all he was worth, wrote a letter to *The Times* in which he said, in reference to the Bill, that a transference of the burden of the tax and the great increase of its amount will certainly necessitate a radical rearrangement of the Sliding Scale which governs the wages of 129,000 workmen, and that from past experience this will involve a very severe struggle between employers and employed, and a great loss to both, as well as to the whole of South Wales. Sir William Thomas Lewis now seemed anxious to secure the fulfilment of his predictions. He is bluffing the workmen to the utmost extent of his power. Nobody knows the weakness of the employers' position better than Sir William and he is trying to carry it off with a high hand. Of course, as everybody down here knows, and nobody better than the employers themselves, Sir William carries the Coal Owners' Association in his waistcoat pocket. If there is a stoppage I do not hesitate to say that it will be the fault of Sir William Thomas Lewis. The men do not want to come out, and will only do so if forced by the employers.'

The irregular stoppages which took place on April 1 in certain districts extended rapidly to others, the ballot on the question of the granting of plenary powers gave an adverse majority of 30,372 (44,872 against 14,500) and the strike became general.

On April 11 the coal-owners posted at the pit-heads the terms under which they were prepared to allow a resumption of work. These terms were less favourable than those embodied under the old Sliding Scale, and with their publication disappeared the last hope of the avoidance of a long struggle. Moreover, to the unconcealed joy of the Associated Owners, the strikers in their pits had been joined by the men working in the Clydach Vale pits of the Cambrian Collieries, although these latter were outside the Association.

The case of Clydach Vale was a special one. In 1893 the Clydach Vale colliers had come out, in violation of an existing agreement, in sympathy with the hauliers. D. A. had then only permitted the resumption of work on the express condition that the men bound themselves never again to disregard agreements. In 1898 the stand he had taken on the miners' side caused the workers in his pits to approach the management with an application for a 20 per cent. advance. As a matter of fact, D. A. supported their demand for an advance at the meeting of the Cambrian Board. The other directors were opposed, however, and it was rejected. What happened at the meeting was, of course, not known to the men. On April 4 the men came out, partly on the ground of this refusal, partly out of sympathy with their comrades in the Associated pits. Throughout the coalfield, D. A., within a few days, became as unpopular as he had been previously popular.

' In every locality ' [declared a local newspaper], ' in the Rhondda Valleys the miners, standing in groups in various parts of the street, condemned Mr. D. A. Thomas, M.P , in most severe terms. Wherever one goes, " What do you think of D. A. Thomas now ? " It is the general opinion in the Valleys that the colliers would not have come out had it not been for the articles and the speeches of Mr. D. A. Thomas. He is blamed for all the present crisis. The miners, although determined to stand out for an advance, feel that they are in a state of great confusion. The men state that Mr. D. A. Thomas knew very well that long contracts had been made, and it was a cruel action on his part to urge the men to demand what he knew the employers at the present juncture could not afford to offer them.   Such are some of the criticisms of the Hon. Member in different parts of the district.   On Saturday last he was idolised by the great bulk of the miners of the Rhondda.'

On April 6, the men having temporarily returned to work pending a general conference of miners fixed for April 9, D. A. went down to Clydach Vale to demand from the Workmen's Committee an early opportunity of rebutting at a mass meeting of the men the charges and allegations made against him.   'Mr. Thomas explained,' states one of the newspapers at the time, 'that he thought that it was only fair treatment to himself to give him an opportunity to meet face to face those who had, as he alleged, maligned him, and he expressed at the same time the hope that his opponents would, like himself, face the music and not run away from him again.'   He was cordially received everywhere, but the meeting did not take place, for, on the 7th, the Clydach Vale miners again came out.

The management of the Cambrian Collieries had excused the irregular stoppage on April 4 and 5, but the men's action in coming out on the 7th was a violation of the undertaking given by the Clydach Vale miners in 1893 that they would not again violate a pledge or come out on strike without proper notice.   On the evening of April 7 the men were informed that 'There will be no more work at the Colliery until further notice from the Company, whatever the workmen may, amongst themselves, decide.'

D. A. himself wrote to the secretary of the Workmen's Committee at the Clydach Vale Collieries :—

'Cardiff, Thursday Afternoon, April 7th, 1898.
' To William James,
    ' Secretary Workmen's Committee,
        'Clydach Vale Colliery.
    ' Dear Sir,
        ' Will you kindly convey to the Workmen's Committee my best thanks for their kindness in affording me an opportunity of addressing a mass meeting to-morrow afternoon,

but in view of the action in coming out this morning without an hour's notice, notwithstanding the resolution on Tuesday last, and thus not only breaking their legal contract with the Company, but their solemn promise to me personally a few years back, I have no desire now to meet them.   My wish was to correct some misapprehensions that appeared to exist in their minds with regard to my action, but after their conduct this morning they are welcome to think of me whatever they please, for in their present strain of mind I shall attach no value to their opinion one way or the other ; be it good or bad, it is a matter of indifference to me.   The general body of workmen in South Wales and Monmouth-shire stand in a different position to those at Clydach Vale ; they have been given notice by their employers, and were entitled morally and legally to come out.   But at Clydach Vale, after pledging me their word of honour not to come out without notice, the case is entirely different.   Had they given notice I should have had no cause of complaint, but as it is, how can we, in future, place the smallest value upon any promise they may make us ?   You will please under-stand that, strongly as I feel on the treatment I have re-ceived at the hands of the Clydach Vale workmen, I am confident that their action is reprobated by all the more thoughtful men at the colliery as strongly as it must be by honourable men everywhere.   Every effort of mine has been directed, especially during the past week, to try and find some means of averting the crisis and enabling the Cambrian Board of Directors to make with the men some mutually satisfactory arrangement to continue work, and show such an example that might be followed by other large collieries with advantage to the district generally and to the workmen in particular.   Until this morning I still entertained a hope that I might succeed, but now the men are determined to close the door.

'Believe me to be,

'Yours faithfully,

(Signed)   'D. A. Thomas.'

In a letter which he addressed to the *South Wales Daily News* four days later (on April 11), D. A. wrote :

' I have the satisfaction of feeling that I left nothing undone to prevent a stoppage at Clydach Vale.   I did not give up hope even at the eleventh hour of averting the strike, until the men broke their contract and rendered me helpless.   Indeed, from information that reaches me to-day I believe that I might have succeeded.   The responsibility now rests on the shoulders of the men.   They are determined to fight.   Be it so ; they have struck the first blow below the belt.   I am myself a man of peace, but there is, I fear, just a little of the old Adam left, and let the men not run away with the idea that the Company will content themselves with silk padded gloves, while they, the men, fight, so to speak, with knuckle-dusters.   The men have come out without notice.   They did not think it necessary to consult me first.   I do not know when they may wish to return ; but this I do know, that they will not return until we give permission.   The next decision lies not with them, but with the Company, both as to the time and the terms upon which we shall reopen the Collieries.'

The Clydach Vale workmen had violated a well-remembered, though not an actually written pledge, and D. A.'s wrath at that betrayal of a moral obligation was accentuated because the action of the men in coming out on strike had followed close on the heels of a strong effort which he had made at the meeting of the directors of the Cambrian Board to concede the workmen an immediate advance.   His firmness had its effect.   Within a few days the great majority of the Clydach Vale workmen frankly admitted their error ; at a mass meeting held on April 13 they passed a resolution recognising ' with regret our breach of faith and promises.'

D. A. accepted this resolution : he met the men and obtained the assent of his fellow directors to a settlement. On Monday, April 18, the Clydach Vale workmen resumed employment with an advance of 10 per cent. and an undertaking from the Company to provide them with any assistance the men might require in the carrying out of a scheme for the deduction of the increased wage from their pay and its subscription to a fund which had been opened for the support of the miners on strike at the Associated Collieries.

There had been no artifice or trickery on the part of either side in the arrangement of this settlement.   It was an open deal in which firmness triumphed on the one side and reason on the other.   The effect on the coalfield was profound.

I

The Cambrian Collieries worked during the whole period of the strike, with the exception of the first nine or ten days. Under the pressure of the demand for coal the pits of the non-associated collieries were, to use the words of one of the colliery managers, 'worked to death.' [1] There was an abundant supply of labour, and the non-associated owners employed as many of the strikers as they could find place for safely in the mines. Double shifts of working were introduced wherever these were permissible by the inspectors of mines as consistent with safety. Under these stimulating conditions the outputs of the Clydach Vale and other non-associated collieries were increased. Wages were increased by another 10 per cent. Although the greater part of the production at the Cambrian and other non-associated collieries had been disposed of under long period contracts concluded in the autumn of 1897, big profits were made on the extra outputs.

Such was the history of an affair which, involved as it was in all the passions and unreason excited by a great industrial struggle, affected profoundly for a long time to come the position of D. A. in South Wales. By the general public outside the area, the circumstances were imperfectly understood ; within it, there were few on either side of the struggle who could retain any impartiality of mind. That D. A. did so was his great offence, and that while the Cambrian Collieries were at work the rest of the coalfield was idle.

Early in June the miners made a renewed effort to settle on the basis of an advance of 10 per cent. and a Conciliation Board to regulate wages. These terms were refused by the employers, and in the ensuing weeks serious disturbances occurred. There were riots in the Aberdare and Merthyr districts, and under pressure from the local magistrates detachments of the South Wales Borderers, 1st Worcesters, and Guards were imported into the coalfield and distributed in various parts of the disaffected districts. Minor conflicts took place between the strikers and the police, but there were no serious attempts on life and property, and before the end of June the troops had been

[1] Most of the non-associated collieries worked throughout the strike.

From a Drawing by J. M. Staniforth]   CHECK!   *[by permission of the 'Western Mail.'*

Collier : "HOORAY! THAT'S MORE THAN A THOUSAND A WEEK TO OUR STRIKE FUND."

withdrawn. In July the Board of Trade sent Sir Edward Fry to South Wales to investigate the position and offer his services in the capacity of mediator or conciliator. He was received as an act of personal courtesy by Sir W. T. Lewis, but only to be informed by him that he refused to recognise Sir Edward in any position as a conciliator, and that the Associated Coal Owners declined to admit any intervention of a conciliator or of any other person appointed by the Government or otherwise.

D. A. deplored this treatment of Sir Edward Fry by the Associated Owners. If, he stated, they had been less precipitate and had recognised Sir Edward in the preliminary stages of his intervention, it would still have remained open to them to refuse any terms offered through the Board of Trade mediator. The workmen's representatives expressed their readiness to accept Sir Edward as conciliator, or, if the employers were willing, as an arbitrator to decide finally between them, but Sir W. T. Lewis and his fellow Associated Owners were immovable.

In a speech delivered on August 6, D. A. suggested as a possible basis of settlement the withdrawal by both sides of all demands made subsequent to February, the inclusion of the Lewis Control Scheme in the new sliding scale, the enforcement of that scheme before the autumn, so that it might be in operation when the 1899 contracts would be arranged, and that it should be given a trial for twelve months. He had not in any way modified his opinions concerning the need of a method to prevent undue competition and the practicability of the Lewis scheme.

In answer to a critic who condemned his intervention in the dispute he wrote :

' I know of no ground for repentance for any action of mine in this matter, for while nothing that I can do to bring this unfortunate dispute to an end shall be left undone I will in the future, as in the past, take every opportunity that offers itself for urging the adoption of some means of preventing cut-throat competition.'

The masters who had defied the Government were not likely to listen to the recommendations of a colliery owner whom they hated as much as they feared, and the strike continued its devastating course.

All that the miners obtained in the final terms of settlement by which work was resumed on September 1 was the recognition by the owners of the principle of the minimum, and an immediate advance of 5 per cent. In the words of Mabon, the employers had driven the miners along the path of humiliation to one of the worst settlements in their experience. All that can be said is that they emerged from the struggle with a hard-won appreciation of the value of unity, and not only established soon afterwards a stronger Trades Union than any which had previously existed in the coalfield, but also became allied to the Miners' Federation of Great Britain.

The 1898 strike was the last struggle of the old industrial feudal spirit against the rising tide of industrial democracy. Sir W. T. Lewis may be described as the last of the industrial barons. The only relationship which he really admitted between himself and the workmen was that of master and man. He had no sympathy with the newer spirit that was agitating labour in all the industrial countries of the world ; he either did not grasp or refused to admit the fundamental equalities and interdependence of capital and labour in the production of wealth ; and he lacked the imagination which would have enabled him to envisage the future developments of industrial action and adopt statesmanlike measures to meet them with a minimum of disturbance to the common interests of employers and workmen.

In this sense he was the antithesis of D. A. Thomas. The latter represented the dynamic and the former the static forces in the world of industry. The one stood for evolutionary progress, and the other for reaction. In the case of D. A., the history of the strike of 1898, and of the part which he played in the events leading up to it, suggests that he was perhaps inclined to set too great a pace to the slow progress of evolutionary development. He advocated a minimum wage ; Sir W. T. Lewis resisted it ; he supported the principle of collective bargaining and encouraged the demand for the creation of Conciliation Boards ; Sir W. T. Lewis refused recognition of trade unionism and set his face

resolutely against any change in the direction of conciliation which involved the intervention of any third party into
the affairs of employers and workmen ; he defended the
Compensation Act, agitated for a restriction of working-
hours underground to a day of eight hours winding, and
held that the cost of these reforms should be transferred
to the consumer ; Sir W. T. Lewis resisted these reforms
with all the resources at his command.   He was a reluctant
convert to such artificial restrictions on economic forces
as were necessary to secure reasonable wages for the workmen and a reasonable rate of profit for the employers, while
Sir W. T. Lewis regarded all such restrictions as arbitrary
and impracticable.   Both were strong personalities ; both
in their way were autocrats ; both preferred to make laws
rather than to obey them.   Regarded in relation to this
conflict of personalities the strike of 1898 may be called the
Battle of the Kinsmen, for the two men were distant cousins.
Poles asunder in their outlook on industrial problems, the
difference between them was that between a man with
vision and a man without.

The triumph for the moment was with Sir W. T. Lewis.
He had defeated, impoverished and humiliated the workmen
and had destroyed the hopes of 1897 that a scheme would be
introduced in South Wales for the regulation of prices and
output.   It was a temporary triumph.   Within four years
practically all the reforms which D. A. had supported or
inspired prior to and during the strike had been established,
in principle if not in form, as permanent conditions in the
wages system in the coalfield.

In October 1898 he prophesied that the August settlement would lead to the death of the Sliding Scale.   That
prophecy was verified with remarkable accuracy.   At the
first available opportunity the miners gave notice to terminate the agreement of 1898, and in its place there was
introduced a system under which a Conciliation Board was
established with an independent chairman, a minimum
wage fixed at 30 per cent. on the standard rates of 1879 ;
and a minimum selling price of 11s. 10d. per ton f.o.b.   Sir
W. T. Lewis had at this time ceased to be a member of
the Sliding Scale Committee.   His disappearance thus

synchronised with a complete surrender of the system for which he stood, and with the concession, even without a day's loss of work, of all the more important of the reforms for which the miners, with D. A. Thomas' support, had agitated in 1898.

The deep personal and public estrangement between the kinsmen continued for many years. The reconciliation of the two men took place under somewhat dramatic circumstances on the occasion of the presentation of the freedom of the Borough of Merthyr to Sir W. T. Lewis on October 1, 1908. D. A. attended that ceremony, and at the subsequent luncheon at Cyfarthfa Castle he said : ' It gives me special pleasure to be here because it has given me an opportunity of re-cementing a very old friendship which has for far too long a time been ruptured, and I now hope that from this day you will find Sir William and myself good, honest, sincere friends.' Enthusiastic cheers on the part of the whole company greeted this graceful expression of good feeling.

At the time D. A. failed in his struggle for the adoption of his plans for the regulation of output, but the object at which he aimed was largely attained by the fixing in 1902 of a minimum wage and a minimum selling price. The effect of those minima was not only to check the downward tendency of prices on a falling market, but also to diminish the influence on prices of the operations of speculative middlemen, and, while since 1898 several factors have contributed towards greater market stability in the coal trade of South Wales, there can be no question as to the superiority of the Conciliation Board over the Sliding Scale system.

It was shortly after this fixation in 1902 that he read before the Royal Statistical Society on May 19, 1903, a paper on ' The Growth and Direction of our Foreign Trade in Coal during the Last Half Century,' for which he was awarded the Guy Medal of the Society. In the preparation of this paper he took infinite pains. He had handled the statistical aspects of the foreign coal trade in his ' Notes ' of 1896. But the tables and the diagrams which accompanied this study were far more comprehensive, detailed and mathematical, and they have secured for it a permanent place in the literature on the subject.

The statistics he had collected showed that, ' whatever may be the cause, there has been a very serious check to the expansion of foreign demand for British produce during the past ten years, and that there is ground for something more than a suspicion that our experts, both in respect to value and quantity, have become, at least for the time being, stationary if not retrogressive.' This result, while disquieting, did not cause him to compromise with his economic conscience, or shake his Free Trade faith.   Thus he wrote :

' Should it prove on a more prolonged observation that this relative retrogression on our part is permanent and that we are being overtaken in the international race, it must not be taken as any argument favouring a change in our fiscal policy in the direction of Protection.   It would prove to be due, I think, to circumstances largely beyond human control and over which man disquieteth himself in vain.'

Moreover he qualified his conclusions by the statement that the period covered—that of nearly ten years—might prove too short to be conclusive of a permanent tendency. In 1913 he undertook the task of bringing the statistics of his 1903 study up to date.   This task was completed in 1914–15, and the statistics were brought up to the end of 1913.   They fully justified the caution he exercised in qualifying his original conclusions, showing as they do that the depression in the export trade of the United Kingdom in the periods 1886–90 and 1896–1900 was only temporary ; after 1900 our exports both in quantity and in value made a greater forward bound than at any other period in the history of the country.

CHAPTER X

The Captain of Industry

By David Evans

The story of the 1898 strike has been told in some detail because it illustrates very clearly D. A.'s general ideas both as to the relations of capital and labour and as to the effective organisation of the mining industry.

It shows him, although an individualist who believed in competition as the indispensable spur to the exercise of individual initiative and the output of individual effort, by no means unsympathetic to the aspirations of labour for better conditions and even a measure of responsibility ; a man of his word, who expected others to be the same, and regarded a violated pledge as a grave moral dereliction, to be treated with granite inflexibility. These views came out again, in relation to subsequent industrial disputes.

In the strike at the Cambrian Combine Collieries in 1910–11, originating at the Naval Collieries, which raged over the question of the guaranteed minimum for men in abnormal places, D. A. was the employer not of 3,000 men, as in 1898, but of 12,000 men : he controlled an output of nearly four million tons per annum instead of less than one million ; but whereas in 1898 he had been independent, he was now (owing to his acquisition, in 1906, of the Glamorgan Collieries) a member of the Owners' Association. This strike, which was one of the most fiercely contested and turbulent in the history of the industry, ended in disastrous failure for the men. It coincided with, and was in part conditioned by, a syndicalist propaganda with which D. A. had no sympathy whatever. It was the direct prelude to the National Miners' Strike of 1912, in which D. A.

—whose colliery holdings had meantime greatly extended— was the master mind on the side of the employers. Again, as in the Clydach Vale affair in 1898, it was for him largely a question of pledges. His view was that the men's demands involved the violation of the coal wages agreement of 1910, which was operative for five years, and that the form in which the miners demanded a minimum wage struck a deadly blow at the only efficient wages system—that of payment by results.

In general he held that the cause of the unrest in the mining industry of South Wales was not any unfairness in the relation of the level of wages to the level of the cost of living. In the South Wales coalfield ' the rate of wages had increased at twice the rate of the cost of living.' True, the British industrial system as a whole as it existed in his day was not elastic enough to secure the prompt re-adjustment of wages to changing conditions of trade and to the ever strengthening demand on the part of labour for a higher standard of living. ' In this world,' he said in 1913, ' half the trouble is due to slowness in adjusting new conditions to altered circumstances, and wages have not been adjusted in some of the biggest industries to the increased cost of living.' But this criticism did not apply to the mining industry of South Wales. Wages rose or fell with every rise or fall in the price of coal qualified by the volume of trade and other factors bearing immediately on the earning power of the industry, and the changes took place at quarterly intervals.

Moreover, while the actual wages earned by miners were higher than the average wage for the country as a whole, and considerably higher than in the railway service, in the building trade, and in many other major industries, and had risen more rapidly than the cost of living, the potential earning power of the miner was materially greater than his actual earnings. The majority of men will work no harder than they must, and he was philosopher enough to realise that the desire for wages above the subsistence level is influenced as much by moral and social as by economic considerations. What he did condemn, and condemn with the indignation of an honest mind, were the dishonest practices of ca' cannyism and malingering. These practices were as injurious to the public interest as they were to the private interests of employers. They imposed an artificial restraint on the production of wealth, and, therefore, on the supply of useful commodities, and while they were inspired by economic opinions as false as they were mischievous, they demoralised those who indulged in them. He had discovered cases where organised ca' canny action on the part of the colliers, employed on a seam of coal for which no price list was fixed, had been responsible for the output of from 30 per cent. to 40 per cent. less coal than that produced by the same men after the price list had been fixed. On one of the many occasions on which he protested against this practice he wrote with a characteristic touch of sarcasm :

' I have often wondered how religious men, as a very large proportion of Welsh workmen are, can reconcile such conduct with their consciences. I do not wish to emphasise the employers' grievances in this matter because the little game is always seen through, and is so well known as to have little influence on the minds of those to whom the settlement of the price list may be referred, but it is an exceedingly short-sighted and silly policy.'

If, then, the cause of the industrial unrest in the South Wales coalfield was not economic, what was its true source ? He traced it partly to the defective system under which the organised interests of the workmen were governed, and partly to the spread of revolutionary ideas for the recon-struction of the social and industrial systems of the country. The principle of trade unionism was in itself perfectly sound. He recognised it officially twenty years before such official recognition was given by the Monmouthshire and South Wales Coal Owners' Association. While not denying to any of his workmen the right to private judgment and full liberty of action, he personally encouraged them to become members of a trade union, and preferably of the strongest or most representative of the trade unions in the industry. But if the principle of trade unionism was sound and even essential for the greater stability of the relations between labour and capital, the medium through which it was applied was marred by all the faults of an ultra-democratic form of government.

' Democratic government ' [he wrote] ' is at best the lesser of two evils. No one supposes that the many are necessarily imbued with supreme wisdom or that the judgment of the people is by any means always right. A standing weakness of democracy is that it is easily swayed and led by the fluent speaker rather than by the man of caution and capacity. Froth rises to the top, and the person who carries his brains in his tongue is the chosen leader.'

Moreover, the great strikes had been preceded by a new propaganda, entirely different from that of trade unionism in the old sense.

' Well nigh every speech of the young and dominant school ' [he wrote to *The Times* in March 1912] ' declares that the industry should be carried on without profit and that the workmen will never be content until the mines are either nationalised or handed over to the workmen, while to secure these ends class war and the Syndicalist method of a general strike and the holding up of the nation to ransom are openly advocated.'

It was idle, he said, to suggest that the pamphlet ' The Miners' Next Step ' was issued by irresponsibles, for the authors of that pamphlet were living in mid-Rhondda, were personally more or less known to him, and the more prominent of them were those unofficial leaders who had ' kept 12,000 men out of work for twelve months at a cost of over a million in wages in opposition to a price list ' which subsequent experience showed ' enabled the colliers to earn on an average 10s. per day.'

Although as a loyal citizen he accepted the decision of Parliament as expressed in the Minimum Wage Act, he believed, with Adam Smith, that there were no two functions more inconsistent than those of the Sovereign and of the trader ; that it was the business of the individual in his private capacity to trade. He was convinced that more injury than benefit had been produced by many of the legislative measures of recent Governments affecting the relations of employers and workmen. The Trades Disputes Act, for instance, by removing the financial responsibility of trade union organisations, had destroyed one of the most effective checks on unconstitutionally aggressive action on the part of trade unions, while the various powers that had been conferred on the Board of Trade to intervene in industrial disputes tended towards the weakening of the local sense of responsibility. It was not, therefore, from the State that he expected a solution. He believed in private initiative and never faltered in that belief.

This same essential continuity is to be found in his more general ideas. Thus, in the plan for the price organisation of the coal trade article he set out in his ' Notes ' in 1896 and advocated in the subsequent years can be seen, already worked out in broad outline, many of the governing principles he applied when he made the great decision that his fortress was in South Wales rather than in Westminster.

First Period

On June 8, 1901, he had resigned his position as managing director of the Cambrian Collieries, Ltd. After his retirement from the Board of that company his only business tie with the coal trade was the partnership he held in the firm of Thomas & Davey, sales agents for the Cambrian Collieries. Until March 5, 1906, he did not rejoin the Cambrian Board. It is within the course of a single decade, *i.e.*, between 1907 and 1916, that there falls the history of achievements, industrial and commercial, that established him as one of the greatest coal-owners in the United Kingdom, and carried his name to the ends of the earth as a symbol of capitalist power.

The beginning of this process seemed insignificant enough. In 1906 the Cambrian Company were working a ' fault ' on the Glamorgan Company's boundary. It was pointed out to D. A. that this fault would enable the Glamorgan Company to obtain a certain amount of coal from the Cambrian property which could not have been obtained by the Cambrian Company itself without the expenditure of a great deal of capital. There was nothing exceptional in this experience. Such difficulties are a normal feature of mining development, and they are either left unremedied and the coal lost or settled by agreements between the owners of the properties affected.

But in this particular case the problem was to be solved along very different lines from those ordinarily followed. D. A. had now turned his back on politics for good ; he was inspired by a determination to find, if he could, in business a scope for the exercise and expansion of his remarkable energies. He had acquired fame as an authority on coal questions, and, within the rather narrow circle in which he moved, considerable prestige as a public man of fearless independence ; but asked for more than that from life, and felt that he could get a great deal more from it by devoting himself to business.

Such was the soil on which the seed of a minor engineering difficulty fell. Possession of the property of the Glamorgan Coal Company immediately suggested itself to him, not only as a solution of the problem of working most economically a particular section of the Cambrian Company's taking, but also as a step in the direction of the acquisition of that power in the world of industry on which he had now set his mind.

The Glamorgan Collieries were not very prosperous. The ordinary shareholders had never received a dividend, and the preference shares were quoted on the market at about one-half their par value. On the other hand, the ties which bound the Hood family to Llwynypia were intimate, and between the Hoods and D. A. there were strong personal antipathies. During the great coal strike of 1898, the proprietors of the adjoining Cambrian Collieries at Clydach Vale had given great offence to the proprietors of the Glamorgan Collieries (which belonged to the Association) by employing their workmen. In 1907 the embers of the controversies of 1898 were still aglow in the private relationship of many of the associated and non-associated colliery owners, and the estrangement between the Hoods and D. A. precluded direct negotiations between them. However, conversations and feelers between their agents, extending over a period of nearly twelve months, culminated eventually in an offer by D. A. to purchase the whole of the Hood interests in the company, and the greater part also of the interests which they controlled for another family (the Walkers), represented by Mr. E. A. Mitchell Innes. Terms were arranged for the purchase of those interests at £250,000, on the basis of £3 for each ordinary share and £7 for each preference share.

An incident that took place within twenty-four hours of the conclusion of the deal reveals a characteristic trait. On the morning after the completion of the deal, Mr. W. Hood telephoned Mr. Llewellyn, colliery manager at Clydach, who had been acting for D. A., complaining that he had had a very sleepless night, and was gravely perturbed as to whether the purchase of the Hood interests, on the basis of £7 for the preference shares and £3 for the ordinary shares, involved the transfer also of the £45,000 debentures. He admitted that what D. A. had bought was ' the whole ' of their interests, but pointed out that what the parties had negotiated over were the terms for the transfer of the ordinary and preference share capital, and he vowed that if D. A. insisted on carrying out the letter of the agreement, and, therefore, on the possession of the debentures as well as the share capital, ' he would hound him for the rest of his life.'

An emergency meeting between the parties was immediately arranged. At that meeting D. A. Thomas stated that although, under the agreement which he had made, he was entitled to the transfer to him of the whole of Hood holdings in the company, still, as neither he nor they had it in their minds that the debentures were included, he agreed that the purchase price should not cover the debentures. It was a typical act. In this case not only did it remove a prejudice, it formed the basis of a lasting friendship between the two men.

The first immediate effect of the Glamorgan deal was to place D. A. in control of an output of about two million tons of coal per annum, and thus provide him with the opportunity of applying on a restricted scale his policy of price regulation. The two properties were placed under a single management, their underground workings were organised so as to allow them to be worked as a unit and not as separate parts, and a common price policy was applied to the coals of both. This extension of his interests also gave him an opportunity of applying the strong views he held as to the rights of shareholders. The position of every director was, he held, in many respects analogous to that of a trustee. The duty imposed upon him was the safe custody and profitable employment of the capital of others as well as his own. Thus, he wrote in 1911 :

'I regard myself as in a fiduciary position in relation to the shareholders, and I intend to do my best for them, having due regard to the fair and reasonable claims of the workmen. If I did not endeavour to the best of my ability to safeguard the interests of those who have shown me their confidence by placing me in this position of trust, I should very properly lay myself open to the charge of having proved an unjust steward.'

It was on this basis that he reorganised the finances of the Glamorgan Coal Company.

While engaged in the Glamorgan negotiations D. A. founded the firm of Lysberg, Ltd., and on the completion of the Glamorgan deal the sales agency was placed in the hands of this private firm. The circumstances which led to the formation of this company were peculiar. The underground timbering in the mines of South Wales is done mainly by pine props imported from France, Spain, Portugal and the Baltic. The bulk of the best pitwood is drawn from the famous Landes district of south-west France, where the pines were originally planted by Bremontier, a contemporary of Napoleon, with a view to arresting the scourge of the west wind-driven sand dunes, advancing year by year to the east and destroying cultivated lands and habitation. The trade in this timber is considerable. Pitwood imports into South Wales in pre-war years amounted to about one and a half million loads per annum, of which nearly a million tons were discharged at the port of Cardiff. Importation of this timber prior to 1907 was almost entirely in the hands of merchants : in that year the leading merchants formed themselves into a 'ring' for the regulation

K

of prices.   The effect of this combination was to drive up prices from 18s. to 40s. per ton.   As timber is the chief raw material of the mining industry the effect of this artificial price was to increase considerably the cost of production at the mines.   The firm of Lysberg, Ltd., was formed to combat the operations of the ring.

D. A. was further primarily responsible for the creation of a Pitwood Consumers' Syndicate, consisting of seven colliery undertakings, who entered into an agreement to obtain their pitwood supplies from one buying agency. The main function entrusted to Lysberg, Ltd., was to buy direct from the growers of timber and sell on a commission basis to the constituent members of the Consumers' Syndicate. The effect of the pitwood operations of the new company was to break the ' ring ' and bring down prices with such rapidity that, within three months of the formation of Lysberg, Ltd., in November 1907 with a capital of £20,000, the price of pitwood at Cardiff was only 17s. 3d. per ton. The success of the company attracted other collieries into the syndicate ; in 1914 its membership represented a coal output of between eight and ten million tons per annum, or nearly one-fifth the total output of the coalfield.   D. A. was chairman of the company, while this was one of the first business concerns on which the present Viscountess Rhondda held a seat as director.   In the course of time, the ramifications of Lysberg, Ltd., extended into many other branches of industry and commerce, and it became one of the most important ship-owning, coal-exporting and pitwood-importing undertakings in South Wales.

Another incident of the Glamorgan deal was the formation of the Cambrian Trust, Ltd., with a capital of £120,000 in £10 shares.   This also was a private company, all the shares in which were held by the Cambrian Collieries, Ltd., and D. A., its founder, handed over to the trust, on the terms he had acquired them, the Hood interests in the Glamorgan Company.

The next big deal, and one which followed quickly on the heels of the absorption of the Llwynypia property, was the acquisition, through the Cambrian Trust, in June 1908, of 67 per cent. of the ordinary share capital in the Naval

Colliery Company at a cost of £100,471. In this transaction D. A. acted in conjunction with Mr. T. J. Callaghan,
managing director of L. Gueret, Ltd., and the interests
acquired were those of Mr. Louis Gueret, who had been a
part proprietor since 1888 in the Naval Colliery.[1]

The 67 per cent. proportion gave the Cambrian Trust
a controlling interest in the share capital of the Naval
Collieries, Ltd., the bulk of the remaining 33 per cent.
being acquired by D. A. and Mr. T. J. Callaghan per-
sonally. In this transaction D. A. purchased jointly with
Mr. T. J. Callaghan, chairman and managing director of
L. Gueret, Ltd., the interest of Mr. Louis Gueret in L.
Gueret, Ltd., which company were owners of the Naval
Colliery. By means of this control D. A. was able to
extend to another big property the economics of administration and working introduced at the Glamorgan Colliery.
L. Gueret, Ltd., retained their ownership of the Naval
Company debentures as well as its coal sales agency, but
in addition to the Chairmanship of the Naval Company
D. A. held the deputy-chairmanship of L. Gueret, Ltd.,
and the direction of the price policy of the Naval Company
became as effective as that of the Glamorgan.

Combined action in the sale and marketing of coal, as
well as in the working of collieries, was by this second deal
extended to joint undertakings with an output of nearly
three million tons per annum.

In the early part of 1909 there was a lull in his activities.
He was laid up at Llanwern by a severe attack of rheumatic
fever. All that happened, however, to the movement which
he had created was an impeded rate of progress, and among

---

[1] The consummation of the Naval deal was probably facilitated by
the memory of a curious little incident which had occurred during the
'98 strike. During this strike the Naval Collieries, which did not belong
to the Coal Owners' Association, were amongst the collieries which continued to work, and in order to prevent under-cutting D. A. came to a
private verbal agreement with Mr. T. J. Callaghan that neither of them
would sell below a certain price. Shortly after this Mr. Callaghan
discovered that a contract which Naval were after had gone to Cambrian
at something below the agreed price. He went round to see D. A., who
had just got down from London. D. A. knew nothing of the deal, but
made inquiries and found that, owing to some misunderstanding, his
partner had concluded the deal. 'How much do you estimate that you
lost by this?' he inquired. 'About £600,' was the reply. He sat down
and wrote out a cheque for the amount.

the developments of that year were the establishment in association with L. Gueret, Ltd., of the coal shipping firm now known as Gueret's Anglo-Brazilian Coaling Co., Ltd., with a view to the expansion of trade with South America, and the acquisition by L. Gueret, Ltd., of a considerable share of the capital of the Albion Steam Coal Co., Ltd., whose pits near Pontypridd had an output of approximately 500,000 tons per annum, and of which L. Gueret, Ltd., became the joint selling agents.

In 1910 the master mind was again active. In April that year he obtained control of the Penrhiwfer and the Britannic Collieries at Gilfach Goch, lying immediately to the west and adjoining the Glamorgan Colliery undertaking, and immediately to the south of the Cambrian Colliery area. Of the Penrhiwfer Colliery, which had been acquired ' for a mere song,' he himself wrote that ' it was an undertaking upon which something like a quarter of a million had been expended, but for which there was nothing to show but two holes in the hillside surrounded by roofless buildings with crumbling walls.' The Penrhiwfer and Britannic Merthyr takings contain some of the more valuable of the steam coal measures.

It was this aggregation of mining enterprises that became known in the coal trade as the Cambrian Combine. The properties worked by the four companies, whose share capital totalled £1,400,000, adjoin one another and form a compact area of 6,868 acres, the greater part of which is situated in the centre of the Rhondda Valley. Their combined output in 1910 was at the rate of about three million tons per annum.

D. A. displayed no less energy in the development of the resources of these properties than he had done in the acquisition of control over them. Within five years, at an expenditure of £260,000, a new pit was sunk at the Naval Colliery, two smaller pits at the Britannic Colliery, and one at the Cambrian Colliery, while a battery of fifty new by-product recovery coke-ovens was constructed at the Glamorgan Collieries—enterprises which brought the total number of the combined collieries up to nineteen pits and three levels, and which were intended to increase the coal output to four million tons per annum, and the coke output to 70,000 tons per annum. Moreover, he gave a practical example of his deep interest in mining research work by establishing at Llwynypia a chemical laboratory as a branch of the by-product installation.

His policy was more that of the attainment of personal control than the actual fusion of trading corporations. The four companies retained their separate identities and traded under their own names, but their properties were worked under a system of collective production, the purchase of materials as well as the control over price policy was centralised, and all the collieries were placed under one supervising management and operated technically as a single unit. In all these administrative respects the combine was an organic whole.

In March 1913 the interests of the shareholders in the four constituent colliery companies of the combine were consolidated. For this purpose Consolidated Cambrian, Ltd., was formed with an authorised share capital of £2,000,000, and a subscribed capital of £1,791,211.

There were only two occasions in D. A.'s whole business career when he was personally identified with public issues of new capital. The first of these was the formation of Cambrian Collieries, Ltd., in 1895 on the conversion of the firm of Thomas, Riches & Co. into a limited liability company, when there was an issue of £200,000 in 4½ per cent. debentures and a portion of an issue of £200,000 in 6 per cent. preference shares. On that occasion the debentures were over-subscribed three times and the preference shares seven times. The other occasion was on the formation of Consolidated Cambrian, Limited, in May 1913. Of the capital of £2,000,000 registered by that company there were issued for sale at par 273,000 6 per cent. preference shares, and during the period of subscription these shares were quoted on the market at a substantial premium and were enormously over applied.

The creation of the Cambrian Combine was only one of his many achievements. The facts concerning the others are in some particulars even more remarkable. Every conquest was a stepping-stone to further conquests ; every successful deal was an inspiration to a greater effort ; and every increase in his power as a coal-master stimulated an ever-expanding ambition.   In April 1910 he completed the combine by the purchase of the Britannic properties at Gilfach. Goch.   Two months later, *i.e.*, June 1910, in conjunction with J. W. Beynon and Leonard Llewelyn, he acquired a controlling interest in the Fernhill Collieries situated at Treherbert.

In 1911 he became interested in collieries situated further west in the South Wales coalfield, and acquired the Duffryn Rhondda in the Afan Valley, and Cynon properties.

Second Period

An economic sphere less favourable than the South Wales coalfield to the employment of the genius of a great man of business, and particularly of a great business man who was under the influence of the more modern tendencies in industrial organisation, could hardly have been found. The mining industry in that district was hidebound by traditions.   The production of coal was more or less universally regarded as one economic function, the sale of that coal as another, and the marketing of it as a third function— all distinct and separate.   The colliery owners undertook the task of sinking and working the coal-mines, the sale of the output of the collieries was delegated to sales agents, whose duty was to sell the coal at the best price they could get consistent with such an arrangement of business as was calculated to secure the maximum regularity of employment at the pits, while the marketing of the coal was left in the hands of speculative middlemen and export merchants.

Again, the coalfield was divided up into hundreds of separate colliery undertakings, nearly all owned and worked by separate companies in active competition with each other, and jealous of one another's prosperity.   It was an industrial system composed in the main of petty businesses, lacking in all qualities of cohesion, and permeated by that distrust and envy usually characteristic of small industrial as of political communities under the sway of narrow parochial ideas, and either remote from, or hostile to, the influences of progressive thought and action. Moreover, it was as unimaginative as it was in the higher sense unprogressive.

D. A.'s achievements cut across all this. Few, if any, other colliery owners in the South Wales coalfield shared his ideas, and though the example which he set was bound in time to affect profoundly the organisation of the mining industry in South Wales and Monmouthshire, time was needed to convince the other coal-owners in South Wales of the wisdom of the policy of which his name became a symbol. In the meantime he directed his energies to the consolidation and extension of the interests which he had acquired in the coalfield, and to the acquisition of new interests in other fields of enterprise.

The position of personal pre-eminence as a man of business which he had acquired brought him offers of directorships from many and varied joint stock undertakings in South Wales. In 1909 he joined the Board of the Taff Vale Railway Company and shortly afterwards the Board of the Port Talbot Railway and Docks Company. In 1911–12 he was elected to a seat on the directorate of the Ebbw Vale Steel and Iron Company, and in 1914 became a vice-chairman of that concern, while he also became associated in a directorial capacity with several other enterprises.

But the feature of his activities in the period 1911–15 was the diversity of their character. He regarded as wasteful any and every system of enterprise which tolerated the existence of middlemen, when the services performed by them could be safely undertaken by the capitalists engaged in the actual production of the commodity. If there were profits to be made in the distribution of goods over the production of which he had control, those profits, he argued, should be retained, as far as practicable, for the benefit of the capital and labour immediately engaged in their production. He admitted that it was not practicable in every case to eliminate the merchant ; on the contrary, he believed strongly that there was a place, even in the coal trade, for the merchant who investigated the potentialities of foreign markets and who, by the marketing of coal on the basis more of analysis than of name, systematically studied and catered for the varied needs of consumers. He was prepared to undertake himself, to some extent, even this branch of the trade, but it was a specialised function, and there was great scope, in his opinion, for the activities of merchants operating on scientific lines. But the middle-man was only to be tolerated in so far as he was an absolute necessity for the most efficient conduct and most rapid development of the production of commodities. It was a logical result of the principles of business organisation in which he believed that he should endeavour to bring dis-tributive and other incidental functions within the purview of his own activities.

One of the first changes which he brought about was the centralisation of the agencies for the sale of the coals pro-duced at the collieries under his control. He placed the agency of the Glamorgan Coal Company in the hands of Lysberg, Ltd., of which he was chairman ; that of the Naval Colliery Company was retained by L. Gueret, Ltd., of which he was deputy chairman ; the sales agency of the Britannic Merthyr Coal Company he secured for the firm of Thomas & Davey, of which he was the principal partner, and also the agency of the Cambrian Collieries, Ltd. ; while Lysberg, Ltd., were given the agency of the Imperial Navi-gation Coal Company, Ltd. His next step was to create dis-tributive organisations, including shipowning, in the various countries with which he traded as coal-owner. In 1908 the principals of Lysberg, Ltd., formed La Cie. Chargeurs Française of Paris and Bayonne, with a capital of £105,000. By 1914 this French shipping company, for whom Plisson & Company, Paris, acted as managing owners, controlled a fleet of 50,000 tons d.w. Another offshoot of this concern was the Anglo-Spanish Coaling Company, Ltd., created for the purpose of establishing coal depots at Spanish ports ; later this company became the largest shareholder in subsidiary distributive organisations in France, Spain and Morocco.

Again, there was an enormous volume of insurance business involved in the various undertakings in which he was concerned as chairman, managing director or big shareholder. He saw no reason why this branch of commerce should not be attached to the great organisation which he had created. He was able to obtain the services of men with considerable experience in the conduct of insurance work, and with their aid, backed by the finances at his disposal, he was associated with the formation of the Plisson-Lysberg Insurance Company, Ltd. This corporation acquired a very great proportion of the insurance business of his undertakings which had previously gone to other insurance companies. He carried out extensive Stock Exchange operations, and these increased as his commercial and industrial engagements extended, and so he became a partner in the Cardiff stockbroking firm of A. Mitchelson & Co. In January 1915 he financially assisted in the formation of the Globe Shipping Company, with a registered capital of £100,000 and the ownership of one steamer. So prosperous was this company that in 1919 it owned and managed nearly 40,000 tons d.w. of steam tonnage.

Appreciating as he always did the value of a favourable public opinion, and the enormous influence which the press exercised in the moulding of that opinion, and in the correction of error and the spread of truth concerning Capital and Labour, he not only cultivated close relationships with the newspapers of his day, but also acquired control of several and founded one or two. Among the journals which he controlled were the *South Wales Journal of Commerce*, *Y Baner*, *Y Tyst*, *Cambrian News*, *Tarian*, and at a later date the Pontypridd newspaper series, and the *Merthyr Express*, and (financially though not politically) the *Western Mail*, Cardiff; while he also partly or wholly controlled the printing firms of Gee & Sons, Ltd., Denbigh, the Cambrian News, Ltd., Aberystwyth, the South Wales Printing and Publishing Company, Ltd., Cardiff, H. W. Southney & Son, Merthyr, and the Tarian Printing and Publishing Company. He attached exceptional importance to publicity on industrial questions, and together with Mr. Joseph Shaw, K.C., was instrumental in the creation of a publicity branch for the Monmouthshire and South Wales Coal Owners' Association. He had intended to either acquire one of the leading London evening papers or establish an evening paper of his own in the Metropolis. The *Pall Mall Gazette* was one of the London evening newspapers which he contemplated purchasing.

' A newspaper in London ' [he told the writer on one occasion] ' is a source of political power and I am prepared to spend some money on it. I prefer that sort of hobby to the ownership of a yacht, or the ownership of a mansion in town. I am not going to deny that I am wealthy now. As a matter of fact, I am a millionaire, and if I lose money I won't mind it, if by my wealth I increase my influence. There is room in London for an evening newspaper, the special features of which would be the publication of articles on economic subjects by experts, my object being to influence the opinions not so much of the man in the street, but those of Parliament and Clubland.'

He frequently deplored the lack of knowledge displayed by London newspapers in their discussion of coal questions, and in a conversation with the writer, during one of the war-period coal crises in South Wales, he repudiated the suggestion made in the newspapers at the time that he was a typical coal-owner, and denied strongly that he was making colossal profits out of the sale of coal. ' I am certainly,' he said, ' making big profits, but from coal the least of all my enterprises. I should say that on an average my coal investments yield me about five per cent., while some of my minor interests yield me 100 per cent. or more.' A point he emphasised was that, in his capacity as coal-owner, he was merely trustee for some 30,000 shareholders, and in that capacity he would be unfaithful to those who placed their interests in his charge if he did not do his best for them.

He was a prolific contributor to the columns of the newspapers. The files of the Cardiff journals teem with his special articles and letters on economic and political questions. On writing for the press he gave the writer this advice :

' In your articles be as simple as you can : spare your readers as much mental exertion as possible, for when you will have grown as old as I am you will find that the nation is composed mostly of fools and that they are either incapable of mental effort or are too lazy to apply it. Now and again, of course, you must leave a little to the imagination of your readers, but don't overload your matter with facts and figures, and it is often better to state your main point incidentally than to develop it by argument.'

With most men business interests would have absorbed practically all their energies, or at any rate left them with little time or inclination for the pursuit of other objects. That was not the case with D. A. He possessed an almost inexhaustible fund of physical, nervous and mental energy. His vitality was amazing. In the midst of the difficult problems which he had to investigate and solve from day to day as an employer of labour, as a capitalist with great European and American commitments,[1] and as a financier and promoter who was always on the look-out for new openings, he interested himself in every phase of the relations between capital and labour in the South Wales coalfield, applied himself assiduously to the discharge of the duties of the various public appointments he had accepted after the outbreak of the war in 1914, and exercised a vigilant and critical watchfulness of the policy and acts of the Government in the regulation of industry and commerce.

Among other positions which he occupied after the outbreak of the war were those of the chairmanship of the Clothing Committee of the Welsh Army Corps, membership of one of the Government War Contracts Committees, the chairmanship of the Departmental Committee appointed by the Board of Trade to consider the position of the coal trade after the war, and membership of the Lord Balfour Committee on Commercial and Industrial Policy. He readily placed at the disposal of the Government the services of the Pitwood Importing Organisation which he had created. In the earlier days of the war those services were invaluable, for they were efficient enough to keep the Admiralty Collieries abundantly supplied with pitwood imported from France and other foreign countries.

A suggestion made, but not adopted, may be recorded in his own words, written in September 1916 :

' A few weeks after the war broke out I recommended the Admiralty, through their representative at Cardiff, to

[1] See Chapter XIII and Appendix.

take over the entire control of the Admiralty Collieries in South Wales, guaranteeing, as they did in the case of the railways, profits equal to those derived before the war and leaving the management in the hands of the various colliery companies. This, I was told, was not practicable, though my own limited experience led me to believe that such control would have been perfectly practicable. Had the Government commenced with the Admiralty Collieries, under a process of evolution, control might have been extended to the whole coal production of the United Kingdom. Had this been done much of the labour trouble in the coal trade, and for the matter of that to some extent, also, in the railway world, would, I am convinced, have been avoided. Much of the unrest of the Welsh coalfields has been due to the discontent among the miners who believed that the coal-owners were making undue profits out of the war, and, in my opinion, had the Government at the outset limited profits to those obtained before the war, and allowed no increase in wages beyond those sufficient to cover the increased cost of living, public opinion would have supported them to the fullest extent.'

THIRD PERIOD

The *annus mirabilis* of his coal-owning achievements was 1916. In that year hardly a month passed in which his name was not connected with the conclusion of deals for the acquisition of new properties or with rumours of such transactions, and by its end he had added no less than six colliery undertakings, producing upwards of $3\frac{1}{2}$ million tons per annum, to those which he already controlled.

The first of these deals was that by which he obtained control over the Elder Collieries in the Maesteg district.

Next, in July 1916, he acquired a controlling interest in the Ferndale Collieries of D. Davis & Sons, Ltd., and by this transaction brought within the ambit of his influence one of the most successful companies and one of the richest steam coal takings in the world. The property is situated in the centre of the steam coal area of the South Wales coalfield, and possessed the almost unique distinction of a fifty years' record of practically unbroken prosperity.

The ink on the agreements under which the great Ferndale Collieries had been transferred to his control had hardly had time to dry when another deal, involving nearly as great a purchase price, was completed by D. A. and the group of financiers who were co-operating with him. On September 8, 1916, the official announcement was made that he had acquired a controlling interest in North's Navigation Collieries (1889), Ltd.

When this property was taken over in September 1916, the collieries at Caereu, Cognant and Maesteg, embracing an area of between 6000 and 7000 acres, had an output of nearly $1\frac{1}{4}$ million tons per annum. There are two estates, the smaller of which is situated at the south crop of the south basin of the coalfield near the Tondu junction, upon the Llynfi and Ogmore branch of the Great Western Railway, and the larger estate near Maesteg in the upper part of the Llynfi Valley, and extending northwards into the Afan and eastwards into the Garw Valley.

The other collieries which fell within the sphere of his directing influence in 1916 were relatively minor undertakings. In October 1916, in association with Mr. A. Mitchelson and Mr. H. S. Berry, he obtained possession of the Gwaun-Cae-Gurwen Anthracite Colliery, and, within a fortnight of the conclusion of this deal, of the International Coal Company.

This was the last of his colliery deals, but they do not exhaust his achievements as a financier and industrial organiser in this the most active period in his life as a capitalist. In November 1916, in conjunction with three other gentlemen, he acquired from the Board of Trade liquidator of enemy undertakings the German-owned shares in Sanatogen, Ltd., at a cost of £360,000, while a week later he also completed negotiations for the acquisition from the Board of Trade of control over the Anglo-Continental Guano Company, Ltd., which was another German property established in this country. In August 1916, acting in conjunction with a number of other capitalists, he made an unsuccessful bid for the Mannesmann Tube Company, situated at Llandore, near Swansea.

In the consolidation of the interests of these new properties he followed the same policy as that which he had adopted in connection with the undertakings acquired between 1907 and 1911. Addressing a meeting of shareholders after the purchase of a controlling interest in the Ferndale Collieries, he said :

' Our chief aim is the standardisation, so to speak, of policy, management and administration. Neither the public nor labour has anything to fear from us. No doubt we shall be able to effect a certain number of economies in management, but there is no intention of forming a coal ring or to put up prices ; on the contrary the tendency of these economies will be towards a reduction in the price of coal. There is no hostility to labour. The effect of a combination of this kind will be to eliminate the speculative middleman but not to interfere with the bonâ fide merchant, to whose enterprise in the development of foreign markets for the distribution of the Welsh product colliery owners owe so much.'

The sales agencies were in these, as in the previous deals, transferred to firms over which he had exclusive or predominant control, and into sales contracts restrictive clauses were introduced which reduced to a minimum the speculation of middlemen. All these different concerns retained their identities and traded independently of each other except in so far as their operations were influenced by a centralised price policy. There was nothing in the nature of a pooling of profits, or of a common agency for the purchase of material, while the pits were far too separated for the application to them as in the Cambrian Combine of a system of collective production. The only really effective tie between them was that D. A. either held a controlling financial interest or directed their several policies in his capacity as chairman of the respective companies.

The view, therefore, entertained rather widely, that these transactions were incidents in the creation of a huge coal trade combination is based on a fundamental misconstruction of the facts. They gave him great power, and had he lived it is very probable that that power would have been used towards the establishment in the South Wales coalfield of an industrial organisation under which prices would be better controlled than they had been in pre-war days ; but while these different colliery undertakings still derived such benefits as are inherent in a directorship that is practically common to them all they remain, subject to a common price policy, distinct trading bodies in active competition with each other.

Certainly these deals gave the movement in the direction of combination a great stimulus, and so extensive have been the absorptions and fusions in the decade ending 1920 that approximately at least three-fifths of the whole output of the South Wales coalfield is now under the control of four groups of allied colliery companies. But the distinguishing feature of D.A.'s activities in the coalfield was their personal and individualistic character. He was in business largely from ' a love of the game.' He revelled in the hard realities of a big business deal ; he was a great hunter pursuing big quarry. Only those who have realised the thrill of the chase can appreciate what business meant to him.

CHAPTER XI

No account of my father would be complete without some record of his public utterances and of the letters which he wrote to the press. He was a great letter-writer. To the end of his life he found it infinitely easier to express himself on paper than on the platform': his pen was his natural medium.

His letters, which dealt very largely with industrial questions, were usually filled to the brim with carefully worked out statistics, and packed with—often somewhat abstruse—economic theory. He had not the journalist's capacity for watering down his ideas with chat ; his writings were as full of stuff as an egg of meat, and not a line could be safely skipped. It might therefore be supposed that they made heavy and dull reading ; they were on the contrary esteemed very good copy by the local papers to which he usually wrote ; for this reason, that whether consciously or unconsciously, he invariably seasoned his dryest fact with the salt of some personal controversy. He loved a pen-and-ink fight. If it was natural to him to take a vivid interest in economic theory, it was even more characteristic to leap to battle. Sometimes he was the aggressor, more often perhaps some unwise antagonist trod on his coat-tail always temptingly outspread. He was a trying opponent, because, whilst he never lost his temper, indeed obviously enjoyed the whole performance with all the zest of a schoolboy in a fight, he had an almost uncanny knack of finding and unmercifully prodding his opponent's tenderest spot.

One must admit that this love of a fight was a handicap to him in his career. He wasted both time and energy upon it, made many unnecessary enemies and acquired a reputation for being difficult. Whilst he did thereby inspire a certain wholesome awe in some opponents, there were often times when he would have been far wiser not to fight. But he never could resist the temptation. He was always lured off the straight path that led to success by any chance of battle. . . . This was not for want of good advice at home. My mother is a peace-loving woman. ' It's not worth your while, David,' she would protest when he insisted on returning fire in the case of an attack from some quite insignificant quarter. Worth while or no, he had no intention of missing a chance of a fight ; he only grinned and went off whistling to spend an enjoyable evening or so in his study making up his reply, bits of which would often be read aloud for our approval and suggestions.

This habit of his was in early days a terrible trouble to his fellow coal-owners. It was one of the things that the older ones never quite forgave him, which seems odd, since he attacked the local labour leaders far more often than he did the docksmen. The labour leaders, however, used to the shrewd knocks of political warfare, forgave him wonderfully quickly. The coal-owners, who had the sensitiveness of those unused to publicity, were hurt in their tenderest feelings. They had still in the 'nineties those Victorian ideas of dignity which involved never making any attempt to enlist public opinion on their side. They had all the expert's contempt for public opinion anyway, and were still under the delusion that they could win without it. As for bandying words with the men ! . . . Their sense of suitability and dignity was outraged by the introduction of this new weapon, even when used on their side—and of course it was by no means always used on their side.

It has not been altogether easy to make a selection from my father's contributions to the press. To have given them all would have been to have filled a couple of volumes. Moreover, the earlier ones dealt largely with the local coal controversies of twenty or thirty years ago, details of which make as stale reading to-day as do last year's fashion-papers. I have therefore deliberately selected the personal parts of the letters, and would ask readers of this chapter to remember that what I have really done is to dish up the sauce without the meat.

The first big batch of letters was written during 1897 and 1898. The Sliding Scale Agreement which had been entered into in 1892 was timed to come to an end on March 31, 1898. For some years things had been bad in the South Wales coalfield. Profits had been very low even in the best collieries ; many of the poorer ones had failed altogether. Wages had been very low. At that time the wages of the South Wales miners compared very unfavourably with those of colliers in other parts of the country, although ten years later this position was reversed. In the summer of 1897 controversy arose both amongst masters and men as to whether it was advisable to renew the old 1892 Sliding Scale Agreement without amendment. My father was for drastic alteration. He had in 1896 put forward a Control of Output Scheme which would, he believed, if adopted, benefit the whole industry enormously. The majority of the coal-owners, however, disapproved of his scheme, largely because it was new ; they were also influenced by the fact that Sir W. T. Lewis (afterwards Lord Merthyr, chairman of the Coal Owners' Association), a second cousin and old enemy of my father's, was strongly against it. In order to dispose finally of my father's scheme Sir W. T. Lewis introduced in 1897 a Control of Output Scheme of his own, which though it differed in detail from my father's was essentially the same thing. My father, recognising his own scheme in another guise, dropped his original demand and proceeded to support enthusiastically Sir W. T. Lewis's version, which was, of course, the last thing that gentleman wanted. The men, meanwhile, were inclined to favour strongly a Control of Output Scheme, and to demand its adoption, but their leaders—more timid then than now—were afraid of going against the owners, and were moreover most indignant with my father for appealing directly to the men without their permission as he had done. My father was in fact a free lance attacking both sides as seemed best to him, and unpopular with the leaders on both sides, although—or rather because— he had considerable following amongst the rank and file.

During the summer of 1897 my father spent more than a little energy in attacking the men's leaders because they had not the courage to fight the owners on the Control of Output issue.   This roused the leaders to intense indignation, and they retorted by violently attacking him at various local meetings.

On September 9 my father replied in a letter to the *South Wales Daily News,* from which I quote a short paragraph.   It was headed :

'MR. D. A. THOMAS AND HIS CRITICS.'

' I appear to have put my foot into a hornet's nest, but I think I may congratulate myself upon having brought about greater unity among the miners' leaders in South Wales than has existed for some years.   I do not remember any occasion upon which they have shown so much unanimity as in their recent condemnation of myself.   They do not specify with precision the particular offence of which I have been guilty in regard to themselves, but content themselves with bringing a number of counter-charges against myself. I gather, however, that my chief crime has been a want of appreciation of the efforts they have made on behalf of the workmen, and in suggesting any unfavourable comparison between the wages paid in this and any other district.'

This letter had naturally enough the result of bringing forth specific charges from the miners' leaders, to which on September 22 he replied in a long letter to the *Western Mail,* from which I quote a few extracts :

'CONTROL OF THE COAL OUTPUT

'LETTER FROM MR. D. A. THOMAS, M.P.

'REPLY TO MESSRS. ONIONS AND RICHARDS

'CRITICISM OF LABOUR LEADERS.

' Mr. Richards accuses me of " making the position far more difficult, for the men did not care a jot for Mr. D. A. Thomas."   If I have made it more difficult to pursue the policy of doing nothing, as advocated by " Mabon " in his July address to the Cambrian Association, I am heartily glad of it, but seeing that " the men do not care a jot " for what I say, I fail to understand how I can in any way have affected the position. . . .

'Let me briefly enumerate the charges with which, as far as I understand, I am charged :

' 1. "Mr. D. A. Thomas is a millionaire." I wish I were. I only wish Mr. Richards would persuade my bankers that such were the case, but I cannot admit the soft impeachment.[1] . . . But were I a millionaire, in what way would it justify inaction on the part of the miners' leaders ?

.   .   .   .   .   .

' 3. Again, " Mr. D. A. Thomas's Colliery was not represented at the last conference." I must confess at once that I did not know it was one of the functions of a colliery owner to see that his workmen sent delegates to labour conferences. Until Mr. Richards' censure I had always thought the duty of an employer to be not to attempt to influence the workmen in such matters.

.   .   .   .   .   .

' 5. Mr. Onions complains that " up to a few weeks ago Mr. Thomas was in perfect agreement with the leaders," but that now I criticise the attitude of some of them. " Mabon " was in a fighting mood in June, and it is true that it was only after his extraordinary right-about-face in July that I began criticising his attitude, and when, through the Cambrian Association, he advised the workmen to rest content with their position and be satisfied with the blessings which they had already received, I cannot see how my criticisms justify inaction on the part of the miners' leaders.

' 6. Allegations have been made that the colliery company with which I am associated have been guilty of underselling. These statements, as I understand underselling, are untrue. They are always put forward whenever I make any public utterance in favour of the workmen. They generally emanate from the collieries of the employers on the sliding-scale committee. This, of course, may only be a coincidence. . . . But if I have been guilty of underselling, then let the employers help me against myself by putting into operation my proposals for the prevention of underselling. My action, in any case, would hardly justify inaction on the part of the miners' leaders.

' 7. My board of directors are charged with not giving the workmen the advance in wages that one of their number thinks the workmen generally are entitled to. A more silly complaint it would be difficult to conceive. I cannot

---

[1] His total fortune in 1897 amounted to about £100,000.

advise them to give any advance until our competitors in the coal trade are prepared to do the same.   They would be exceedingly foolish, in my judgment, to do anything of the kind, and would be untrue to the interests of the shareholders whom they represent.   But can this justify inaction on the part of the miners' leaders ? '

After this letter there seems to have been a lull for some weeks, possibly due to the fact that the attitude of the men's leaders had stiffened considerably, and my father had at the moment no fault to find with it.   Mabon and his colleagues, however, who had by no means forgiven his attacks, were keeping up a running fire of abuse, and in a speech made at Pontypridd, which was reported in the *South Wales Daily News* on December 7, he retorted :

' The curious part of the affair was that while Mabon was pursuing him week after week, and day after day, with these vindictive misrepresentations relating to matters of private and personal concern, Mabon was at the same time whining to his friends at the " cruel persecution " of Mr. D. A. Thomas, trying to pose, in short, as St. Mabon the Martyr.   He (Mr. Thomas) never went into Mabon's family affairs, but he only dealt with him as a public man and confined himself to his public actions and utterances.   Let Mabon follow the same rule and give up listening to the *clichés* of disappointed competitors.   (Hear, hear.)   He hoped that nothing that he had said would prevent Mabon from continuing to give the world his views upon the coal trade, for those discourses afforded an endless fund of amusement to merchants on 'Change.   (Laughter.)   His description last week of the half-million wagons—rather more than twenty times the number of wagons full and empty employed in that particular trade—of coal waiting to be tipped, and the 1s. 6d. increase in the f.o.b. cost that had resulted from the rise in freights was inimitable. (Laughter.)   By all means let him continue those entertainments, but let him confine his imagination to general matters.'

This speech, perhaps naturally, displeased Mabon considerably.   He described it as

' . . . such a tissue of libellous insinuations that no honourable man would touch it unless he was compelled to for the purpose of disinfection ' (*South Wales Daily News,* December 11, 1897).

After this somewhat heated interchange the papers record nothing further until March 1898, by which time the attitude of the leaders had further stiffened, and the position had considerably altered. In an interview with a *South Wales Daily News* representative on March 5, my father is reported as saying :

' The action of the miners' representatives upon the Sliding Scale Committee commends itself thoroughly to my mind. I think they have acted discreetly, and have fully justified the authority given them by their constituents. On the other hand, I regard the proposals of the employers as, under the circumstances, little short of impertinence.

' *The Reporter* : If you say such things of the employers they will call you hard names again.

' Well, my skin is getting pretty thick by this time. Whenever I do anything to support the action of the workmen I am always denounced by the employers and threatened with dire consequences at the next election.'

By this time Sir W. T. Lewis was and had been for some time busy repudiating the scheme which he had hatched merely to scotch my father's proposals. He desired, as he always had, to go on with the old Sliding Scale Agreement unaltered. My father, however, had no intention of letting him drop the scheme without a struggle. In season and out of season he reminded him that it was his (Sir W. T. Lewis') own scheme that he was repudiating.

In a letter to *The Times*, reproduced in the *Western Mail* on March 11, he wrote :

' It does not appeal to me as right that Sir W. T. Lewis' claim to the authorship of the control scheme should be overlooked, or fair that the workmen and myself should be denounced as unreasonable and revolutionary, when we are only asking Sir W. T. Lewis and the employers in general to adopt their own proposals.'

The controversy, which was conducted not directly with Sir William, who adhered to the older tradition and did not care to adventure personally into the public press, but for the most part with the South Wales correspondent of *The Times*, continued during March.

D. A. Thomas was of course accused by his enemies of deliberately trying to bring about a stoppage. In an interview with a *Western Mail* reporter, published on March 28, it would seem that, he had begun to give up hope of the Control Scheme being adopted :

' *The Reporter :* Do you think there is any chance of the Control Scheme being adopted ?

' *D. A.:* No ; I fear that now Sir William Thomas Lewis, who leads the employers by the nose, repudiates his own scheme, there is no hope for it at present, but we must go on preparing the soil for it.   A number of employers are in favour of it, even some on the sliding-scale committee. I cannot see why the employers should hesitate to avert the present crisis by giving a trial to the scheme, which, it must be remembered, would not come into operation if the price of coal is maintained at anything like the present figure.

' It has been said that a strike would benefit those firms which are not in the associations ?

' A strike would be the very worst thing that could happen to me from a financial point of view, but I cannot go into the private affairs of the Cambrian Company.   The general stoppage whether we worked or not would cost me personally many hundreds of pounds.

' In what way ?

' Suppose we went on working, some of our large contractors could come down upon us for double the monthly quantities at low prices, and we should not be able to take advantage of the rise to the extent of a single ton.   It must also be remembered that in the event of a general stoppage at the associated collieries the cost of production would go up.

' What do you think about the question of plenary powers ?

' The representatives of the men must, of course, be given some authority to negotiate, but I think the workmen would be very foolish to give plenary powers, and the leaders would be equally unwise to accept them.   The men should give the representatives, in my judgment, authority within certain limits.   If I were a workman I would most decidedly refuse to give authority to bind me for several years to the present scale. I would say to the leaders, " Do the best you can to get these amendments for me, but under no circumstances agree to the masters' proposals or to the scale as it now stands." '

Early in April came a curious development of the situation. The Cambrian workmen asked for an advance of twenty per cent. in wages. The Cambrian Board refused to give any advance at all, declaring that they would give nothing which the Associated Owners did not give. The Cambrian workmen came out on strike. The result of this unexpected development was that my father, who up to this time had been immensely popular with the rank and file, became in a day the best hated man in South Wales.

He was always held responsible by the general public for the actions of the Cambrian Board, but as a young man he was very far from being able to sway it. On the contrary the very fact of the popular misconception that he controlled the actions of Cambrian went against him inside the board room. On this particular occasion several of the directors, notably my father's elder brother, John Thomas, an innate Conservative, had been watching his proceedings during the past six months with deep disgust. His attacks on the Coal Owners' Association, his bandying words with the miners' leaders, his egging on of the men to insist on their rights, all these things went against every prejudice they had. When the Cambrian men asked for an advance these directors saw their chance to administer a just snub not only to the Cambrian men, but to my father, and to range themselves and their colliery on the side of the owners : they took it. My father, who was in favour of giving an advance (though not the whole twenty per cent. asked for), was overruled. Providentially, however, John Thomas went off to Biarritz before the next board meeting ; a reasonable compromise was then agreed to and the men came back to work.

The last letter of the Control controversy period, from which I propose to quote, is one to the *Western Mail* evoked by a speech made by Mr. Lester Jones, President of the Cardiff Chamber of Commerce and a firm supporter of Sir W. T. Lewis.

'. . . In criticising my action it was hardly necessary for Mr. Jones to say that " his own opinion was very much in accord with that of Sir William Thomas Lewis." It is well known that the Monmouthshire and South Wales Coal Owners' Association is a one-man affair, and that Sir W. T. Lewis carries the Association, so to speak, in his waistcoat pocket ; it was hardly necessary, therefore, for Mr. Jones to put his little beak—and Mr. Jones will not I am sure take offence where no offence is meant—for a moment over the edge of the pocket to chirp " Here I am still quite in accord," for nobody ever doubted it. . . . Last week Mr. Jones was loudest in his jeers because the Cambrian Colliery had not seen fit to give an advance ; this week he cannot contain his indignation because they have. It is impossible to please some folks.'

The next batch of letters came during the Cambrian strike of 1901. My father had really very little to do with this strike, which began in January 1901 and lasted for four months. When it broke out he had been on the verge of giving up his Cambrian directorship in order to devote himself more completely to politics. He held his resignation up, however, until the strike was over, and it was he, of course, who was singled out for attack by the men's leaders. The owners, still very sore at his behaviour during the strike of 1898, looked on with satisfaction. The *Western Mail's* introductory remarks to an interview with him will sum up the situation :

' THE CLYDACH VALE STRIKE
' MR. D. A. THOMAS TAKES UP THE CUDGELS
' " EVEN THE WORM WILL TURN "
' REPLY TO THE REPRESENTATIVES OF THE MEN.

' Mr. D. A. Thomas, M.P., has at last consented to give his views of the strike at the collieries with which he is closely associated at Clydach Vale—the Cambrian Collieries. These were the collieries which were kept in full swing throughout the disastrous general strike of a couple of years ago, and coal-owners, colliers, and general public are looking on with keen interest.'
. . . ' " Mabon," said Mr. Thomas with a laugh, " when

he assumes the rôle of fighting leader, reminds me of the ' Duke of Plaza-Toro,' who

> ' In enterprise of martial kind,
> When there was any fighting,
> He led his regiment from behind :
> He found it less exciting.' " '

' Mabon ' replied more in sorrow than in anger :

' . . . not until " D. A." himself spoke would I believe that they who have so often heard the workmen before and encouraged them to bring their grievances to them would now condemn them without a hearing. As to " D. A." himself, the workmen, my colleagues, and myself were led to believe, somehow, that he was ill and away from home. To this supposed fact we attributed the reluctance of the directors to receive our deputation. In him was our hope. We thought that when he returned something would certainly be done to bring both parties together and have the unfortunate dispute brought to an end. And again shall I say that unless he had himself spoken it would not be believed that all these hopes would be so soon and completely shattered.'

My father refused to interfere in a matter concerning the safety of the miners, which lay within the province of the colliery manager :

' . . . The Clydach Vale dispute is not going to be settled by a newspaper controversy, and the matter really rests in Mr. Llewelyn's hands and not in mine. I look upon Mr. Llewelyn [1] as a very promising young mining engineer, who, I venture to predict, will attain a very prominent position in the South Wales coalfield. He is perfectly competent to deal with this dispute himself.'

During the course of the strike many further letters and interviews appeared. At its conclusion he left the Board in order to devote himself more completely to politics, and amongst other activities threw himself with much energy into the task of building up an efficient Liberal Organisation for South Monmouthshire with a view to defeating Colonel Fred Morgan (the sitting Conservative M.P.) at the next election.

[1] Now Sir Leonard Llewelyn, K.B.E.

In December 1901 some remarks made in a speech at a Liberal meeting at Cwmbran raised the ire of Mr. Joseph Lawrence, Conservative member for the Monmouth Boroughs, and led to an amusing interchange of personalities. My father had suggested that Colonel Fred Morgan owed his seat not so much to his own personal qualifications as to the fact that he shone in the reflected popularity of his brother Lord Tredegar, and had remarked that :

' . . . he had taken the trouble to go through the Hansard reports of the House of Commons, and had come to the conclusion that Colonel Morgan was not an obstructionist by speeches. His record for twenty years had been three seconds per annum. (Laughter.) Since then he had made another speech, which had raised the record to five seconds per annum.'

On December 13 Mr. Joseph Lawrence took exception to these remarks (and also apparently to some reference to himself (not reported), which he described as being clumsy and witless), complained that they were in extremely bad taste, and alluded to my father as a ' sort of playful hippopotamus of politics.' He further referred to the fact that there had been trouble between my father and his ex-colleague in Merthyr Boroughs, Mr. Pritchard Morgan, a Liberal Imperialist.

My father replied in a speech delivered at Newport on December 18 :

' Mr. Lawrence had once said that he regarded consistency as a virtue of small minds ; consequently, his constituency must not look to him for that virtue.[1] (Laughter.) But if the converse were true, if to be everything in turn and nothing long, if to be consistent only in inconsistency was a true measure of intellectual greatness, and he had nothing to gain by flattering Mr. Lawrence—Newport was represented in Parliament by nothing short of genius. (Laughter.) On another occasion he would amplify this view by reference to the opinion expounded by Mr. Lawrence at Llantrisant and Newport, to convictions firmly held at Cardiff and

---

[1] This was a reference to the fact that Mr. Lawrence, who had begun life as a Liberal, had now changed his political convictions.

opposite convictions held with equal firmness a few months after at Monmouth.   Mr. Lawrence reminded him more than anything else of a quick change artiste (laughter), and it was marvellous the variety of wardrobes he was able to pack in his mobile carpet-bag.'

But perhaps the most interesting portion of the speech was that devoted to explaining the reason of the trouble between himself and Mr. Pritchard Morgan :

'. . . He felt sure, however, that Mr. Lawrence should not suggest that his treatment of Mr. Pritchard Morgan was other than what it should have been.   No one appreciated more than he did the generosity of his late colleague, but he was not sure whether in the excitement of a general election, it had received a full meed of public recognition.   What happened was this—a couple of days before the poll the walls of Merthyr were covered with this advice : " Vote for Keir Hardie and D. A. Thomas—both pro-Boers." [1] (Laughter.) Virtue carried to excess became a vice, and when, notwithstanding modest efforts at concealment, he discovered that the poster was issued by Mr. Pritchard Morgan, he (the speaker) said that such self-abnegation on the part of his colleague should not go unrecognised. (Laughter.) He thought it was only due to himself to say that he left no stone unturned to give publicity to his late colleague's generosity (loud laughter), a generosity all the greater because on another poster he (Mr. Pritchard Morgan) described himself as a Liberal Imperialist.   Mr. Morgan had wished to do good by stealth, and naturally blushed to find it fame. (Laughter.)   It was significant of the confidence with which Mr. Morgan had inspired the electors during a period of twelve years' representation of Merthyr that they took his advice, and voted as he had directed them. . . .' [2]

Mr. Joseph Lawrence was perhaps naturally annoyed by parts of this speech, and on December 21 retorted in two

---

[1] This was during the Khaki election of 1901, when pro-Boer was the most opprobrious epithet which could be used.   Incidentally Mr. Keir Hardie, who was then standing for Merthyr for the first time, was regarded as a wild and dangerous extremist, to be bracketed with whom might well prove fatal to any Liberal candidate's chances.

[2] That is to say my father and Mr. Keir Hardie were returned, whilst Mr. Pritchard Morgan was at the bottom of the poll.

long letters to the *Western Mail*, the opening paragraph of the first of which ran :

' The *Western Mail* once said Mr. D. A. Thomas was the most sinister figure in Welsh politics. It didn't distress him. If you wish to instil into some men's minds elementary ideas of the decencies and amenities of public life you must first trepan them. Other men you must club well, when a rapier fails to penetrate their hides.

' Mr. D. A. Thomas, relying on the impunity from castigation I once accorded him when he vituperated me, has this time presumed too far. He pleads he is without a sense of humour. His " paper bullets of the brain " prove it. I am neither awed nor edified by his ill-mannered behaviour— thrice repeated—in attacking other members with personalities in their own constituencies contrary to all the accepted canons of public life.'

In a later portion of one of the letters he—perhaps rather unwisely—compared himself to Disraeli.

To this rebuke my father replied in an open letter :

' Llanwern, Dec. 21, 1901.

' DEAR LAWRENCE,

' I have read your amusing letter in to-day's paper, and cannot help feeling that something I have said has annoyed you. Should any opportunity occur of dealing with the many important matters you raised, you may rely upon my doing it in a spirit of good temper, " an angry man stirreth up strife, and a furious man aboundeth in transgression."

' In the meantime, please do not run away with the idea that because I occasionally find it difficult to take you seriously on the coal trade, I am not at one with your London Correspondent in the *South Wales Daily Telegraph*,[1] when he says : " Mr. Lawrence, as all the world knows, is not by any means an ordinary man."

' I shall look forward with pleasure to your maiden speech in Parliament, and also when later, as you promise, " history will repeat itself," and " after the manner of Disraeli," you delight the House of Commons.

' I have long felt that what the Tory Party needs is another Disraeli, and I venture with confidence to predict

[1] This paper was believed to be owned by Mr. Lawrence.

it is not the Welsh Members only who will " relish " and " Hail " your appearance in that rôle.

'Wishing you the compliments of the season,
'Believe me,
'Yours very faithfully,
'D. A. Thomas.

'P.S.—I am sending this to the local press, as I might be thought lacking in courtesy were I not publicly to acknowledge your references to myself.'

In 1904 there was a further and prolonged press controversy over the candidature of Mr. Guest (now Lord Wimborne) for Cardiff.

Presumably disagreements had been going on for some months behind the scenes before the matter burst into print. At the time that Mr. Guest was proposed as Liberal candidate for Cardiff he was actually still sitting Conservative member for Plymouth, but during the Tariff Reform controversy had, with the rest of his family, followed Mr. Winston Churchill across the floor of the House. My father, with a number of other Cardiff Liberals, took strong exception to the idea of his candidature. His first letter on the subject appeared in the *South Wales Daily News* on May 21, 1904.

I quote extracts :

'The General Purposes Committee of the Cardiff Liberal Association are preparing to mark the height to which the flowing tide of Liberalism has risen, and to signalise what Mr. Herbert Gladstone promises will be the greatest victory of modern times, by selecting as their candidate " the sitting Conservative member for Plymouth." He is the most suitable man they have been able to find to represent the metropolis of Wales. On the face of it the selection would not appear to be an ideal one, but they explain this seeming incongruity by an assurance that Mr. Guest's past must be attributed to the folly of youth, out of which he will grow to political maturity, and if we only give him time he will abandon his opposition to English Disestablishment and his affection for the House of Lords, just as completely, just as readily, as he has abandoned other principles of Tory faith, and become all that we look for in a Radical representative.

'I do not question that his education is progressing,

or that it will make rapid strides under the stimulus of the opposition that is now being offered to his candidature. But I very much doubt whether the hon. member himself will be prepared to adopt unreservedly the plea put forward by his friends in mitigation of his former attitude towards Liberal and Labour reforms, for he claims to have made a close study of political questions for years past. . . .'

To the *South Wales Daily News*, May 31, 1904 :

' Before dealing with the attitude of Mr. Guest towards Labour, may I be allowed in this letter to refer to the criticisms that have been directed during the past week at those of us who are opposed to his candidature, and let me renew my appeal to Mr. Guest's friends to conduct the controversy without heat. Gentlemen, let us be calm ; let us try to discuss the points of difference in a philosophic spirit, free from prejudice, appealing only to reason. Nothing can be gained by calling names or ascribing unworthy motives. The issue between us is one upon which Liberals may honestly differ ; it is that of loyalty to party *versus* loyalty to principle. We are accused of disloyalty because we decline to discard our principles. True there are minor points on which we are at variance, such as the methods adopted in the selection of the candidate, the question whether the Labour Party should have been first consulted, and whether a sitting Tory member makes the best possible Radical candidate immediately his opinions become modified. But the main issue is that of party *versus* principles. Mr. Lewis Williams and Mr. Allgood deem loyalty to party to be paramount over every other consideration. They say, in effect, let us have a candidate who calls himself a Liberal whatever his antecedents or principles may be : the label is the great thing. We Radicals on the other hand place principle first, and further believe that in so doing we in the long run best serve the true interests of the Progressive Party. We are ready to subordinate our opinions on questions of policy and tactics to those of the recognised leaders of the party, but we are not prepared to abandon principles at the behest of anyone. Party organisation is only a means to an end, and not the end itself. If Party Unity can only be secured by the sacrifice of principles for the promotion of which the party is organised, the whole purpose of party is defeated. It is only fair to add that the friends of Mr. Guest state that he is at the moment in a very plastic condition, and that if sufficient and prolonged pressure is applied he will ultimately develop into a pronounced Progressive. Let me at once admit that the rapid results of the pressure already applied tend to corroborate this view and greatly encourage us to continue the squeezing process. But assuming Mr. Guest's friends have fully and correctly gauged his political character, I cannot help thinking that the suitable and dignified candidate for the Radical metropolis of Wales is the man who already holds the principles of the party from conviction, rather than one who only adopts them under pressure. Sir Edward Reed has been accused of being an indiarubber politician ; I don't know that the substitution of putty for indiarubber is necessarily an improvement.

.   .   .   .   .   .

'I accept the kindly advice of my friend Mr. Lloyd George in the spirit in which it was given, and I do not presume for a moment to question his authority on the subject of " political wrecking." No one appreciates Mr. Lloyd George's intelligence more fully than I do, and I may therefore be allowed to reciprocate his kindly advice by suggesting that with his marvellous gift of fluency he might convey an equally strong and possibly not less lasting impression upon the more thoughtful of his hearers were he to sometimes moderate his language and avoid attributing to others motives which they disavow.

'There is one statement made by Mr George on Friday night in which I cannot help thinking his memory must have betrayed him. He is reported to have said, " During the Education Act (presumably during the passage of the Bill through the House of Commons) he (Mr. George) had conversations with Mr. Guest, Mr. Churchill and some others. They did not like the Act. It is true they obeyed the party Whips, but that with a great deal of reluctance." Mr. Guest has told us that his conscience has for long been his only guide and not the crack of the party Whip. Mr. George made that statement in order to show that Mr. Guest's conversion was not the political somersault some of us supposed, but had been a slow mental process extending over years. Now I decline altogether to believe that Mr. Guest could have been guilty of telling Mr. George in private that he was opposed to the Education Bill and only supported it under pressure, while at the same time in public he was declaring to his constituents that it was an " admirable instrument," " a great educational measure," which they must " be determined to put their shoulders together " to pass into law, that " the compromise introduced into the Bill was fair and the only right one," and that those who shared the views of Mr. Lloyd George were " blinded by secular animosity," were " proposing an unjustifiable fraud," were guilty of " wily and insidious attacks," and were " wicked and wrong to declare that the Bill was an ecclesiastical or sectarian Bill."   I have not an exaggerated opinion of Mr. Guest's political consistency, but I feel sure my friend has unwittingly done Mr. Guest an injustice, and now that his attention has been drawn to it I feel sure he will take the earliest opportunity of correcting the error into which he has only fallen in his friendly anxiety to portray the Tory member for Parliament as a tried and trusted Liberal of long standing.'

South Wales Daily News, June 3, 1904 :

' Whatever may be the qualifications of a sitting Conservative member for the position of Radical candidate, it is only fair to say that they are in no way affected by the methods adopted by certain members of the General Purposes Committee of the Cardiff Liberal Association in their recent selection, and Mr. Guest cannot of course in any way be held responsible for the refusal of the Executive to consult the recognised leaders of Labour in Cardiff before the recommendation was made.   The Executive alone is responsible for what can hardly fail to be regarded by impartial men as a distinct and deliberate snub to an important section of the Progressive Party, namely, that of organised Labour in the town. . . .   What course the Trades Council will now take remains to be seen, and, in the meantime, we may quietly call to mind Mr. Guest's services to Labour in the past, and consider his qualifications to represent Labour in the future.

'The officials of the Liberal Publication Department who favour his candidature have acted wisely from their point of view in refusing to furnish the Trades Council with copies of the record of Mr. Guest's votes : they would hardly have helped him with Labour. . . .

'Mr. Guest's sympathy with Labour may be judged from

M

the following indications : he voted for the Corn Tax, a tax paid largely by the poorest of the poor ; for the Coal Duty, which has proved so prejudicial to the wages of the colliers in South Wales and Monmouthshire, and to the trade of the great port Mr. Guest now seeks to represent in Parliament. He voted against " an attempt to secure the more vigorous administration of the existing laws designed to secure better conditions for railwaymen." Last year he voted against Mr. Shackleton's Trades Disputes Bill, though it was not a party measure. This year, after his selection by the Cardiff Liberal Association, he voted for Mr. Paulton's Bill, but with an additional clause for safeguarding the funds of trades unions. He now declares, in respect of the somewhat wider measures of Mr. Paulton, that " trades unionists only asked that they should be restored to the position they occupied under the legislation of 1876, and which they occupied till recent decisions in the Law Courts. He did not think that was an extreme or unreasonable demand." As one of those whose names appear on the back of Mr. Paulton's Bill, and who was therefore responsible for its introduction, I thank Mr. Guest for this testimonial to our moderation, but, why, holding such views, did he vote against the more modest proposals of Mr. Shackleton last year ? It was all very well to dissemble your love, but why did you kick them downstairs ? The explanation, I fear, is that in the case of the Conservative member for Plymouth

" A merciful Providence fashioned him hollow,
In order that he might his principles swallow."

The process of conversion on this matter since Mr. Guest was first mentioned for Cardiff is more amazing than instructive. Space will not permit me to give details of the process, but they go to prove that his expression of opinion made to-day is only of value as indicating what it will not be to-morrow. . . . He is so afraid lest the country should lose a day of his valuable services that he clings closely to the old love of Plymouth until he is on with the new at Cardiff. . . .'

These protests were of no avail. Mr. Guest was adopted as Liberal Candidate, and in the election of 1906 Cardiff was lost to the Liberals and a Tory member, Lord Ninian Stewart, returned.

CHAPTER XII

LETTERS AND PRESS CONTROVERSIES, 1906 TO THE END

SHORTLY after the election of 1906 my father rejoined the Cambrian and other Boards and began to devote himself more completely to business than ever before.

In October 1906 he was once more engaged in controversy with one of the miners' leaders, this time Mr. Watts Morgan :

Western Mail, October 20, 1906 :

'ATTACK ON MR. D. A. THOMAS
'STRONG REMARKS BY MR. WATTS MORGAN
'TALK ABOUT RUSSIA AND THE CZAR.

' He (Mr. Morgan) wanted to warn Mr. D. A. Thomas that as long as the company were inviting non-Unionists into the colliery they were creating friction with the workmen. . . . One other point which would appeal to Mr. D. A. Thomas was the autocratic way in which the management dealt with the workmen. Talk about Russia and the Czar, indeed.'

Western Mail, Tuesday, October 23, 1906 :

'MR. D. A. THOMAS AS THE CZAR
'CHARACTERISTIC REPLY TO MR. WATTS MORGAN
'SHARP ATTACK MET BY A COUNTER-ATTACK.

' May I be allowed in self-defence to refer to the attack made by Mr. Watts Morgan upon myself, and reported in your issue of Saturday—an attack which I cannot help feeling was as uncalled for as it was unprovoked.

' Only recently I rejoined the Cambrian Board, for whose action I am no more or less responsible than any other individual director. But because I happen to occupy a public position Mr. Watts Morgan has lost no time in attempting to go behind the back of the colliery agent, who is more immediately responsible for the safe working of the mines, and by administering a series of warnings and threats to my humble self, he seeks to induce me to interfere in the agents' province and to betray the trust confided to me by the shareholders of the company. He has mistaken his man.'

He had indeed mistaken his man if he expected my father to do anything but abide absolutely by the verdict of the colliery manager. All his life he carried complete trust in and loyalty to his subordinates almost to a fault. In return he demanded a very complete loyalty from them, and usually got it. Loyalty was perhaps the virtue he prized most of all.

' Let me pass on to the case which, according to Mr. Watts Morgan, is " one of the most brutal that have taken place anywhere in the Rhondda." " He hoped that he would never have to call attention to a similar case again." Well, I hope that if he does that he will not attempt to mislead the public. His attitude on this occasion is the more inexcusable in that Mr. Llewelyn only a few days ago furnished the press with full particulars of the case. Let me briefly summarise the facts of this " brutal case " as given by Mr. Llewelyn. It is that of a man named John Martin, who has been employed at the colliery for a number of years, and latterly as lamp examiner and locker of No. 2 pit by night. In June of this year one of our overmen detected a defective lamp in the workings and called Martin's attention to the fact, pointing out to him that he had passed the lamp without having detected the defect. Martin admitted the mistake, attributed it to his failing eyesight, and expressed regret at the occurrence. The matter was reported to the manager, who gave instructions that Martin could not be allowed to retain his position as lamp locker, but that he should be employed in some other occupation. Several employments underground were then offered to Martin, but these he refused for one reason or another to accept. When Mr. Watts Morgan pressed for his reinstatement it was pointed out that this involved grave risks to the lives of hundreds of workmen. For this

Mr. Llewelyn was called an autocrat, and I am likened to the Czar of Russia. . . . Mr. Watts Morgan will, I feel sure, accept this little advice from the Little White Father in the spirit in which it is given.'

This reply seems to have annoyed Mr. Watts Morgan considerably. In his next speech he referred to 'A pawky, scraggy, squeaky coal-owner of Mr. D. A. Thomas' type.'

My father promptly replied :

Western Mail, Monday, October 29, 1906 :

'LITTLE WHITE FATHER CONTROVERSY
'MR. THOMAS' REJOINDER TO MR. WATTS MORGAN
'POLITICAL BLACKMAILING—A PROTEST
'LAST YEAR'S EXPLOSION AT CLYDACH VALE.

' The temperature displayed by Mr. Watts Morgan leads me to suspect that I have said something which has caused him annoyance. Apparently, it was a reference to his intellectual calibre. I once heard so great an authority on Parliamentary etiquette as the late Mr. Gladstone make a similar reference to a gentleman of Cabinet rank who happened at the time to be seated opposite him, and if in following the precedent set by that illustrious statesman I have wounded the susceptibilities of Mr. Morgan I am sorry. But, frankly, the report of his speech affords me no ground for revising my estimate of his mental qualifications. Mr. Watts Morgan has almost persuaded himself that it was not he who commenced this controversy, but it is idle for him now to attempt to excuse his unprovoked onslaught on my humble self by arguing that his description of me as the Czar of Russia was restricted in its application. Even the worm will turn, and he must not get angry when he discovers that there are limits to the endurance of even so peace-loving an individual as myself. . . . Mr. Watts Morgan avers that I claim not to be asked to reconcile my private actions with my public views. No, what I have done is to protest against political blackmailing, to which Mr. Morgan and his friends have endeavoured to subject me. When the governor of a certain island was asked why he had not obeyed the instructions given him to fire a salute on a particular occasion he replied : " I have a hundred reasons.

In the first place I have no guns." "That is enough," was the answer, "we can dispense with the remaining ninety-nine." So when I am charged by Messrs. Rees and Thomas with having deliberately brought about the lock-out of 1901, I can produce many reasons in disproof of this grave charge, but I hope it will suffice if I point out that there was no lock-out at the Cambrian Collieries in 1901. There was a strike of five months' duration caused by the men coming out without notice. True I may have been responsible in some degree for the prolongation of the struggle, because I considered that once the struggle had been forced upon us the occasion was a favourable one for modifying several long-standing disabilities under which the company laboured. Mr. Morgan's references to the case of Martin are amusing, but in the interests of accuracy I must repeat that he asked for Martin's "reinstatement" in a position involving the safety of the lives of hundreds of workmen after the man had acknowledged himself to be physically incapacitated for the office, and Mr. Morgan's suggestion that he should be found work on the surface was merely a belated afterthought.

'I was a friend of the Federation when most of its present leaders in South Wales were stoutly resisting the introduction of its policy into the district, and I have remained a friend ever since. When I require references for my attitude towards Labour I shall not need to go to Messrs. Watts Morgan, Noah Rees or John Thomas, but I shall rely on Messrs. Burt, John Wilson, Mabon, Fenwick, Bell and other leaders whose testimony, I respectfully submit, will carry hardly less weight with a discriminating public than would anything that could be said by Messrs. Morgan, Rees and Thomas.'

There are no further letters during 1906, and 1907 seems to have been a blank year, but December 1908 finds them at it again :

South Wales Daily News, December 12, 1908 :

'THE LLWYNYPIA STOPPAGE

'"THE LITTLE WHITE FATHER AND THE GREAT TROMBONE."

'Once more the Rhondda Valley resounds and reverberates with the intellectual note of the Great Trombone ; and it becomes necessary for the Little White Father to

raise again the still small voice of common sense and reason.
I had almost begun by advising Mr. Watts Morgan to confine his public utterances to matters within his own range
of information, but to restrict his opportunities within
such very narrow limitation would, I feel, be unduly taxing
his patience.   So I forbear.

.   .   .   .   .   .

'There is only one point more with which I should like
to deal.   Mr. Morgan resents the generosity of the company
in providing free meals for the children.   The local leaders
try to draw off attention from their illegal action in advising
the men to come out without notice—Mr. Morgan free from
blame, of course, in this particular—by exciting public
sympathy in favour of the little ones who suffer as a consequence.   The company felt it was very hard the poor
children should suffer, however blameworthy their parents
might be, and took practical steps to prevent it.   Whether
those parents are morally justified in saying they would
see their offspring starve as a result of their own stupidity
rather than accept food at the hands of those whom they
(their parents) have tried to injure, I will not stop now to
discuss.   But after this exposure of their cant and hypocrisy
I hope we shall hear no more whining about the sufferings
of the children from Mr. Hopla and leaders of that kidney.'

The next controversy took place once more on the
political field, and arose during the election of January
1910.   My father, attracted once more by the chance of
an interesting fight, had left Merthyr with its huge, safe
majority in order to try to win back Cardiff (then held by
Lord Ninian Stewart) for the Liberals.

A catechism was on that occasion addressed to my
father by the *Western Mail* (the Conservative paper).   I
give some of the questions with his replies.   The first is
interesting as showing that the animosity felt against him
for his action during the strike of 1898 had not, even in 1910,
died down.

'*Question* :
'Who encouraged the workmen to persist in their demands
in 1898 and made a fortune by working the Cambrian
Collieries at the same time by prolonging the strike, which

resulted in an enormous loss to thousands of workmen at Cardiff and Penarth Dock thrown out of their employment ?

' *Answer* :

' I accept the fullest responsibility for the action of the Cambrian Company in 1898. We were not at the time, and never had been, members of the Employers' Association. Personally I was strongly opposed (and am still) to the regulation of wages by an automatic sliding scale which make prices—over which the workmen can exercise no control—the only factor. I was also opposed to the whole attitude of the employers at the time. . . .

' The stoppage was due to the mistaken policy of the South Wales employers, encouraged, if my memory serves me, by the *Western Mail.* The *Western Mail* must, therefore, take its share of the responsibility for the disastrous results its action produced, and not seek to shift the blame on innocent shoulders.

' *Question* :

' Who was requested by the workmen at Aberdare to give up the representation of Merthyr and Aberdare Boroughs owing to his attitude towards the Clydach Vale workmen in June 1901 ?

' *Answer* :

' There is no truth in the allegation. During the whole of the twenty-two years I represented the Merthyr Boroughs I have never had any vote of want of confidence passed upon me by the workmen of the constituency, much less have I been asked by them to resign. On the contrary, in 1906, the general election next following the date mentioned in your fable, I was elected—the great majority of the voters being workmen—by a higher percentage of those on the register than any member in England or Wales, though a direct Labour and another Liberal were candidates for the Merthyr Boroughs at the time.

' *Question* :

' Is it true that Mr. D. A. Thomas and his partner in the Cambrian Collieries made above £472,000 as profits in the nine years ended 1907 ; that they divided 30 per cent. profit in the second half of 1908, and have made enormous profits in the year 1909 ?

' *Answer* :

' I am glad at last to come to one suggestion that is well founded. I cannot deny the soft impeachment that we make profits at Cambrian, and that these were really excellent in 1908.   If it will be any information to the Editor I don't mind admitting that is mainly the purpose for which the company was first formed and continues its existence.   We not only pay the highest rates of wages in the coalfield, but under the played-out system of Free Trade we last year paid 20 per cent. dividend to our ordinary shareholders after placing substantial sums to reserves, etc.   Tell it, not in Gath, but I am paid as Managing Director a salary—I confess by no means adequate—for the despicable duty of looking after the interests of the shareholders, and my ambition is to make the company a regularly paying 20 per cent. concern.   I am not without hope that my ambition may be realised.'

In December 1910 my father retired from Parliament but still continued to take an active interest in politics, as may be seen from many of his public utterances.   I quote one made in reference to Sir Edward Carson in November 1913 at the time of the threatened Ulster rebellion :

' He was a kind of man who, if he were on a football field and found the game going against him, would lead a rabble on the ground against the referee.'

Most of the letters and speeches at this period, however, related to industrial matters.

Western Mail, Thursday, November 27, 1913 :

' NEED TO CONSERVE COAL
' MR. D. A. THOMAS' POOR IDEA OF OUR STATESMEN.

' He [D. A. Thomas] said that between 1700 and 1751 the population of England and Wales was practically stationary, but during the last 150 years—since the growth of the production of coal—the population had grown six-fold.   The countries which were following closely in England's wake were countries which produced coal.   Coal was not nearing the point of exhaustion in South Wales, neither would within the next 400 years ; but it would become dearer and dearer, the thinner seams having to be worked.   As far as possible they should conserve their resources.   Was it right for this generation to work out from the ground that which the centuries had put there, and leave their successors to face a National Debt with no coal ? Statesmen should carefully consider the question, but there were not a dozen in the House of Commons who understood coal, and not many more who understood political economy.'

In March 1912 an amusing accusation was made by Mr. Vernon Hartshorn, which he promptly denied.

' I am one of those [said Mr. Hartshorn] who think that men like Mr. D. A. Thomas are less concerned about fighting the workmen, less concerned about resisting the minimum wage, than about something else. I will tell you what I think D. A. Thomas is after. I do not think there is another man who knows so much about mining in all its branches from the commercial standpoint as D. A. Thomas does. He has organised the industry commercially as no other man has done, and I give it as my opinion that his chief concern in this movement is to bring sufficient pressure to bear upon the Government to compel them to take over the Cambrian Collieries and to pay a big price for them. I say that in all sincerity. I think it is his little game, and if it proves to be correct it will be quite in accord with all the other little games he has played, at any rate during my lifetime. (Laughter.) Well, that is a matter for the Government and not for us. If the Government choose to buy their collieries out and ensure to the workers what they are asking for, very well. But what we do want the Government to do, if they do anything at all, is to see that either under the State ownership or private enterprise, the home life of the miners shall be safeguarded against poverty, want and misery, such as has characterised their life in the past.'

Western Mail, Monday, March 4, 1912 :

' WITHOUT FOUNDATION

' MR. D. A. THOMAS DENIES MR. HARTSHORN'S STATEMENT.

' Mr. D. A. Thomas, interviewed on Sunday with regard to Mr. Hartshorn's reference to the Cambrian Collieries, made the following statement :

" I am sure my friend Mr. Vernon Hartshorn expressed the opinion in perfect sincerity, but there is no foundation for the suggestion in fact. If the shareholders in any of the Cambrian Combine Collieries wish to dispose of their property I should much prefer them to sell to Mr. Vernon Hartshorn and his friends, who might then put the guaranteed individual minimum wage, irrespective of work done, into operation.   It would prove a most interesting object-lesson."

In January 1914, in a speech delivered up in the Rhondda, he made a very typical defence of his point of view.

Western Mail, Friday, January 30, 1914 :

'Mr. D. A. Thomas on his Defence
  'Syndicalist Movement in Wales
 'Production per Workman decreased.

'Mr. D. A. Thomas said he had heard that a coloured gentleman had recently been trying to collect a few coppers from the Cambrian workmen as they left with their pay. The speaker observed that he might have a black face, but he had not a black heart like D. A. Thomas.   (Laughter.) He (Mr. Thomas) believed he had a skin like a rhinoceros, and if people were not saying nasty things of him he would feel that he was neglecting his public duties.   But he was going to defend himself against that charge.   Over the past five years during which the trade had been more than usually prosperous, the amount distributed in dividends to colliery ordinary shareholders in South Wales was only about 8 per cent. of the amount paid in wages to the colliery workmen.   Moreover, the total amount paid in capital in what was essentially a hazardous enterprise amounted only to about a seventh of the increased earnings received by the workmen during the past twenty-seven years.   (Cheers.)

'Increase in Average Wage

'Since 1907, when the Cambrian Combine acquired the Glamorgan Collieries, the population of the district in which the Cambrian Combine Collieries were situated, and which constituted about one-third of the inhabitants of the administrative area of the Rhondda Urban District Council, had increased by over 22 per cent., the number of workmen employed in the four combined collieries had grown from 10,500 to over 12,700 or by about 21 per cent., and the amount of wages paid at those collieries had increased by over 25 per cent.   The Combine's annual wage bill amounted

to about £1,250,000, and since 1907 the average weekly
earnings of every man and boy employed above and below
ground had increased from 27s. 8d. to 42s. (Cheers.) The
increase in the average wage had not been accompanied
by a proportionate increase in the efficiency of the workmen.
On the contrary, and in spite of an additional capital
expenditure of £350,000, the production per workman had
decreased considerably, for the increase in the total output
of the combined collieries had only grown about 7 per cent.
The prospective output of course was very considerable,
and they hoped that in the course of the next few years
they would produce at least a million tons a year more than
now. And this was going to be good for the district. In
addition the Combine made large quantities of coke and
bricks. In helping themselves they had helped others as
well.

' Syndicalist Movement

' Mr. Thomas added that he was not a Socialist or a
Syndicalist. Every man was of course entitled to his views.
He claimed that the advent of the Combine had done much
materially to benefit the district. Syndicalism was going
pretty strong. He had shown his side of the balance sheet,
but what had the Syndicalists done on their side ? They
were instrumental in bringing about the strike which lasted
twelve months, had cost the Cambrian Combine workmen
nearly a million in wages, had entirely depleted the coffers
of the South Wales Miners' Federation, and in the end the
workmen had returned to work on the terms on which they
had come out. (Cheers.) Then came the national strike,
in which the Cambrian Combine workmen alone had lost
another £135,000, and Mr. Thomas estimated that it would
take the workmen ten years to recoup themselves for that
loss out of the increases that they had obtained under the
Minimum Wage Act. Further comment than that implied
in this simple statement of facts on the futility of the policy
of Syndicalists he thought was unnecessary. (Applause.)

' Fairly Good Times Coming

' Referring to the future, Mr. Thomas expressed the
opinion that the coal trade was in for a fairly good time
during the year. The collieries would be kept well employed, and he thought there was no fear of wages being

reduced in the next twelve months. He was sometimes accused by fellow employers of being too frank, but he thought that having the facts large on their side they should make them known. If the public heard only one side, public opinion could only be formed on that one side. He maintained that he himself and any fairly large colliery owner had done more to provide wages and the means of subsistence for the men and their families than all the miners' agents in South Wales had done, or were likely to do if they lived to be one hundred.'

In these later days personal attacks upon him had become comparatively rare. Perhaps because, as the Americans would say, 'It's ill work monkeying with a jigsaw.' In March 1916, however, Mr. Tom Richards ventured in.

Western Mail, Saturday, March 11, 1916 :

'Colliery Profits
'A Criticism of Lord Rhondda
'What the Workmen Think
'By Mr. T. Richards, M.P.

' The most interesting of these reports is undoubtedly that of the Consolidated Cambrian Collieries Company as given at their annual meeting by Lord Rhondda. Not because, as one would have expected, it shows the best results on the year's trading, but that there is contained in it many illuminating features not to be found in any of the other reports. One such feature was the expressions of sympathy with the poor shareholders. These expressions of sympathy were accompanied with a five per cent. bonus on their shares, which, as Lord Rhondda stated, " would help them to bear with less hardship the very trying times through which they were passing."

' Then there was a statement of the earnings of the miners—without the sympathetic expressions—and these were given as " averaging for all workmen and boys employed 8s. 11·72d. per day," followed by Lord Rhondda's stock ingenious comparisons of the amount received respectively by Capital and Labour from the joint production. " Labour," he says, " receives 20s., while Capital only receives 1s. 6·81d." Evidently from this statement, even by this ingenious method of calculation, things are improving for the shareholder. It is not long ago that we were told by the Commoner Mr. D. A. Thomas, " that for every shilling Capital receives Labour receives one pound." That is over 50 per cent. advance in a few months, an item which is not to be despised even by wealthy capitalists, and which, as Lord Rhondda states, must " prove a boon and help to the poor shareholders."

' The members of the Conciliation Board have just been told by their new independent chairman, Lord Muir-Mackenzie, that " figures are like the chameleon, which takes its colour from the ground on which it is standing." I think it will be interesting to test this statement by removing the 20s. received by Labour, and the 1s. 6·81d. received by Capital from the Great Western Hotel, London, to a mass meeting of the Naval Collieries workmen in the Rhondda Valley, and allow them to be handled by the horny-handed grimy collier in the rough-and-ready manner he has of considering these matters, and see whether he will arrive at the same conclusion as his lordship, that he " did not think that the ordinary shareholder was getting more than his fair share of the joint production of Capital and Labour." The first thing the collier would ask would be, When did Capital produce anything ? But without pausing to argue that issue we will suppose him to be one of those in receipt of 6s. 6d. a day ; there are many hundreds who receive that amount in the collieries of the Cambrian Combine.

' Lord Rhondda told the public that 12 per cent. of the men earned over 12s. per day. Why did he omit giving the percentage of the workmen—and the percentage would be very much higher—who earn (or at least are paid) less than half that amount per day ? There is no reason that I know of for this omission other than that given by Lord Muir-Mackenzie, that the figures must have relation to the colour of the ground upon which they are handled, and to cite these hard-worked, poorly paid workmen would not harmonise with the expression of sympathy with the poor shareholders who were only to receive 15 per cent. upon their investments, coupled with the explanation that were it not for the restrictions of the Government in commandeering their coal it would have been very much higher.

' What the Workmen Think

' I would not be accorded the space necessary to produce even a tithe of what the Naval workmen think of all this at the present time, when, as Lord Rhondda says, " the relations between the employees and the company were good, more friendly, indeed, than they had been for years," to say nothing of the not-so-long ago when they were fought to a finish to keep up this fair ratio between Capital and Labour.   I will select as an illustration one of the poor shareholders referred to by Lord Rhondda, say the holder of £1000.   He may be living in the same street, or close to the 6s. 6d. per day workman.   He drew his 10 per cent. last year, or £100 ; this year he receives £150 as his share for the great effort and labour entailed in allowing his £1000 to remain in the company.   Of course, as Lord Rhondda fairly stated, " colliery enterprises are risky undertakings, and the life of a coal-mine is comparatively short," and he may lose his big thousand pounds after only drawing his " salary " of a hundred or hundred and fifty for forty or fifty years." '

The reply came in the form of an open letter to Mr. Richards.   (They had, of course, known each other for twenty years or more.)

' My dear Tom,
' I am sorry I incurred your displeasure by what I told the shareholders of the Cambrian Combine at their annual meeting last month, and I must ask you to make some allowance for the position in which I found myself.   I was endeavouring to give an account of my stewardship, and vainly attempting to justify in some measure a salary which you will be the first to admit is out of all proportion to the services I render the company—services you would yourself, I feel sure, readily undertake to discharge more efficiently at half the remuneration that I receive.
' Now, what was it I said that so offended you ?   You take no exception, so far as I can gather, to my statement that the average wages of colliers at all the collieries of the Combine amounted to little short of 12s. a day, and that the average of all persons employed above and below ground, including boys, amounted to a fraction under 9s. a day, or to my further statement that a considerable percentage of the men, when they attended regularly to their work, were getting over £4 10s. 0d. per week : none too much, to my mind, when they earn it.
' But what did so much excite your indignation was (1) my

suggestion that, having regard to the uncertainty of colliery enterprise as investment, and the comparatively short life of colliery undertakings, a participation of one-twelfth, or to the extent of a penny in every shilling, in the joint production of Capital and Labour, was not an undue share for the ordinary shareholder to receive in an exceptionally prosperous year ; and (2) my unfortunate expression of satisfaction that the relations between the company and their employees were good, in fact better than they had been for years.

'Tut, tut ! When did Capital produce anything ? you say, having in mind, no doubt, the experience of the South Wales Miners' Federation when they invested the funds of the " grimy collier," if I may be permitted to quote your description, in a North Wales Slate Quarry—presumably you believed up to that time that Capital was productive, since you deemed it wise to throw these surplus funds of the Federation into the Quarry ? The experience, however, of all capitalists has not been so unfortunate as that of the Federation.

'If Capital plays no part in production, I agree its employment is certainly not entitled to any share of the proceeds of industry : if, however, it renders no help, why in the name of commonsense employ it at all ? Why does not the Federation forthwith open up new collieries without regard to Capital ? Just imagine the earthly paradise wherein all proceeds went to the workmen, and no more money was wasted on employers, miners' agents, strikes or Trade Unions !

'My dear Tom, I can remember you in your unregenerate days, when you were one of the most bitter enemies of the Federation. I can also remember in the not very distant past when you professed to be a Liberal, but now that you have become a convert to Socialism I am afraid you haven't learnt your lesson properly. The orthodox Socialist does not deny the necessity for or the utility of Capital, but only asserts that in the public interest this should be provided by the credit of the community or that of the State, and not by individuals.

'I am not a Socialist myself, but I readily acknowledge there is much to be said for the creed, and were it not for the inherent and consequently ineradicable selfishness of the average man, and my belief that such selfishness when kept within limits is a stimulus that probably makes for

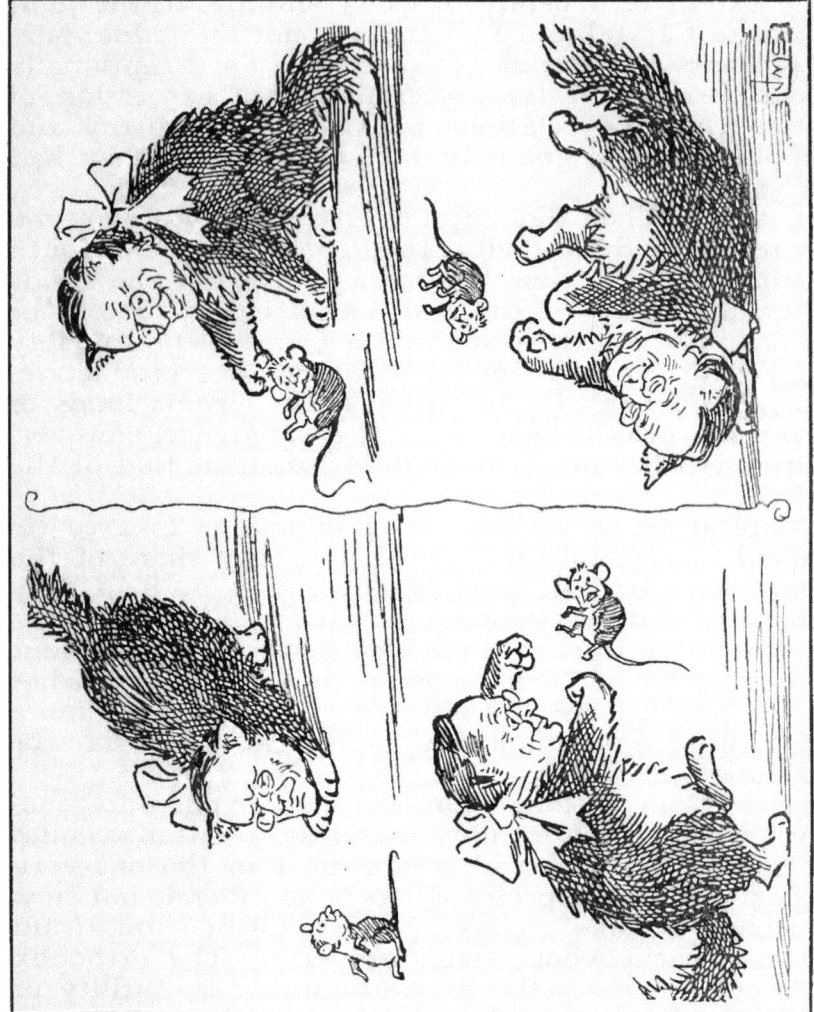

A GIANT AT PLAY

From a Drawing by
J. M. Staniforth

material progress, in other words, did I conceive it likely that a scheme of government could be evolved by which the average man might be made an altruist, and be induced to work as hard for the community in general as he will now do for himself, I might become a Socialist.   For, believe me, I am not out for the accumulation of wealth merely for its own sake, but desire, as you do, to make the best use of whatever talent has been entrusted to my care.

' The only value of wealth is the influence and power it places in the hands of its possessor to do good in his time and generation according to his lights.   Honestly, what I should fear under a Socialist régime is that instead of labour getting 11d. in the shilling, as it does now, at the Cambrian, the whole production would not amount to tenpence, and, consequently, even when Labour secured all, the workman would receive less than he gets now.

' You say you will not pause to argue the issue that Capital produces nothing, and there, if I may respectfully say so, you give evidence of your wisdom   You proceed, however, to assert that the man who invests £1000 in Cambrian ordinary shares is not entitled to receive more by way of interest than the equivalent of the minimum wage— 6s. 6d. per day—paid to certain Cambrian workmen, and you complain that I did not in my speech give the percentage of men who " earn (or at least are paid) " less than 7s. 6d. per day.   The qualification in brackets, by the way, is yours, not mine.

' Let us examine your proposition a little more closely. Your contention I take to be, that the method adopted hitherto by economists of the old school of regarding the capital expended in an enterprise as a unit on the one hand, and the whole of labour employed as an entity on the other, is entirely fallacious, and that the proper mode is to have regard only to the remuneration of individual investors and workmen.   But even on that assumption I don't quite understand why you fix upon the shareholder with a holding of £1000 and compare him with a workman who earns— I beg pardon, who " at least is paid "—6s. 6d. per day.   I should rather have expected you to have compared the holder of the smallest number of shares with the minimum wage workman, or the largest registered holder, who happens in this instance to be myself, with the most highly paid workman, or, better still, the average shareholder with the average wage earner.   If you are entitled to pick out any shareholder at hazard, as you appear to have done, you would surely have made out a better case from your point of view, and with equal logic, if you had compared my dividend with the earnings of the lowest paid workman.

' It may, for future guidance, interest you to have some information relative to the holdings of the ordinary shareholder in the Combine, though for the investment of a shilling you could have obtained the fullest particulars at Somerset House. The average holding is £504. The directors and their personal friends hold considerably more than half the ordinary capital, and if the holdings of these are deducted, the average holding of the remaining shareholders is £235 each, or less than one-fourth that of the holder you selected for purposes of comparison. There are 228 shareholders each with a holding of less than £50, and with an average of £22 each. The smallest holder has precisely £1, and the dividend for the year on his investment amounted to 3s.

' Now, my dear Tom, if you will only pursue your studies on previous lines, you will find that the lowest paid capitalist in Cambrian receives for the whole year less than one-half of what the lowest paid workman receives every day ; in other words, the minimum wage workman " at least is paid " for four hours' occupation as much as the poor capitalist receives in twelve months ! Then take the 228 shareholders whose average holding is £22 each, and for expressing sympathy with whom I incurred your unsparing castigation —they each receive on an average in twelve months as much as the minimum wage workman is paid in two weeks. Would it be impertinent for me to ask if the Federation only hoped at most to receive for the thousands of pounds they invested in the North Wales slate quarry a dividend equal to the wages of a single quarryman in their employ ?

' Another point I should like to have made clear is this. Suppose the holder of £1000 in Cambrian Ordinary, who you .contend is not entitled to a dividend higher than the equivalent of 6s. 6d. per day, varies his investment and puts £100 into each of ten companies, is he according to the new economic school of which you are so distinguished a disciple entitled to collect 6s. 6d. per day from each venture, if they prove sufficiently profitable, or ten times as much as when he invests all his capital in one enterprise only ?

' In your last article in the *Western Mail* you condemned Mr. Shaw for accepting too high a remuneration. The chairman of the P. D. is well able to take care of himself, but you have on other occasions commented adversely on the amount of my director's fees. A fault confessed, they say, is half redressed. Let me, then, frankly admit that my chief, indeed my only claim to distinction is that I am the most overpaid man in the country, with the possible exception of certain miners' leaders. But what would you have me do, when people are so ill advised as to pay me these excessive fees ? Would you yourself refuse them were you in my unfortunate position ? Let me beg of you to have compassion on a poor creature whose business reputation is immeasurably beyond his real merit.

'You will not, I know, suggest that every Member of Parliament is worth £400 a year. Why, there are some that both you and I would consider dear at £2 a week. To carry your argument to a logical conclusion, does it not follow that even you yourself are not entitled to more than 6s. 6d. per day ?

'The other statement you resented in my speech to the Cambrian shareholders was that the relations between the company and their employees were good, and, in fact, better than they have been for years. I had that on what I consider unimpeachable authority, and I expressed my satisfaction at the altered condition of things, a gratification which those present at the meeting shared to the fullest extent. Would you have had us feel otherwise ? I am sure you would not, for you are not one of those, of whom there are but too many in political life, who, while preaching peace and goodwill among men on the Sabbath, devote the rest of the week to stirring up strife and ill blood in the community, and whose work in Parliament largely consists in trying to remedy grievances of their own creation. To such men a better understanding between employers and workmen spells loss of occupation. You, my dear Tom, are not of that type.

'You have freely criticised me ; may I be allowed to make just one criticism in return ? In your article in the *Western Mail* you assumed the attitude of champion of labour, and throughout suggest that I am antagonistic to its best interests. I know you honestly think so. Now I take an entirely different view, and I would in all serious-ness suggest that when you have done a tithe—did I say a tithe ?—rather would I say a fraction of one per cent.—as much for the welfare of the men as I have done, I mean in providing them with the means to pay for the food and clothing of themselves and their families, it will be time enough for you to begin comparing your services to labour with mine.

'It is hardly for me to advise the member for West Monmouth, but I cannot sometimes help feeling when reading your articles that they are a little too acrid in tone, and calculated to irritate rather than to convince those whom you are anxious to convert to your own way of thinking. May I suggest that you would better serve your purpose were you more to avoid the imputation of evil motives in those from whom you differ, and content your-self with appeals to reason rather than to prejudice ?

'Believe me, my dear Tom, to be

'Yours very faithfully,

(Signed)   'RHONDDA.

'Cambrian Buildings, Cardiff, March 21, 1916.'

Mr. Richards, perhaps not unnaturally, replied with some heat and at some length. More interesting, however, was Mr. Hartshorn's comment.

South Wales Daily News, March 28, 1916 :

'LORD RHONDDA

'IS HE A NATIONAL PROBLEM ?

'LABOUR LEADER'S DIAGNOSIS

'(*By Mr. Vernon Hartshorn, J.P.*)

'Lord Rhondda's open letter to Mr. Thomas Richards, M.P., has interested me greatly, as it must have interested any other Socialist who read it. Between Lord Rhondda and those who hold the Socialistic faith there is a great deal of affinity, paradoxical though this assertion may seem to those who do not understand. Lord Rhondda is one of the " awful examples " which are available to the Socialistic propagandist in expounding his doctrines, for his lordship is—and he himself is aware of it—one of those men whom nature meant for the public service, but whom the system of private ownership has diverted to less worthy ends. Lord Rhondda is fast becoming a national problem, and it will soon be time for a Royal Commission to sit upon him in the national interests. He is potentially one of the most valuable national assets that we possess, but the community has not yet had the sense to devise an economic and social organisation in which his business talent might be utilised fully for the public good. He has consequently been doomed to use his talents, not on behalf of the nation, which inspires the highest ideals of service to mankind, but on behalf of a crowd of useless shareholders, whose commonplace, if not sordid outlook must be really objectionable to the idealism of Lord Rhondda, who is out " not for the accumulation of the wealth for its own sake, but to make the best use of whatever talent has been entrusted to his care," because he believes that " the only value of wealth is the influence and power it places in the hands of its possessor to do good in his time and generation according to his light." It is a noble ideal. But it is not the ideal of the speculative market. It is not the ideal of the Stock Exchange. . . . Would not the position be far more stimulating and dignified ? Would it not be a far more attractive position to a man with Lord Rhondda's ideal ? It is really pathetic that Lord Rhondda should throw the cloak of his own organising talents over the mediocrity of shareholders to protect them against the charge of uselessness. The possession of capital does not confer natural talent or genius or even average intelligence upon the possessor ; even the shrewdness or cunning which enables a man to invest his money in a paying concern has no inherent social value.

' It amazes me that Lord Rhondda can assert that men will work better for private shareholders than they will for the nation. These are days when the deeds being done for the social ideal of mere nationality eclipse anything ever attempted on behalf of capitalism.

' When Lord Rhondda went to Canada and the United States on behalf of the Ministry of Munitions did he give the nation less efficient service than he gives the shareholders of the Cambrian Combine ? We all know that he did not. It seems absurd to even imagine that there could be such a strange human being as a man who would give less efficient service to the nation simply because it is the nation than to a mixed medley of shareholders, most of whom, perhaps, he has never seen. Human nature is not quite so irrational as that. The tragedy of Lord Rhondda's position is that he is devoting to the services of uninteresting shareholders the talents that were meant to be used for the common good ; that ideal which has inspired the best men in history.'

Sketches of him were becoming frequent in the local press. I quote one other.

South Wales Daily News, October 26, 1916 :

' D. A. as We Know Him
' *By an Old Hand on 'Change.*

' We know him best as " D. A.," and although he is now called Lord Rhondda on the Exchange floor he will never be anything but D. A. Thomas, with the surname as superfluity. How many are there who recognise his many-sidedness ? Yesterday, or the day before, we were reading of the sale of his pedigree cattle, and also that he had given the highest price of the season in the sale of one of the best Hereford herds. A week or so ago it was an account of his driving the motor in a ploughing experiment—demonstrating the advantage of using the motor instead of horses. He is the largest landowner in Monmouthshire, excepting Lord Tredegar, and puts into his land interests all those qualities and the energy that are shown in the sphere of commerce and finance ; and speaking of finance, who now remembers that he worked a while in London as a stockbroker ?—no bad apprenticeship for the man who since has had to do some of the biggest deals of all times against the acutest business brains of Yankeeland !

' It is more than twenty years ago that he came to the Docks, and my first business dealings with him were in a little room at the back of the house opposite the Taff Vale Station. In those days we all had to work in old dwelling-houses—clerks in the kitchen, accountants in the bedrooms, principals in the parlours, for it was before the proper office accommodation had been built, except in the Exchange building itself, which was utterly inadequate to supply the demand. " D. A." was then, as he is now, always approachable and kindly. We did not at that time realise how very gifted he was in foresight. I remember spirited controversy with him at a later date—that was just before the boom of 1900–1901. He was strongly optimistic. My own ideas, derived from the earlier days when best steam coal was about 9s. or 10s. a ton, were quite contrary : but he stood almost alone in anticipating the good times coming, and proved to be a true prophet, doubtless making a good pile out of his own perceptive power.

' That he should have devoted so many years to politics —a devotion he now apparently regards as misplaced— was only in keeping with his mind and character, for " D. A." was always a fighter. . . .

' He has a quality of mental detachment which must stand him in good stead at the present time, when his engagements are so numerous and varied. I remember one thing in the old Exchange—before we became so wonderfully respectable with polished floors and cushioned seats—that he stood for ten minutes or a quarter of an hour talking of the doings of the rooks and crows at Llanwern, and invited me to spend a week-end with him to see the cattle and crows out there (why didn't I go ?) ; and then as one after another came up to him he talked coal business with them, immediately resuming the discourse on feather and flock. Perhaps this faculty accounts largely for his clear-sightedness in affairs. It may account also for the irritation he causes in the minds of men—that is, the majority—who live in illusion, taking the ostensible for the real, observing conventions, afflicted with dogma no less in business than in religion.

' " D. A." goes right to the heart of the matter, seeing it in (wasn't it Bacon who used the term ?) " dry light " free from mist and distortion. . .

' Whatever Lord Rhondda attains to, or in whatever association he may reach, he will always be " D. A."—the man we have known, criticised, sometimes fought against, yet always esteemed.'

It was particularly true to say that he saw things in a ' dry light.' ' His reasoning faculties were well insulated from his emotions ' : it was one of his most notable qualities and one which made him unpopular with the average sloppy sentimentalist of whom he had a peculiar horror.

I quote *in toto* a letter to the *Western Mail* which I think is of some interest. He had always been in favour of Woman Suffrage in the somewhat bored way which was not infre- quent amongst the men with strongly feminist women folk, but he was definitely opposed to militancy, as he was to every form of unconstitutional action (passive resistance, the Ulster Rebellion, Fenianism, etc., etc.). Although my mother and I were both strongly in favour of militancy this never caused any family dissension, mainly no doubt because he never interfered with other people's beliefs, he would have considered it an impertinence—certainly he listened with the greatest interest to accounts of stormy street corner meetings, and with considerable enjoyment to my description of an encounter with a well-known Cabinet Minister. Most of the militant leaders stayed at Llanwern at one time or another. Nor was he very seriously put about when we went to prison, in fact on each occasion he took the trouble to come and see us in the dock, and afterwards confided to me that he ' felt very proud of your old mother, she answered the magistrate very well.'

Western Mail, November 18, 1916 :

' LORD RHONDDA
' LABOUR BARGAIN AND WOMEN'S WORK.

' Sir,
' In your summary of the few remarks I made at the meeting of the Cardiff Business Club which was addressed by Mr. Frank Hodges last night you report me as having said :

" He ' thought ' the bargain between the Government, the employers and the workmen made before the war . . . should be fully carried out."

' The agreement I refer to was that come to between the Government and Trade Unions " after " the outbreak of war. I did not say I " thought " it should be kept ; I said it " must " be kept. It is not a matter of thinking, hesitation or doubt ; when a bargain is made it has to be kept.
' Again you say, referring to the question of women :

" His Lordship said that 40 per cent. of the women would be drones and parasites."

' What I intended to convey and I think I did convey to my audience, was that it was absurd to say, as it is too often said, that the proper place for a woman is the home, attending to her husband and children, when we know that under existing conditions something like 40 per cent. of the women of this country do not marry. This large number while remaining at home can take little or no part in the production of the means of subsistence necessary for their support, and consequently, though often unwillingly, live a life of idleness dependent on the work of others.   It is in that sense that they become drones and parasites.

' This condition of enforced idleness is repugnant to all right thinking women, and I contend that women who have no families requiring their attention should be encouraged to engage in occupation which they are in many cases as well qualified or even better qualified than men to perform. In this way the aggregate quantity of commodities to be distributed among the whole community would be increased and the share of each would be larger.

' I would, however, insist that no distinction should be made in the remuneration paid to men and women.   In other words, equal work for equal pay.

' I am, etc.,
' RHONDDA.'

He was accused of many things in his time, but it was perhaps rather hard for so convinced an individualist to be held responsible for promoting Socialism.

Western Mail, November 27, 1916:

' LORD RHONDDA
' RESPONSIBILITY FOR THE GROWTH OF SOCIALISM.

' The Rev. W. F. Philps, Tenby, who fought West Glamorgan as an anti-Socialist at the last general election, writes to *The Times*:

' " Lord Rhondda should be the last person on earth to suggest that your correspondent is ' saturated with Socialism.'   His Lordship himself once told the South Wales miners that had he been a collier he would have been a Socialist and a revolutionary one at that. Quite recently also he declared that no one should use the war for private profit.   Time and again for reasons best known to himself he has piped to the Socialists in South Wales, and it is not for him to complain now that the miners are preparing to dance to the same tune. Lord Rhondda's share of personal responsibility for the growth of socialist opinion and propaganda in the South Wales coalfield is greater than that of any other individual, and his present attitude is too cynical for words." '

My final quotation is from an article of his published in the *Daily Chronicle* on December 7, 1916, only two days before he was asked to join Mr. Lloyd George's Ministry. It was one of his last contributions to the press.

' Prospect of an Era of British Combines
' A Reply
' By Lord Rhondda.

' Under this heading an anonymous correspondent, in your issue of Saturday last, draws attention to what he conceives to be possible dangers that may accrue to the community after the war as a consequence of what he is pleased to term " Lord Rhondda's activity." I shall be glad if you will allow me to point to a few of the misconceptions under which he labours, and which, if allowed to pass unnoticed, might lead the less informed of your readers to wrong conclusions.

' Before doing so, however, I may perhaps in self defence be permitted, even at the risk of being thought egotistical, to remind him that I devoted nearly a quarter of a century of the best years of my life to public work in the House of Commons, and also to say that my happiest and proudest memory is the knowledge that I enjoyed the confidence of the miners of South Wales over a longer period and in a larger measure than any man now living, miners' agents not excepted. It was not until the conviction was forced upon me that under no circumstances did my political leaders wish to avail themselves of my service, and that I could be of more use to the community by helping to develop the resources of the country than by perambulating the Parliamentary lobbies at the back of the Party Whip, that I decided to return to commercial life.

' Control of the Collieries.

' I hope your readers will not doubt my sincerity when I say that I am out for the game and not for the stakes, and while I admit I find business a very fascinating game, I contend that by increasing the means of subsistence of the people I have in the aggregate contributed more to the material happiness and well-being of Welsh colliery workers and their families than have all the miners' leaders combined, though moved by the best intentions.   That is an expression of opinion, however, to which I hardly expect them to subscribe.

'Your correspondent writes, quite honestly, I am sure, under misapprehension in several particulars.   He thinks I have made huge profits out of the war, and that with these I have been enabled to enter upon what he considers a campaign of activity most dangerous to the State.   I have made no huge fortune out of the war.   I do not, however, feel called upon to disclose my methods of acquisitiveness, and thereby invite the competition of your correspondent, but I will say that what I have done in the way of acquiring control of Welsh collieries, the South Wales Miners' Federation might have far more easily done with the large sums at their disposal, had they been so minded.   If instead of squandering the funds of their powerful organisation in a North Wales slate quarry, and in a rash newspaper enterprise (very speculative investments at best, and of which they can have had little knowledge), they had anticipated me and obtained the control of collieries at home, in the efficient management of which they claim to have a far better knowledge than they concede me, they might have secured for the members of their already wealthy federation the profits they now so much grudge the poor outside investor.

'But be that as it may, I think I can best refute the charge levelled against me of wishing to make a profit out of the necessities of the nation by reminding your readers that soon after the outbreak of hostilities I recommended the Government to take over the control of the Admiralty collieries, only leaving the proprietors the income they had been receiving prior to the war, but this I was told was impracticable ; while I have since repeatedly and publicly expressed the opinion that no man should be allowed to make profit out of the war—consequently your correspondent's charges leave my withers unwrung. . . .

'Your correspondent refers to a proposal I put forward some twenty years ago to prevent undue competition among coal sellers.   I well remember it, and shall always look back with pride and pleasure on the numerous and enthusiastic meetings of colliery workmen I addressed throughout the coalfield in support of the proposal.   Unfortunately I failed to secure its adoption, but the educative value was such that never since has the price of South Wales coal been so low as it then was, with the result that the foreigner has not been able to exploit the follies of coal-owners and obtain his requirements at below cost of production, while the wages of colliery workmen are double what they were formerly.

' Your correspondent very generously admits that I am " doing nothing more than I am legally entitled to," and predicts that I may plead justification in the general public welfare. I certainly do. I believe if we are to meet industrial competition on equal footing after the war, it will be best done by large undertakings efficiently managed in the most up-to-date methods and equipped with the most modern appliances. Only in this way will it be possible to pay high wages with low costs of production.

' While I am prepared to accept and indeed to advocate State control in competent hands during the exceptional conditions created by the war, and in order that all efforts may be concentrated on winning the war, the more I observe the results of State intervention in times of peace, the more individualistic do I become. That involves a point of principle and policy upon which I differ from my Socialist friends in South Wales who advise (cf. " The Miners' Next Step," page 26) the lodges to adopt the " scientific weapon of the irritation strike by simply remaining at work, reducing their output, and so contrive by their general conduct to make the colliery unremunerative," and advocate " that a continual agitation be carried on in favour of increasing the minimum wage and shortening the hours of work until we have extracted the whole of the employers' profits " ; so that they may " build up an organisation that will ultimately take over the mining industry and carry it on in the interest of the workers." '

CHAPTER XIII

AMERICAN INTERESTS : THE 'LUSITANIA'

MY father's American interests could be divided into two groups—his interests in Canada and those in America.

The Canadian position was this. He held the controlling interest in a company which had for its object the development of certain districts in Northern Alberta and British Columbia. A railway was projected which should run from Kittamaht on the coast in British Columbia via Findlay Forks, Peace River Crossing, Vermilion and Fort McMurray to Prince Albert in Saskatchewan, and thus open up a large tract of fertile northern country. This railway was, however, never completed. Further, he had bought up the Peace River Development Corporation which owned certain stores and some land on the Peace River at Peace River Crossing, and at Fort St. John and Fort Vermilion, and owned a couple of boats which in summer made a regular service between these places. He did not enter into these enterprises so much in a spirit of money making as in a spirit of adventure. 'It is my way of amusing myself,' he would say, 'and I can afford it.' Undoubtedly his enterprise helped to open up the Peace River country.

I have asked Mr. August Rust Oppenheim to give me some account of my father's American plans, with the details of which he was more familiar than myself. He writes :

'I first became acquainted with your father in the early summer of 1913, when he came to this country to investigate the American coal business in all its phases : the many qualities of coal and the method of production, transportation and sale.

'He visited the West Virginia coalfields, the Pacific Coast, and I believe also the Middle-West coalfields, and studied particularly carefully the efficient loading and discharging devices at the very modern coal terminals of the Great Lakes coal-handling ports. While he was on the Pacific Coast he made an investigation of the coal reserves of British Columbia, and a careful examination of the Western Fuel Company.

' He returned to England in July. He then came back to America in the early spring of 1914 with a well-developed plan of co-operation between British and American coal interests with particular reference to Welsh coal and New River and Pocahontas coal.

' He had some very interesting maps prepared, showing the more important coal properties in the New River and Pocahontas districts, and giving their vital statistics. He also had competent engineers prepare for him a considerable number of reports on various coal properties which he thought of bringing into the international combine. One phase of his plan was to form a great selling organisation into which he planned to put certain important British Coal Sales Agencies, controlled by himself and associates, with docking and storage facilities in many ports in the Mediterranean and South America.

' Meanwhile I had been in close touch with your father, journeying with him to England on the same steamer in 1913, for the purpose of arranging in London for the financing of the Western Fuel Company, in which your father was to become interested, and which was to be acquired by Messrs. Imbrie and Company, whose foreign manager I was. This transaction was independent of the proposed big combine.

' The further object of my trip to England was the advisability of establishing a London Branch of Imbrie and Company, Investment Bankers of New York. Your father took a great interest in this plan ; so much so that he expressed himself desirous of becoming a partner in the prospective London business of Imbrie and Company if satisfactory arrangements could be made.

' I left for America and took this matter up with Imbrie and Company, pending your father's return to this country, but when he arrived it was found that no arrangements satisfactory to your father could be made with Imbrie for a London partnership. He had, however, meanwhile decided that it would be highly desirable for him to have a central organisation for his many activities in the form of an investment banking house or private house in London, which should be an organisation capable of underwriting securities and participating in such underwritings. It was then that he made a partnership agreement with me which was terminated by the war, but which he desired to revive just as soon as conditions warranted.

'Your father then returned to England in the late spring of 1914 and I followed him early in the summer. His plan for the co-operation of the American and British coal industries had taken more definite form, and we planned to work this matter out in England in great detail, putting it through if possible, upon his next return to the United States. It is evident that if this plan had been in operation during the war it would have been of very considerable benefit to the Allies ; in fact, it would even be a great thing to-day.

'While he was in this country he became interested in the Peace River enterprise, and with these you are as well or better acquainted than I.

'Please permit me to mention a few human touches which I had so often the opportunity to observe. He was a keen student of American business developments and a great admirer of intelligent American business aggressiveness. He was very fond of the theatre in New York. He loved a good joke. He had little patience with people who bored him and who were what he called "mentally quite ordinary." He was so very young in his outlook on life and always liked to be considered as one of the younger men. I still recollect, with a chuckle, that he declined to give a position to a young man of your acquaintance because this youngster had the poor taste of accentuating the difference in age between the two, persistently using the term "sir" in conversation with your father, when "Mr. Thomas" would have done just as well. I can still hear your father say "Sir, sir,—does that silly ass think I am an octogenarian ?" This, of course, was the summer of 1914, before he was burdened with the tremendous responsibilities of his war activities.'

There were also certain schemes in connection with a barge service on the Mississippi which did not, however, turn out successfully.[1]

In the spring of 1915 various business matters obliged

[1] See Appendix D, Notes on his American interests, by David Evans.

O

him to pay a short visit to New York, and I joined him there for the last fortnight of his stay. We enjoyed ourselves thoroughly. He would take more time off from work in America than he ever did at home, and in the intervals of discussing plans for the navigation of the Mississippi and various other schemes we used to motor about and lunch at various country clubs. On one occasion we were driven out to Princeton. I remember it specially because of the speed at which we were driven. He was always a little nervous in a car and preferred a very slow and careful driver, but I would defy any normal person over twenty-five to have been happy on that trip, although I am bound to admit that our hosts seemed perfectly at ease. We must have averaged about sixty miles an hour, and several times we were travelling at over seventy. American roads are not amongst the best features of that country; we slowed up for no crossing . . . it was shortly before we sailed, and I remember my father saying that the *Lusitania* (there was already much talk about her) would feel safe compared with this.

We stayed at the Waldorf-Astoria and in the afternoons when there was time we would walk up Fifth Avenue and across Central Park, which—always beautiful—was then looking its best with the trees budding and the wistaria just out. Once or twice we went into the shops. He was always much struck with shops when he went abroad and loud in their praises, and would enlarge on the superiority of the way they did things in America, unaware, since he never entered an English shop, that there was not really much difference between New York and London. I never could convince him, he thought my attempt was due to patriotic prejudice. I always supposed that he had once forty years earlier entered a London shop and so made his comparisons with that. He was just as bad in Paris or Chicago.

During our fortnight in New York we went to the theatre (which we both loved) every evening except two. He was the most satisfactory man I have ever known to go to theatres with, because contrary to the usual male custom he hated revues or musical comedy, and liked good straight comedy best of all ; tragedy he disliked, partly because he cried very easily at the theatre. One evening we dined with some friends who took us to their box at the opera (' Madame Butterfly '). I have seldom seen a man so bored as he was—though I think he hid it from our hosts quite successfully. Our hostess, who was old and delicate, retired before the end of the evening, leaving us to enjoy the finish, but with one accord we rose and fled. I heard him explaining to some other friends at lunch next day how he disliked the opera, how no really musical person could like the opera, which was based on artificiality, and how he knew he was musical because he loved a barrel-organ. I listened with some relish, as our friends were musical experts who loved opera, and the struggle on their faces was worth watching. I could have wished, however, that he had not added (though I must admit it was true) ' and my daughter Margaret entirely agrees with me.' He often seemed curiously unknowledgeable about things which were outside his immediate scope, due I think to the fact that he never cared to take a thing up at all or even learn its rudiments unless he meant to study it seriously.

Part of the joy of New York on that occasion was that there was no war there, and to come from England to America was like stepping from under a thundercloud into brilliant sunshine. After the strained tension of life at home the relief of this care-free place was just wonderful—it may seem heartless to have been able to find relief at such a time, I only know that one did. Had America been against us it would scarcely have been possible to relax as one did, but New York at all events, for all the reiterations of neutrality, was pro-ally with an exuberance of enthusiasm scarcely to be found even at home ; every spy play ended with an allied victory, proof that pit and gallery as well as stalls preferred that ending ; as for Belgian refugees, I who had had some dealings with them at home found a certain difficulty in rising to the American attitude—they believed them all to be saints as well as martyrs.

It was, I think, a great relief to my father to find that the unbiased press and public of this neutral country were as convinced of the righteousness of our cause, of the cleanness of our fighting and of the horror of German atrocities as we ourselves ; we, once in the war, had forfeited our right to impartiality, and were bound to hold such views, but that a nation which still retained the right to take impartial views, and which never failed to remind us of how iniquitous it had considered the South African war, should back us so whole-heartedly gave one great confidence.

We decided to sail on the *Lusitania* on May 1—my father was anxious to be home for that perfect third week in May which he never passed away from home if he could help it. Rumours concerning German intentions were current for some while before she sailed, and there was much talk of the safety of cancelling one's passage and sailing on an American liner (still safe in those days) instead. I believe, however, that not one British person did so (and for that matter very few Americans). Feeling ran strong, and that we should be driven off our own boat by German threats, to take shelter on one of a neutral nationality after we had already booked our passage, was unthinkable. An illogical but typical attitude.

On the morning of May 1 appeared the German warning against sailing on the *Lusitania* underneath the Cunard Co.'s advertisements in all the papers. The steerage passengers were already fixed aboard, but the first and second class passengers read it in time to take the warning if they chose. ' Typically German,' said someone, ' steerage don't count.'

We walked round and round the deck as the ship drew slowly down the Hudson, remarked on the unusual number of small children on board, and agreed that we would not have taken children across on that voyage.

There was tension on board—the passengers were frankly anxious. Many of the British posted farewell letters at New York to come over in a different ship. Conversation turned largely on the possibilities—a young girl who sat at the same table as ourselves said she couldn't help hoping we would have ' some sort of thrill ' going up the Channel. One lady who had beautiful jewels carried them about with her in a handbag for two days before we were struck. She forgot them when the explosion came though. Maybe they are sitting on the saloon table still.

Reproduced from the ' New York Herald,' May 1, 1915.

Curiously enough, we were all convinced that it would happen at night, the last night before reaching Liverpool, going up the Channel. My father and I had just finished lunching when it occurred. As we strolled out of the saloon he said to me, ' I think we might sit up on deck to-night to see what happens.' We stepped into the lift, and at that moment it did happen. A dull thud-like noise, not nearly so loud as I had imagined, but quite unmistakable. We stepped out of the lift and I ran upstairs to my cabin for my lifebelt. My father, who like most men on board (expert or otherwise) did not believe that a single torpedo could sink us, went off to look out of one of the portholes. The ship heeled over almost instantaneously. He went up on deck soon afterwards to look for me, but in that crowd of two thousand people he failed to find me (he and I never met till we reached Queenstown), and then realising that he had no lifebelt he went off to get one. Someone (a steward I think) gave him a Gieve. He tried to blow it up, but it would not blow, and so he went down to his cabin to get one off his bed, but they had all been taken. Finally he found three Boddy belts in his cupboard (the regulation ship's life-belt and a most effective one). He came up on deck again on the near side just as the last boat (half empty) was being launched. The *Lusitania* A deck was by this time level with the water and already the boat was about a foot away from the edge of the ship. A woman holding a small child hesitated whether to dare step over to it. He gave her a shove and sprang after her himself. As the boat drew away the ship slowly sank, and one of her funnels came over to within a few feet of the boat. It seemed as if it must sink it, but she was sinking by the bow as well as rolling over and the funnel, passing within a few feet of their heads, sank just beyond them. My father had timed the explosion, and he looked at his watch when she had disappeared. The whole thing had taken $12\frac{1}{2}$ minutes.

As he settled into the boat someone leant forward and warmly grasped his hand. It was his secretary, Mr. Evans.

The boat, which was only half full of people, was also half full of water; however, they baled it out and picked up some more people out of the water, and after rowing about for two and a half hours were taken on board by a small steamer and brought to Queenstown, which they reached about six o'clock. There my father chanced on a Catholic priest, to whom I shall always be grateful, who took him off to have some dinner and plied him with brandy. My father protested that he had not tasted alcohol for fifteen years, but was in no state to withstand the firm reply that in any case he was going to have some now. He confided to the priest his dilemma about my mother. He must wire to let her know he was safe, yet he could not wire without mentioning me, and he gravely feared, though still uncertain, that I was lost. Together they composed a telegram. It ran, ‘ Landed safely, Margaret not yet, but several boats still to come.’

The next few hours must have seemed like a lifetime. Boat after boat came in with its big load of dead, its smaller load of living. He waited on the quay. . . .

It was eleven o'clock before I reached Queenstown. After floating about in a lifebelt for some hours unconscious I had finally been picked up. I met my father at the end of the gangway as I struggled off the boat. He had engaged a room at the local hotel (kept by a German by the way) which he made over to me, and I shared with a complete stranger for beds were scarce. He himself slept, or rather lay, on the drawing-room floor along with some twenty or thirty others, amongst them a riotous Canadian who had taken considerably more than was good for him and talked and sang the night through. At three in the morning my father got up and took him off for a walk to keep him quiet.

We spent the next night again in Queenstown, a curious heterogeneous party of complete strangers whom this great catastrophe had shaken into a temporarily close intimacy. It was a time when people told the truth. One heard many things. . . .

The hotel was filthy and badly managed beyond description ; never in any country have I met one to approach it.

Someone who met my father just then said that his face seemed for a few weeks to have turned into that of an old man, but I noticed nothing except that for a few days his temper with strangers was very bad.   I remember a drunken inhabitant who one evening just after nine o'clock came up to us and confidingly asked whether by any chance there were any pubs still open.   ' No, thank God ! ' retorted my father.   I am always glad to remember that his temper was still sufficiently out of hand to tell the German hotel-keeper all he thought about his ' damned dog kennel ' before we left.

He, like every one else with us, was aware and intolerably sore to think that the accident could very possibly have been avoided and that in any event the loss of life had been pretty well doubled by lack of organisation on board.   (I remember that as I stood beside a young American girl watching the scene on deck before we sank I said to her, ' Well, I always imagined a shipwreck was a well-organised affair.'   ' Yes,' said she, ' so did I—but I've learnt the devil of a lot in the last five minutes ! ')

It was easy enough when one had been close to the horrors of that ghastly event, when one had seen the results at close range (only 29 per cent. of the children on board were saved), to realise as one had never done before what German brutality meant, and to swear as many did that they would not rest till they had paid the debt they owed (numbers of the surviving crew went straight off to enlist). It was not so easy to remember that for the moment at least no good purpose was served by inveighing against the intolerable British stupidity which had made the catas-trophe so much worse than it need have been.   My father at least found it very difficult and at first well-nigh im-possible.   It is one of the many disadvantages of war that it forces one to suppress wholesome truths about one's own side.

One or two incidents of the time remain in my mind. One relates to the poster displayed by the Cardiff *Evening Express* of May 8.   It ran :

' Great National Disaster
' " D. A." Saved.'

This somewhat equivocal compliment tickled my father immensely.   He secured a copy of the poster, which is still a prized possession of ours.

CHAPTER XIV

THE MUNITIONS MISSION

HE had only just got back to England when Mr. Lloyd George asked him to go to America and Canada, in connection with the supply of munitions from that country. He never seriously hesitated, but frankly he disliked the idea. One does not recover from such a disaster as the *Lusitania* in a few weeks. To cross the Atlantic again so soon was the last thing he had looked for. Moreover, he was, I think, a little surprised at Mr. Lloyd George's choice. Finance he understood, and he had been in touch with many of the big business men of America, but he was totally ignorant of munitions. However, the Minister for Munitions was insistent, and he agreed.

Mr. Lloyd George gave Mr. Harold Begbie the following account of the interview :

' My fight with Rhondda had been bitter, very bitter ; it had been a long fight too, extending over many years. But he was a man who rose superior to memories of that order, particularly in a great cause. I remember so well our meeting in the summer of 1915. It was in the streets of Cardiff. I went up to him, put out my hand, which he took immediately, and said to him : " Look here, Thomas, I want you to do some work for the Government. I want you to help the country." He answered at once, " I'll do anything you ask me : what is it you want me to do ? " I replied, " I want you to go to America." His face fell : there was an expression on it of real pain. Remember he had only just survived the *Lusitania* crime : remember too, that it was that fearful experience which nearly killed him in the end. He replied to me, like the brave man he was, " Isn't there anything else I could do ? I don't mind telling you that the thought of crossing the Atlantic frightens me. To be perfectly frank, I funk it—I funk it badly. I can't get the *Lusitania* out of my mind. I dream of it." I told him that there was nothing more urgent just then than the mission I asked him to accept. There, in the streets of Cardiff, I told him how our magnificent soldiers were being slaughtered for the want of shells, and how we were not getting the help we wanted from the manufacturers of America, simply because of the confusion that existed out there.

' Well, he accepted. It was a noble act on his part, and a very brave one. He went to America. He organised a supply of munitions from the States and from Canada. He got the right men round him. He chose the right men, and he set things going. There were all sorts of quarrels and difficulties, but in every case he simply said, " I know only one thing : our need of guns and shells." And he inspired the whole heart of America with the flames of liberty. From that hour the supply never wavered or checked. It was Rhondda who gave to America and the Allies a breathing space and a chance. That service of his cannot be over-estimated.'

One curious little incident sticks in my mind. He was given no credentials of any sort. He had nothing with him to show that he was the accredited agent of the British Government. The Ministry of Munitions when asked said that this was not necessary. Possibly they were simply in a hurry, possibly they feared to give him too much authority. Just before he started, however, Mr. Lloyd George made a speech in the House of Commons in which he said :

' I felt, in consequence of the great importance of the American and Canadian markets and of the innumerable offers which I have received directly and indirectly, to provide shell munitions of war from Canada and the United States of America, it was very desirable that I should have someone there who, without loss of time, which must necessarily take place when all your business is transacted by means of cable, should be able to represent the Munitions Department in the transaction of business there and find out exactly the position. I propose to send over, on behalf of the Munitions Department, a gentleman who was once a member of this House—a very able business man.   He has business relations with America on a very considerable scale, and I propose to ask Mr. D. A. Thomas to go over to America for the purpose of assisting us in developing the American market.   He will represent and exercise the functions of the Munitions Department, both in Canada and in the United States, and he will be given the fullest authority to discharge the responsible duties with which he is entrusted.   Mr. Thomas will co-operate with the representatives of the Government, both in Canada and the United States of America.   There is not the slightest idea of superseding our existing agencies there.   They have worked admirably. They have saved this country, I believe, millions of money. They have enabled us to develop the resources of that great Continent for the purpose of aiding us in a way which would have been quite impossible without their valuable assistance. Mr. Thomas will co-operate with Messrs. J. P. Morgan and Co., the accredited commercial agents of the British Government in the United States of America, with a view to expediting in every way the supply of munitions.   While invested with full powers, he will, no doubt, act in consultation with the authorities at home, except in cases of special urgency.'

My father with a chuckle bought twelve copies of the 'Hansard' containing this speech, and armed with this, his only visible authority, set off to America.   My mother, mindful of possible submarine dangers, insisted on accompanying him.

I quote from a letter I received from my father dated July 13, 1915 :

' On starting we were convoyed out of the danger zone by a couple of formidable-looking destroyers, which created much interest on board among the passengers.   Only a very few were disposed to resent as an insult to the American flag that an American boat should be protected by British warships.   The Captain told me he did not know why they were there, and said that neither did the officers on the destroyers, but the cause began to be suspected before we had proceeded very far and the mystery dispelled.   All the Americans I spoke to expressed themselves as grateful for the added security.

' We encountered a violent storm on the 30th June, and

the *St. Louis*, twenty years old, creaked and groaned and pitched and rolled in a most alarming fashion. We experienced another storm off the Banks, then a good deal of fog, and finished up at the pier in a considerable thunderstorm accompanied by a deluge of rain. It was not altogether an uneventful passage, and I was glad when we landed.

' The British Ambassador very kindly met me on the boat and came up to the hotel. He had been at J. P. Morgan's when the attempt was made on Morgan's life, and had helped to take the pistol from the lunatic's hand.

' At the instance of my friends, I go about constantly guarded by detectives. This is not at all a pleasant experience but I have now gotten [1] quite used to it.

' On Saturday I called on Thomas Edison, the inventor. He is an exceedingly nice, kind-hearted, and wonderful old gentleman : sixty-eight years of age.

' Yesterday your mother, Nina and myself, after stopping the night with the Marstons, called on John D. Rockefeller, and I walked around with him while he was playing a game of golf on his private course.

' The weather has been quite pleasant up to the present, but to-day it promises to be very warm.

' Bankers and business men over here have received me very well, and appear to welcome my visit, but I expect before I am many weeks older to have made a goodly number of enemies among disappointed commission agents and others.'

The following account of his mission has been given to me by Mr. Ralph Carr :

' Less than two months after his escape from the *Lusitania*, Mr. Thomas was asked by Mr. Lloyd George, who had just assumed responsibility for the supply of munitions, to return to America on behalf of the Government for the purpose of investigating the arrangements for the purchase of munitions in Canada and the United States.

' For months past London had been besieged by agents, or so-called agents, of American firms endeavouring to secure contracts for the supply of shells, rifles, small arms

---

[1] The letter was dictated to a typist, which probably accounts for this Americanism.

ammunition, etc., many of whom alleged that their principals declined to negotiate through Messrs. J. P. Morgan and Co., the official purchasing agents of the British Government in the United States. Mr. Lloyd George, while retaining full confidence in the ability and integrity of Messrs. Morgan, felt that it was desirable that these allegations should be fully investigated on the spot by a business man whose qualifications for such an investigation were unimpeachable. He also wished to learn more of the possibilities of obtaining an increased supply of munitions from Canada, and of the methods and capabilities of the Shell Committee, a body set up by General Sam Hughes, the Canadian Minister of Militia, with the concurrence of Lord Kitchener, for the purpose of arranging and supervising contracts for the manufacture of munitions in the Dominion. He selected Mr. Thomas for this purpose, not only on account of his wide business experience, but also because his commercial connections with America had already brought him into contact with most of the big business men of that country. In communicating the arrangement to the House of Commons on June 23rd, Mr. Lloyd George said that Mr. Thomas would represent and exercise the functions of the Munitions Department both in Canada and in the United States, and would be given the fullest authority to discharge the responsible duties with which he was entrusted (' Hansard,' vol. lxxii. No. 67, p. 1203).

' Before leaving England Mr. Thomas took the precaution of selling out every share that he held in any Company engaged in the manufacture of munitions, in order to dispose of any suggestion that he might be partial to the interest of any particular firm.

' He left Liverpool on June 25th by the American Line steamer *St. Louis*, which was escorted through the danger zone by two British destroyers, to the surprise of many of the passengers, who were at first unaware of Mr. Thomas's identity. His party consisted of Mrs. Thomas, Miss Jameson [1] and Mr. V. Lloyd Owen,[2] in addition to Major-General R. H. Mahon, C.B., C.S.I., who acted as his technical adviser, and Mr. R. H. Carr of the (Munitions) Contract Department of the War Office. Inspector Hester of Scotland Yard (C.I.D.) also accompanied him in order to

---

[1] Miss Nina Jameson, a cousin of my mother's.
[2] A Canadian friend who was acting as his secretary.

watch over his personal safety and that of the confidential papers which he carried. The importance of this precaution became evident when the news was received by wireless some two days out from New York that Mr. J. P. Morgan had been shot and seriously wounded by a German at his country house. On arrival at New York in the early hours of July 5th, the party was met by the British Ambassador, Sir Cecil Spring-Rice, who had motored over direct from Mr. Morgan's house, where he was staying when the outrage took place.

' Mr. Thomas installed his party at the Plaza Hotel and converted a suite of rooms there into offices, which he retained throughout his stay in America. These rooms were on the twelfth floor, a pleasant and airy situation which was found to be not without its drawbacks when on one occasion an important memorandum containing some secret information was blown by a sudden draught through the window, and sailed across the roofs on the opposite side of Fifth Avenue. In spite of a prolonged search by detectives the paper was not recovered, but there was never any reason to suppose that it fell into enemy hands.

' The offices in the Plaza were filled daily from morning till night by a horde of brokers and commission agents, attracted by the hope of securing direct contracts from Mr. Thomas, or of reaping commission by introducing would-be contractors to his notice. Mr. Thomas wisely took the line from the first of refusing to talk business with anyone who was not either a principal or the duly accredited agent of a firm equipped to produce munitions of war. He also declined to negotiate direct contracts and insisted that all business must be done through Messrs. J. P. Morgan and Co. By taking this firm line he protected the Government against irresponsible agents whose intervention would not only have raised prices but have exposed the British Government to the risk of contracting with firms which had no direct facilities for manufacture. In one case he was asked by the War Office to investigate the capacity for making rifles of a firm which he discovered to be exclusively engaged in the manufacture of toys and teddy bears !

' Mr. Thomas' detailed and careful enquiries established beyond a doubt that there was no single manufacturing firm of repute in the United States whose principals objected to negotiating through Messrs. Morgan. Their export department, under the exceedingly able management of Mr. E. R. Stettinius, late President of the Diamond Match

Company, was found to be fully competent to handle the enormous volume of business involved in the supply of munitions from the United States. The reduction of prices resulting from their direct negotiations with the big manufacturing firms was a remarkable testimony of the advantages of conducting business through a single channel, and in every case the greatest care was taken before an order was transmitted to the War Office to establish the financial and technical capacity of the firm to carry out its undertakings. The contract between Messrs. Morgan and the British Government, however, laid no obligation upon the firm to supervise the progress of contracts, and after conferring on this point with the partners and with Mr. Stettinius, Mr. Thomas found it necessary to set up a British Munitions Board for the purpose, under the Presidency of Lieut.-General L. T. Pease, who had been sent to America previously on a special mission by Sir Stanley von Donop, the Master-General of the Ordnance. With him were associated Mr. Henry Japp, of Messrs. S. Pearson and Co., Mr. J. P. Sneddon, an American consulting engineer of high repute, Mr. F. W. Abbot, an Englishman who had served as manager of some big commercial undertakings in America and elsewhere, and Colonel C. E. Phipps, C.B., and Capt. B. C. Smyth-Pigott, the chief representatives in America of the War Office Inspection Department. The Board served a valuable purpose in following up the performance of contract, and reporting progress from time to time to the Ministry of Munitions in England.

' During his stay in the United States, Mr. Thomas visited the works of several of the most important firms manufacturing munitions, notably the Bethlehem Steel Works, over which he and his party were conducted by Mr. Charles N. Schwab and by Mr. Grace, the President of the Works. He also paid a special visit to Mr. T. A. Edison and conferred with him on the manufacture of certain constituents required for explosives.

' The pressure of business in New York allowed little time for social duties, but Mr. Thomas found time to attend a dinner given in his honour by the Pilgrims Club, where he particularly enjoyed a topical song by a deafening Coon Band, the refrain of which ran :

> " Mr. Tahmus wuz the kid
> That built the Pyramid.
> The hell he did ! "

' Recognising from the outset the importance of giving priority wherever possible in the award of contracts of Canadian over American manufactures, Mr. Thomas was anxious to proceed at the earliest date to Canada, but at the time of his arrival in New York both Sir Robert Borden and General Hughes were in England, and anticipating their early return he considered it advisable to defer his visit to Canada until he could accompany them. Their return, however, was considerably delayed, and when reports reached him indicating that his prolonged stay in New York had given rise to some uneasiness in Canada he proceeded to Ottawa on July 25th. On the evening of their arrival the party had the honour of dining with T.R.H. the Duke and Duchess of Connaught at Government House, on the occasion of the Duchess's birthday. Throughout the whole of his stay in Canada Mr. Thomas was greatly helped and encouraged by the constant interest taken by the Duke in the affairs of his mission, and derived much benefit from his wide and intimate knowledge of men and conditions in the Dominions.

' There was a marked difference between the American and Canadian aspect of the mission. In the United States its character was purely commercial. Mr. Thomas' function there was to investigate from the point of view of a business man the methods by which the purchase of munitions on behalf of the British Government was being effected, and to consider by what means deliveries could be expedited. In Canada, on the other hand, the character of the mission, though chiefly commercial, was necessarily influenced by conditions of a political nature in order to secure that the application of business methods did not conflict with Imperial considerations. The supply of munitions from Canada had to be regarded not as a mere mercantile transaction between a seller and a buyer, but as a spontaneous contribution by an integral and loyal part of the British Empire to the forces engaged in protecting her interests. In the United States, again, the paramount consideration, as far as the distribution of orders was concerned, was to place them where they could be executed most cheaply, rapidly and effectively. In Canada, on the other hand, it was impossible to ignore the economic condition of the country and the advisability of distributing the orders in such a way as to alleviate the industrial depression which preceded the war, and but for the creation of munitions industries might have developed into a disastrous commercial crisis throughout the Dominion.

' These considerations had materially affected the policy of the Canadian Shell Committee. Instead of placing the bulk of the contracts with big firms in Canada which were best equipped at the outset to manufacture shells, the Committee adopted the plan of splitting up War Office orders into small quantities and assigning them to a large number of different manufacturers. This involved the organisation of an elaborate scheme for the manufacture of separate components of fixed ammunition in different factories, and for the assembling and loading of these components. By this means the War Office orders were spread over hundreds of manufacturers instead of being concentrated in the hands of the large firms. The plan was undoubtedly not the most economical that might have been devised, but it had the advantages of familiarising a very large number of firms with the processes of shell manufacture and of distributing orders over a very wide area. The Shell Committee were evidently determined to resist all forms of graft and political pull, and although allegations to the contrary were made from time to time, Mr. Thomas found no reason to believe that the Committee were actuated at any time by narrow political considerations, or that they exercised any undue discrimination as between one firm and another.

' The effective working of the Shell Committee was hampered, however, by the fact that their organisation was not expanded sufficiently with the growth of the business with which it had to deal. In this respect conditions were not dissimilar from those which had obtained in England before the responsibilities of the War Office for manufacture and supply of munitions were transferred to the new Ministry of Munitions. The Shell Committee, moreover, acted not as the agents of the British War Office but as contractors with them, the four manufacturers on the Committee accepting contracts from the War Office at the price fixed on each occasion by that Department. They then placed sub-contracts with individual manufacturers at prices which allowed a sufficient margin for the assembling of components and the costs of administration, and placed any surplus to a reserve fund, with the intention of subsequently returning the accumulated surplus to the British Government. This mode of procedure did not commend

P

itself to Mr. Thomas, and on Sir Robert Borden's return from England he advised him that the Committee should be strengthened and reconstituted as direct agents of the Ministry of Munitions, for the purpose of placing contracts on their behalf with the individual contractors, in the manner adopted by the Ministry of Munitions in England. The negotiations involved by this proposed change of procedure necessarily occupied a considerable time and unduly prolonged the length of Mr. Thomas' stay in Canada. Ultimately, when his departure could no longer be delayed, Mr. W. L. Hichens, the chairman of Messrs. Cammell, Laird and Co., was sent out to Canada by Mr. Lloyd George for the purpose of carrying through the changes which Mr. Thomas had initiated, and of acting as provisional chairman of the new organisation, pending the appointment of a permanent Canadian chairman. Mr. Hichens and the Hon. R. H. Brand reached Ottawa on October 28th, and Mr. Thomas returned for the last time to New York a few days afterwards, having placed at Mr. Hichens' disposal the whole of his Canadian correspondence and papers.

' Although the limited time at his disposal did not admit of his completing the conversion of the Shell Committee into the Imperial Munitions Board, which was very ably carried out by Mr. Hichens, Mr. Thomas had not only laid the foundations of that reorganisation under exceptionally difficult conditions, but had successfully allayed the disquietude which existed in Canada with respect to the allocation of British orders between that country and the United States. In accordance with his recommendations the Ministry of Munitions guaranteed to Canada continuation orders for field artillery ammunition, and also a definite proportion of the new orders for large shells of 6-inch calibre and upwards. He succeeded in arranging with Sir Thomas Shaughnessy of the Canadian Pacific Railway that Mr. Fitzgerald, the head of the company's great buying organisation, should be seconded to supervise the purchase of munitions. Lastly, Mr. Thomas' insistence on the introduction of a system of competitive tendering for the big shell contracts, in preference to the issue of orders at prices fixed by the Shell Committee, though at first unpopular, undoubtedly led to very substantial economies being effected.

' The only contract personally negotiated by Mr. Thomas in Canada deserves special mention. During his visit to Hamilton, Ontario, he inspected the works of the Canadian

Cartridge Company, and received an offer from the proprietors, Mr. Bailie and Mr. Wood, two business men, who without any previous experience had managed to surmount all the practical difficulties involved in the manufacture of brass 18-pounder cartridge cases, to supply an additional million cases at cost price when their existing contract was completed. Alternatively they suggested, in order not to embarrass other manufacturers, that the contract might be made at the current market price on the understanding that on completion they would return the difference between the contract price and the bare cost of labour and materials, as certified by a Government Accountant. The offer was ultimately accepted in this form, and some months afterwards Mr. Thomas was gratified to learn that the million cases had been delivered and that a cheque for many thousands of pounds had been refunded to the Imperial Munitions Board.

'A considerable part of Mr. Thomas' time in Canada was spent in inspecting the work of factories engaged in the production of munitions. Early in August he undertook a tour of 2500 miles in the Eastern Provinces, in the course of which he visited factories in Montreal, Quebec, New Glasgow, Sydney, Halifax and St. John, New Brunswick. For the purposes of this tour and several of his later journeys in Canada the Dominion Government placed the Prime Minister's private railway car at his disposal. Later he visited Toronto, Hamilton and other places in Southern Ontario, and it was a source of keen regret to him that time could not be found for a trip through the Western Provinces to British Columbia. The necessity of keeping in direct touch with affairs in the United States and Canada concurrently involved frequent journeys between New York and Ottawa, and the sixteen-hours run between the two Capitals involved a considerable strain on Mr. Thomas' energies. His health caused him some anxiety throughout his stay in America, and he was constantly under medical treatment, culminating during his last visit to New York in two operations, which, although neither of a very serious character, necessarily involved a certain amount of shock to his nervous system. He had a great faith in American doctors, and had been warned by them that although there was nothing radically wrong with his health or constitution his prospects of long life were not very good. He did not, however, on this account spare himself any exertion which he considered necessary in the interests of the work on which he was engaged.

' Throughout his visit to America his relations with the Press, both in Canada and the United States, were excellent. Reporters found him full of interesting " copy," while his faculty for talking freely to them on the most important aspects of his work without committing himself to the slightest indiscretion kept his staff in a state of perpetual anxiety and admiration. He was always ready to be interviewed even at the most unreasonable hours, and on one occasion, when he arrived with his party by train at Toronto at 7.30 A.M., after a bad night, he walked happily up and down the platform for the best part of an hour with a reporter on each arm, to the dismay of the rest of the party, whose only thoughts were of baths and breakfast. He was a voracious reader of newspapers at all times, and his pockets were invariably bulging with them.

' Canadian Ministers, from Sir Robert Borden downwards, treated him almost as one of themselves, and he was soon on the most friendly terms with men of every shade of political thought in the Dominion, including Sir Wilfrid Laurier and the leaders of the French-Canadian party in the province of Quebec. To the big manufacturers and business men his presence and his active interest were specially welcome. His imagination was fired with the openings that Canada offers for commercial enterprise, and with its vast natural resources. He was never tired of discussing projects for the extraction of its mineral wealth or of picking up information as to the development and use of its water power. Herein lay the secret of his popularity with Canadians, whose natural pride in their country makes them apt to test visitors by what they say of it, and quick to discriminate between mere flattery and genuine admiration. He used to say that if he were only twenty years younger he would throw up all his connections in the home country and start afresh in Canada, and he even meditated at times on the possibility of making his home there after the war. Until then he realised that there was still work for him to do in England, and he had a premonition that office in the Government would be offered to him, realising that that independence of political thought and action which had kept him out of party Governments would be no bar to his employment by a Coalition, which believed in entrusting business affairs to business men.

' The work of the American mission was no bad preparation for the Ministerial offices which he was destined to fill
in the later years of the war.   He had been accustomed
previously to read all letters addressed to him and to dictate
replies, but the size of his daily letter bag in America soon
obliged him to abandon that practice and to trust to his
staff to deal with everything that did not demand his personal attention.   He quickly learned also that where public
affairs are concerned, careful attention has often to be
directed to matters which a business man would dismiss at
once as trivial or unremunerative.   His task interested him
chiefly because it brought him into contact with his equals
in the spheres of industry, commerce and finance, and
because of the magnitude of the operations in which he was
able to take a hand.   As usual he was fascinated by figures.
One afternoon in New York he assisted the Morgan partners
in settling a series of contracts for shells to be supplied to
the Russian Government, and found to his delight that the
aggregate value of the contracts amounted to a sum sufficient
to buy up the whole of the South Wales coalfields or to pay
half the cost of the Panama Canal.   He enjoyed the possession of the plenipotentiary powers entrusted to him with
respect to contracts for munitions, though he was never
tempted to use them unwisely, and would have liked
similar powers to handle other problems on behalf of the
Government, especially in relation to the exchange.   Within
an hour after reading the news of the South Wales coal
strike of July 1915, he secured options for the supply of
many thousands of tons of American coal weekly to the
British Government, and, when reproached for having
acted on his own initiative in a matter which did not concern
him, replied that as the option had cost nothing he saw no
reason for making a fuss about the matter !

' The work of the mission was not without its humours.
A packet of white powder arrived by post one day without
any covering letter or other indication of its nature, and
was hastily emptied into the drains by a nervous detective,
who was not unaware that certain kinds of explosives are
detonated by contact with water.   The mystery was solved
a few days later by a complaint from a personal friend that
the receipt of the valuable sample of white talc powder
which he had forwarded at Mr. Thomas' special request
had not been acknowledged !   More than one lady of
humble origin and penurious circumstances wrote in affec-

tionate terms saying that after seeing Mr. Thomas' portrait in the newspapers she felt convinced that he was a long-lost relative, as her late husband had claimed Welsh ancestry and believed himself to be entitled to a fortune. Among the numerous inventions submitted (on paper) the most remarkable was a hydro-aero-triplane, noiseless and invisible, carrying range-finders by means of which the pilot could see the rivet of a battleship, and enough fuel for a flight of 10,000 miles or more. It was claimed that in one day a single machine could blow up the whole of Essen, the bridges over the Rhine, Berlin, and the Kiel Canal. The total cost of the machine was put as only fifty thousand dollars, and it was to be completed in a month. Mr. Thomas transmitted this offer for the amusement of the Ministry of Munitions, who actually treated it as a serious proposition, and suggested that he should send a representative to San Francisco to meet the inventor ! Another mysterious invention was that of a Polish chemist who claimed to be able to drive any motor engine on salt or fresh water with the addition of a handful of powder, the ingredients of which could be bought for a few pence from any drug stores. Some trouble was taken to follow this up, but when it was found that the inventor would not experiment with any engine supplied by the prospective purchaser or allow anybody to look on while he mixed the powder with the water, Mr. Thomas declined to waste further time on the project.

' During the enforced confinement to a nursing home which followed the operations to his nose and foot in New York, Mr. Thomas was much gratified by the receipt of a cable from the Ministry of Munitions, expressing the hope for his speedy recovery and early return, adding that the Ministry were looking forward to congratulating him in person on the great success he had obtained both in the United States and in Canada in the very difficult work he had undertaken. During his five months' absence from England the Munitions Department had not only sprung into existence, but developed into a vast purchasing and manufacturing organisation, directed by men many of whom were unknown to him, and he sometimes doubted whether his work in America was known or appreciated on the other side. The cable dispelled his doubts, and after recovering from his operations he sailed for Liverpool on November 29th, feeling that he had satisfactorily completed the mission with which he had been charged.'

During his stay out there he was very much interested in his private affairs, which he had left in my charge, and would from time to time dictate me long letters about them. Most of these letters referred to private business matters of ephemeral interest. I give two quotations only :

'Ottawa, 4th October 1915.

' I would very much like to get hold of the Pen-y-coed property with the old castle and wood in which the heronry is, also those two wood-clad hills near Magor, if they form part of the property, and if they could be bought at a reasonable figure. At the same time we must not go too fast, and what with the heavy increase in income-tax and increased cost of living, expenditure for putting up the Tommies at Llanwern, visits to the U.S., etc., on the top of the purchase of the *Cambrian News*, Poole's property and capital invested in the Paint Works, etc., etc., also my enterprises on this side, I am afraid I shall not have much money available for the Perry-Herrick property. However, I shall be glad if you will make enquiries as to what property is for sale, and start negotiations before the property is publicly advertised, if you think it advisable, and at the same time see what can be done in arranging for a mortgage, as it is quite likely you might be able to borrow the whole amount at a reasonable rate of interest and for a period of years if you offered as security at the same time the Llanwern property on the flats.'

I did negotiate for the Perry-Herrick property, an estate of about 4000 acres which adjoined his own in Monmouthshire, and it was finally bought whilst he was on his way home. He was greeted with the news of his new acquisition on his arrival at Liverpool.

'New York, 11th November 1915.

' I am very glad you bought the trees on the Milton farm, and if Hambury is going to sell the land, I would like to buy it myself, if we can scrape together enough money. If some speculative builder bought it, he would probably put up unsightly villas upon it and spoil the whole of the surrounding country. I would not mind if a bit of architecture were put into the buildings, but the average builder is quite devoid of taste and erects the most hideous structures. I saw some most pretty detached little houses in the suburbs of Toronto, and only wish the architect who designed them would go over to England and help us a bit there.

‘ You are quite right to refuse to guarantee an overdraft for X——.   I make a standing rule not to guarantee any account in which I am not personally and largely interested, and I want you to hold fast to this rule under all circumstances.   I quite appreciate your difficulty in saying “ No.” That is one of my particular weaknesses also.   The best way is to make up your mind beforehand definitely.   I cannot understand Mr.—— advising you to guarantee X——. He ought to have known my strong objection to giving guarantees.   Please tell him I am surprised that he should have so advised you.   Another time when you have a difficulty in saying “ No ” just put it on to me, and say you are acting under my very definite instructions.

‘ The enclosed is a paraphrase of a message I have recently received from Lloyd George, and from this you will see that he appears pleased with what I have accomplished over here.   I am rather pleased myself with what I have done, and feel that my time has not been wasted.

‘ I was under an anæsthetic for an hour and a half, and am told I said some nice things about you when I was regaining consciousness, which is evidence how largely you bulk in my thoughts.

‘ I got back to the hotel yesterday, and though I felt a good bit exhausted by the time I reached my room here on crutches, I am quite all right this morning, with both pulse, respiration, and temperature all normal.’

(*Enclosure*)

‘ The Ministry of Munitions hope that you will be able to return at an early date, and are looking forward to congratulating you in person on the great success you have obtained, both in the United States and Canada, in the very difficult work you have undertaken.   They are so glad to learn that your operation has been successfully performed, and trust that you will make a speedy recovery.’

He reached England early in December, and was given a peerage for his services, which was gazetted in the following New Year's honours list.

He asked permission of the Rhondda District Council to take the title of Rhondda. I remember we took some time in deciding what his motto should be. We wanted something which brought in his three initials, D. A. T. Some one finally suggested ' Diligentia absque Timore,' which he liked, and he took that.

A year later he joined Mr. Lloyd George's Ministry as President of the Local Government Board, and after six months in that office was transferred to the Ministry of Food in June 1917.

CHAPTER XV

THE MINISTRY OF FOOD UNDER LORD RHONDDA

By Sir William H. Beveridge, K.C.B.

THE appointment of Lord Rhondda as Food Controller was announced on June 15, 1917. It was two or three weeks after that date before he took up his new duties in earnest and left the Local Government Board.

Notoriously, he did so with the greatest reluctance. He was deeply interested in the project for a Ministry of Health, upon which he was at that moment engaged, and his own health was giving great cause for anxiety. He refused the post of Food Controller when it was first offered him : he accepted it a week or two later only because all efforts to find a suitable alternative had failed. The difficulty experienced by the first Coalition Government in persuading anyone to be Food Controller in November 1916 was repeated in the case of the next Government in the following June. The official lives of Food Controllers in other countries had been generally unpopular and short, and nothing had occurred to suggest that a different fashion could be set in this country. The revolution effected by Lord Rhondda in the popular estimation of food control is the most obvious testimony to the success of his work.

The Ministry of Food, at the time of Lord Rhondda's appointment, was a relatively small department best known to the public by its successive appeals for voluntary economy. The Wheat Commission and the Sugar Commission, which had both been established before the Ministry itself, were indeed already fully developed and at work ; the former, under the Wheat Executive Agreement, made with France and Italy in November, had set on foot the system of joint

Photo: J. Russell & Sons.

AT THE MINISTRY OF FOOD

purchasing and distribution of cereals which was one of the most notable feats of inter-allied co-operation during the war. The policy of the Output of Beer Restriction Acts of 1916 had been carried a step further by a drastic restriction of brewing announced in February 1917. The policy of increasing the percentage of flour to be extracted from wheat, initiated by an Order of the Board of Trade on November 20, 1916, had also been continued, and ' war bread ' had been introduced both by successive further increases in the extraction and by compulsory ' dilution ' of wheat with barley, maize, and other cereals. To facilitate this, and for other purposes, the flour-mills had been taken over. Much valuable preliminary work had been done in formulating alternative schemes for rationing and for sugar distribution : proposals on these points had, indeed, just been submitted to the Cabinet and had been approved by them, subject to confirmation by the new Food Controller when he should be appointed. No general control of supplies, prices, or distribution of food had been attempted.

Lord Rhondda's first task was to unify and to organise his new department. Despite the establishment of the Ministry of Food, food questions were in June 1917 still being dealt with by a number of independent bodies and trade organisations, with somewhat uncertain powers and responsibilities. The Ministry of Munitions were in charge of oils and fats, including the materials for margarine. The Board of Trade controlled imports of meat and cheese, and had begun to deal in frozen fish. There was an arrangement under which representatives of the Home and Foreign Produce Exchange announced maximum prices (of no legal validity) for provisions, and there was an inchoate scheme for partially regulating tea prices under a committee of traders. The Admiralty, the War Office, and the Navy and Army Canteens Board obtained most of their supplies independently. The War Savings Committee undertook a large part of the food economy campaign. The Board of Agriculture undertook food preservation, and the control of oats was shared between the Board of Trade and the War Office.

Most of these outlying activities were brought by Lord

Rhondda directly under the Ministry, and food control was substantially, if not formally, unified. The Board of Trade, indeed, continued to import most of the frozen meat, which was largely required for Army purposes. The two Royal Commissions retained to the end their formal independence. In each case, however, arrangements were made which secured, as a rule, a sufficient measure of co-ordination and the predominance of the Food Controller on questions of policy. The difficult division of responsibilities between the Ministry of Food and the Board of Agriculture (with the Food Production Department) remained, but here also the constitution of various Inter-Departmental Committees provided for regular consultation, and reduced the points of difference to those larger issues of policy which had necessarily to be referred to the Ministers or to the War Cabinet itself.

The internal organisation of the department was no less important. Lord Rhondda's first official act was to appoint as Permanent Secretary to the Ministry of Food and Chief Administrative Officer, Mr. U. F. Wintour, a Board of Trade official whom he had met as Director of Army Contracts, and of whose abilities he had formed a very high opinion. Mr. Wintour was Lord Rhondda's right-hand man throughout the period of his office, and was thus responsible under him both for building up the new Ministry of Food and for the conduct of its work.

In the appointment of Mr. Wintour, and in many other appointments that followed it, Lord Rhondda signalised his belief in the value of permanent civil servants for initiation and control of administrative work. He was careful to combine with the civil servants in his department men of experience in all the main trades that came within its scope. Upon this deliberate blending of governmental and business experience rested the efficiency of the machine which he created.

The organisation of the department, however, was only a means to an end. The proof of a Food Controller is his policy. Lord Rhondda's policy may be summed up in the single word ' thorough.' Half-measures of food control— in particular the fixing of prices without mastery over supplies—had been proved failures in other countries and in our own. Lord Rhondda adopted full measures of control over supplies, prices, and distribution alike ; the success of his administration rested on its completeness.

Three days after his appointment (on June 18, 1917), he issued an announcement in the following terms :

' It would obviously be premature for me to make any definite statement of policy until I have had an opportunity of more fully informing myself on the food position and of becoming acquainted with the organisation of the department I am taking over. This will necessarily occupy a few days.

' In the meantime I can only say that I have been given very ample authority by the Government to deal with the whole situation. I am empowered, should I find it necessary, to take over the food supplies of the country, and to adopt strong measures to check all speculation in the necessaries of life. The man who seeks to profit by the necessities of his country at this hour of our peril, when thousands are cheerfully making the supreme sacrifice in the cause of liberty, is nothing short of a blackmailer and must be treated as such.

' My first effort will be directed towards securing a reduction in the price of bread. This I consider to be the urgent need of the moment. I intend to be as fair as the conditions of war will permit, but frankly my sympathies are with the consumer. I want the help of local authorities in the matter of distribution, and I confidently count on the advice and active help of the co-operative societies and other distributing agencies.

' Before leaving the Local Government Board, the Prime Minister kindly gave me his assurance that in respect to the establishment of the Ministry of Health and the Bill relating to child welfare, the position would be safeguarded. I trust, therefore, that this statement will completely allay the anxiety that has been expressed in many quarters lest my retirement from the Local Government Board might delay these measures of health reform. On the contrary, I think they will have been expedited.

' In view of the fact that I have accepted the position of Food Controller only at the pressing request of the Prime Minister, I feel I am entitled to claim the wholehearted support of the public, of Parliament, and of the Press. I am sanguine that with such support it will be found practicable to effect reductions in the price of the necessaries of life, but without it any effort on my part in that direction will be of no avail.'

While this statement mentions each of the three main branches of food control—supplies, prices, and distribution— the emphasis is clearly on the second. A reduction in the price of bread is definitely promised ; control of profits is made a main feature of the programme. The district commissions, which during May and June inquired into industrial unrest, had indicated the cost of living as a principal source of discontent. Lord Rhondda was at this and at all times profoundly impressed by the effect which rising food prices have upon popular feeling. He took up office with a fixed determination that prices must, and should, come down.

It is interesting to note also, that, though distribution is referred to in the statement, it holds quite a subordinate place, while rationing is not mentioned at all. The Government at that time were bent on avoiding rationing at all costs, through fear of its effects both upon public opinion here and as an encouragement to the submarine campaign of the enemy. The universality of the ration book and the dramatic disappearance of the queues have sometimes caused Lord Rhondda's name to be identified almost entirely with rationing. This is quite a mistake. The changes which he brought about were at least as wide-sweeping in other directions. To get a fair view of his achievement, it must be considered under the three main headings of supplies, of prices, and of distribution and rationing.

Control of Supplies.—Apart from the work of the Wheat and Sugar Commissions, the only cases in which, before Lord Rhondda's appointment, the Ministry of Food assumed direct control over any food supplies, related to the requisitioning of a number of beans and peas in transit to this country and the purchase of a special consignment of New Zealand butter. With Lord Rhondda's arrival there was adopted a regular policy by which, ultimately, the great bulk of all the essential foods actually passed through the hands of the Government and were at one time in the ownership of the Ministry of Food. This policy was carried out most completely in the case of imports. Cereals and sugar were already being imported by the two Commissions. Under Lord Rhondda all bacon, hams, lard, cheese, butter and similar provisions, all oils and fats (edible and otherwise), condensed milk, canned meat, canned fish, eggs, and tea brought to this country came to be directly imported by the Ministry of Food or requisitioned on arrival. This control extended even to minor imports, such as jam, apples, oranges, and dried fruits. In respect of home supplies the control was only slightly less complete. All home-produced meat, and cheese, and most of the butter was bought and sold by the Government, as also, through the control of flour-mills, was all the home-grown wheat and most of the barley. Even the whole potato crop of 1918 was taken over under a scheme framed under Lord Rhondda, though not actually put into force until after his death. Ultimately 85 per cent. of all the food consumed by civilians in this country was actually bought and sold by the Ministry of Food. The only important exceptions were milk, fish and fresh vegetables. The total turnover of the Ministry's trading business (including the two Royal Commissions) came to nearly £900,000,000 a year.

To a large extent this control of supplies was not merely national, but international. The Wheat Executive dealt with all cereals for the United Kingdom, France, and Italy alike, and arranged purchases, shipping, and distribution on an inter-allied basis ; its scope gradually widened to cover other allies and even neutrals. In August 1917 a Meat and Fats Executive was established, and, later, an Oil Seeds Executive. Though in neither of these cases was international co-operation on the lines of the Wheat Executive aimed at or possible, in effect the principal European allies came to have a single programme for all important foods and to buy through a single agency or at least in close consultation.

So far as this country is concerned, the success of the policy of insuring supplies by direct purchase was un-questionable. The United Kingdom came nearer than any other European country to maintaining during the war the pre-war standard of supplies, and at the same time achieved a more equitable distribution.

Control of Prices.—Upon control of supplies was founded an even more extensive control of prices. One of the first acts of Lord Rhondda's administration was the establishment of a Costings Department to determine the proper margins of profit to be allowed to all the various classes of traders— importers, wholesalers, blenders, retailers, and the rest— for the services rendered by them in preparation, transport, and distribution. Once the margins had been determined, effect was given to them by Statutory Orders fixing the prices or the profits to be allowed at each stage. The possibility of profiteering, *i.e.* of exploiting a scarcity, was thus absolutely excluded. These Orders for the most part fixed prices and profits at all stages from the importer or producer to the retailer, and in many cases had to be of considerable complexity, so as to provide for the varying methods of distribution in each trade. In a limited number of cases Lord Rhondda contented himself with fixing retail prices only, particularly for articles of minor importance, or articles of which he did not actually control the supply. Of everything consumed in this country by way of food and drink 94 per cent. was subject to fixed maximum prices. Almost the only articles exempt were fresh vegetables, canned fruits, honey, salt, pepper, vinegar and spices, aerated waters and meals in restaurants. Even such articles as tallow, desiccated cocoanut, and beehive sections were controlled. Only the Armistice saved the Ministry of Food from fixing prices for soap and candles.

The successful solution of the problem of fixing maximum prices is really in its way almost as notable as anything else that Lord Rhondda accomplished. It was, indeed, the side of his work to which he directed most personal attention and interest. At the time of his appointment there was a distinct tendency to say that any fixing of maximum prices must check supply and tend to the disappearance of the article in question. Lord Rhondda secured himself against this by controlling the supplies to start with and only fixing the prices when the supplies were assured. It is true that in one or two cases, of which the ' disappearing rabbit ' is the most familiar, it seemed that the fixing of a maximum price had had the result of driving the commodity off the market. In fact, it is worth while pointing out that the Order which fixed the maximum price for rabbits was made at a time when in any case rabbits would have disappeared from the market owing to the breeding season. The Order at most hastened a natural process.

It was, no doubt, possible even under controlled prices for particular traders to make large profits. Lord Rhondda at an early date laid down the principle that, so far as possible, the existing channels of trade should be maintained. This meant that the margins allowed to each class of trader had to be such as to enable even those with the smallest turnover or the least efficient system to make a living ; on such margins the bigger or more efficient traders could and did do very well indeed. This was an inevitable consequence of trying to fix a flat price for essential articles wherever bought. No doubt in normal times a small corner shop lives by charging its customers more than the big shop ; they pay at a higher rate for the privilege of buying in small quantities or getting credit, or they pay at the same rate for an inferior article. The administration of the Ministry of Food was essentially and necessarily democratic ; it secured to all equal supplies for equal price.

The price was thus often higher than the cut price to which free competition with abundant supplies might have reduced it for those who could deal with the bigger shops. It was much lower than would have resulted from competition in a time of scarcity. The general effect of price control was well illustrated in some charts issued by the Ministry of Food towards the end of 1918, comparing the course of food prices in this country with that of prices of textiles, coal, soap, and other articles, and with that of food prices in other countries. In the three years from July 1914 to the time of Lord Rhondda's appointment the prices of bread, beef, butter and milk increased more rapidly in the United Kingdom than in any other important belligerent or neutral country except Austria ; from that time to the cessation of hostilities they increased far less rapidly than elsewhere. The rate of increase in the price of all the principal foods from July 1917 to October 1918 was only a quarter of the rate of increase from July 1914 to July 1917 ; it was far less than the corresponding rate for clothing, coal, soap and household oils. These results were in part due to the introduction of the bread subsidy. But even if allowance be made for this and bread be entered at what would probably have been its price on a commercial basis, without a subsidy, the influence of control in checking the rise in food prices is still clearly visible.

It was, indeed, recognised that mere ownership of the supplies in bulk did not avoid all the risks attendant on the fixing of maximum prices. In a time of real scarcity particular districts or classes of traders or consumers might readily absorb an undue proportion of any article, and this danger would be increased by the fixing of prices.

Distribution and Rationing.—The third element, accordingly, in Lord Rhondda's policy was the systematic control of distribution and, where necessary, of consumption through rationing. He took steps to secure not merely that the largest possible supplies in the country were assured and were sold at fixed prices or with limited margins of profit : he also made certain that these supplies were properly distributed so that every one should have an opportunity of getting his fair share at those prices.

Two distinct principles of distribution were applied to various articles of food. They may be described briefly as distribution on the basis of registered customers and distribution according to a datum period. The former was the more thorough and detailed, and applied only to articles which were either rationed or for whose supply customers were tied to particular retailers. This was the case with meat, bacon, lard, butter and margarine, sugar, tea and jam. For all these articles the supply to each retailer was based upon the number of customers registered with him ; he also was tied to a particular supplier or suppliers (usually a wholesaler), who in turn had to buy from a particular first-hand supplier (manufacturer, importer or agent) and could only buy enough just to meet the retailers' demands upon him. For other articles, such as cheese, fish and condensed milk, the less elaborate ' datum period system ' proved sufficient. Under this system the aim was merely to secure that each retailer had for distribution the same percentage (25 per cent. or 50 per cent. or 75 per cent., according to the supplies available) of the quantity which he had received in some period before the establishment of control, *i.e.*, the year 1916 in the case of cheese, or 1915 in the case of sugar (till the introduction of sugar rationing). This system, of course, was less effective than the other, because it did not allow for changes of population or the starting of new businesses since the datum period, and it gave no guarantee of supplies to the individual customer.

The control of distribution and rationing involved the establishment of the extensive local machinery of Food Committees, Food Commissioners, and Livestock Commissioners. As both this and the rationing system itself will be dealt with in more detail below, they are merely mentioned here.

The general policy adopted and the results achieved by Lord Rhondda have been briefly summarised above. It may now be worth while to set out in historical order a few of the practical problems with which he had successively to deal, and the measures taken by him. In doing so his tenure of office can conveniently be divided into two parts.

During the first five months—to about the end of November 1917—the matters calling for most attention were the establishment of the local organisation of the Ministry (with which was involved the sugar distribution scheme) ; the introduction of the bread subsidy ; the fixing of cattle prices ; and the establishment of that general control of supplies which has already been mentioned. This period was also in a sense a period of preparation. In the next period up to about the end of April (when Lord Rhondda practically retired from active work) the renovated Ministry of Food was put to the test ; it passed through and surmounted the main food crisis and the peril of the queues.

In setting up the Food Committees and Food Commissioners and introducing the first household sugar distribution scheme, Lord Rhondda was merely giving effect to proposals which had been approved by the War Cabinet in the interregnum preceding his appointment. These proposals provided :

(a) For the setting up by the Local Authorities of Food Control Committees (nearly 2000 in number).

(b) For the appointment, directly under the Ministry of Food, of about twelve Food Commissioners, covering between them the whole of Great Britain.

(c) For the introduction of a scheme of preferential sugar distribution based on the registration of households with particular retailers.

No substantial alteration was made in this scheme by Lord Rhondda before putting it into force, though the drafting of some of the documents was amended. Lord Rhondda's experience at the Local Government Board, however, and the value attached by him to local autonomy were important factors in securing that a real measure of responsibility was given to the Food Control Committees, and that the work of the Ministry of Food was through these Committees and also through the Commissioners effectively decentralised. The Ministry of Food, at any rate, did not make the mistake of attempting by correspondence from Whitehall to settle administrative details from Land's End to John o' Groat's House. It provided in the executive officer of each Food Control Committee a functionary who became almost universally known as the ' Food Controller ' in his district, and effectively screened the Food Controller in London from daily complaints.

The actual circular inviting Local Authorities to appoint Food Control Committees was issued in the early part of August, and in the same month most of the Food Commissioners were appointed. The Ministry of Food was most fortunate in being able to secure for these posts men of high local standing and abilities.

Practically the Commissioners became the general representatives of the Food Controller in their divisions, and the regular channel of communication with the Food Control Committee. They were an essential link in that chain of personal connection between the Ministry of Food in London and individual consumers throughout the country, which enabled difficulties at all stages to be ended by oral discussion in place of being prolonged by correspondence. The Food Committees were numerous enough and near enough to make a personal visit of inquiry or complaint possible for any individual householder or his wife. The officers of the Committees were constantly meeting the Food Commissioner of their Division and his staff. The Food Commissioners were few enough in numbers to be summoned frequently for meetings in London or to pay individual visits, and keep in touch with the various branches at head-quarters. While the Committees and Commissioners were being appointed in Great Britain, a considerable measure of Home Rule was accorded to Ireland, by the setting up at the end of August of an Irish Food Control Committee with extensive powers and responsibilities.

The month of August witnessed also the introduction of the subsidised sale of flour and bread. The retail price of the quartern loaf was fixed at 9d., and that of flour at a corresponding figure. The price which the Ministry had to pay for imported wheat and the price guaranteed to the British farmer for home-grown wheat were in each case much above the level corresponding to this price of bread. The difference was met at the cost of the Treasury, and has amounted to something like £50,000,000 a year. This artificial reduction in the price of bread was, of course, a question of large Government policy. The great majority of European countries, neutral or belligerent, were driven to adopt similar measures.

While the price of bread was thus being reduced at the cost of the Treasury, measures were taken to reduce the price of the next most important article of food, namely, meat, but in this case without a subsidy. A descending scale of cattle prices was fixed beginning at 74s. per live cwt. in September, and running down to 60s. per live cwt. in the following January. This particular measure of Lord Rhondda's has been the subject of great controversy ; though here, too, as in the case of the first sugar distribution scheme, he was, to some extent, merely following out a policy already laid down.

An Army Purchase Committee had been appointed in

March to consider the prices for home-fed cattle to be slaughtered for the Army from August onwards. They proposed a descending scale which was finally applied also to cattle for civilian consumption by the decision of a Cabinet Committee. One effect of the descending scale of prices undoubtedly was to induce farmers to hasten as much as possible the fattening of their cattle and to send them to market before the price reached its lower levels. This, combined with a shortage of feeding stuffs, led to the production of relatively large supplies of meat in the months of November and December, and the corresponding depletion of reserves for the early months of the next year. In October the scale was revised and the price for January raised to 67s. per cwt., but the change came too late to have much effect on the position. The farmers had already made their arrangements for feeding and slaughtering.

It is probably fair to say that in this case Lord Rhondda was driven, largely by circumstances beyond his control, to depart from the main axiom of his policy, namely, that prices should not be controlled without also controlling supplies. The scale of cattle prices was fixed and in operation for some months before the elaborate machinery required to regulate the bringing of cattle to market and their sale and distribution could be established. Public opinion, however, was urgently demanding a reduction in the inflated price of meat and would not have tolerated the delay of all action till the full machinery was available.

Ultimately Lord Rhondda's policy was justified by success. The scheme for the control of livestock and distribution of meat, both home-grown and imported, though it had necessarily to be extemporised under conditions of great urgency, was in fact set up in time for the introduction of rationing, proved workable, and accomplished its end. A difficult situation was retrieved almost at the eleventh hour.

The complete control of supplies described above was naturally only accomplished by successive stages, and some of the minor foods were only included after Lord Rhondda's death. In respect of essentials, progress was rapid. During September and October, 1917, the Ministry of Food took over the sole supply of bacon, hams, lard, butter and cheese. The Oils and Fats Branch of the Ministry of Munitions had been transferred to the Ministry of Food in July, and its operations were gradually extended during the next few months to cover practically all oils and fats (edible or otherwise) and their products. As early as August 1917 Lord Rhondda decided to purchase all tea brought into the country ; a scheme for this purpose was prepared and put into force in consultation with the departments concerned and the growers. Imports of condensed milk were taken over in April 1918.

The purchasing arrangements of the Ministry of Food were naturally world-wide. A steadily increasing proportion of the total food supplies, however, came from North America. The first purchases of bacon (at the beginning of September) were made through the American representative of the Co-operative Wholesale Society, whose services were placed at the disposal of the Ministry. Almost immediately afterwards a special department of the Ministry was established in New York, with offices also in Washington and Toronto, to deal with all foodstuffs other than cereals (for which an organisation already existed in the Wheat Export Company) and sugar.

The purchases of the British Ministry of Food in America were made in accord with the other Allies, and the Head of the British Department acted as Chairman of the ' Allied Provisions Export Commission ' in America. The work of this Commission reached very large proportions. From October 1917 to February 1919, when buying practically ceased, the purchases made amounted to 2,207,000 net tons of food, and the expenditure was approximately £267,000,000. The total cost of administration was about 1/15 of 1 per cent. on the turnover.

While the control of supplies was being established, the first experiment was also being made in the systematic control of distribution on the basis of registered customers. The newly constituted Food Control Committees were called on to put into force the Sugar Distribution Scheme approved by the Cabinet before Lord Rhondda's appointment. This was a distribution scheme pure and simple ;

it did not amount to rationing. Every household in the country was to be registered (with the number of its members) at one particular shop, and the supply of sugar to each shop was to be based upon the number of persons so registered at a given rate per head. Each person was entitled to get that given quantity from the retailer with whom his household was registered. There was, however, no rule to prevent any customer from getting more than that quantity or buying it from a retailer with whom he was not registered, if the retailer was willing to sell. Being merely preferential, the scheme did not provide either for changes in households or for removals. Its sole object was to bring the distribution of sugar among retailers into general accord with the number of their usual customers.

During September and October the Food Committees carried out the first stage of the scheme with rather noticeable smoothness, having regard to their recent constitution and the novelty of the task. It soon became clear, however, that the public expected something more than a loose distribution scheme based on registration of households. Lord Rhondda came to the conclusion that provision must be made for persons who did not live in households at all and for removals, and further, that the public expected and demanded definite rationing. Early in October, accordingly, he decided to recast the scheme before it should come into actual operation in January.

The changes made involved not merely the gradual substitution of individual for household rationing, but also the constitution of a single central register of all sugar consumers, *i.e.* in effect of the whole population of the United Kingdom. The change over from one system to the other necessarily gave some additional work to the retailers and the public. Those who had already filled in one application form on registering their households for sugar, were now required to fill in a further form at their retailers. This gave rise to a certain amount of good-humoured criticism. Mr. Punch published a cartoon of 'Alice in Rhonddaland,' where Alice was depicted as asking a mad grocer for sugar, and on being told to fill in a form, said that she had already done so and was looking for sugar. She gets the reply

' You don't get sugar, you fill in another form.' The *Westminster Gazette* also had a pathetic picture of John Bull looking worried because he was playing the sugar-card patience and the sugar would not come out.

In spite of these criticisms, however, the change over was very adroitly made during the last two months of the year, and caused no serious difficulties. The rationing of sugar was launched successfully on January 1, 1918, and provided a valuable indication of the readiness of the public to submit to restrictions if only they could be assured of fair supplies.

It may be added that the arrangements for distributing the sugar through the retailers in accordance with the requirements of their customers remained unchanged from the very beginning, through all the variations of the sugar scheme itself. The central register of sugar consumers, begun in November 1917, was ultimately abandoned in the following spring, when the success of more difficult forms of rationing (meat and margarine) through Local Committees was assured.

The second period of Lord Rhondda's administration witnessed the development of the food queues and their abolition by rationing. In September and October of 1917 a shortage of tea supplies began to show itself, owing to insufficient shipping during the first half of the year, and rapidly reached an acute stage. A little later came a shortage of bacon and then of butter. The main factor here was the failure of supplies from Denmark and Holland. Action was already being taken to remedy the bacon shortage by purchases from America (which now became practically the sole source of supply), and to replace butter by increasing the production of margarine. The results of this action, however, could not be felt for some time. Meanwhile a serious situation in respect of all these articles developed, and, in the absence of any system for distributing supplies among retailers, began to show itself during November in the characteristic form of queues. It is interesting to note that, though sugar had long been in short supply, and though serious and continued complaints arose in regard to it, actual sugar queues were seldom seen.

In November also the shipping situation began to cause

acute anxiety. It became clear that the total imports that could be brought into this country during 1918 would fall much below the level of 1917 ; there must be drastic cuts in the importation programmes of the various departments concerned—Ministry of Munitions, Ministry of Food, Board of Trade, and the rest. The possibility of having to ration not merely sugar or tea but all foods could no longer be excluded.

The prospective and immediate difficulties were attacked by Lord Rhondda along two lines.

On the one hand, the preparatory work for the introduction of a national rationing system was begun. A centralised system was at that time contemplated, and the Registration Clearing House, which from November onwards dealt with removals under the Sugar Distribution Scheme, had been established with a view to becoming ultimately a central register of the whole population of Great Britain. Authority was sought from the Cabinet to establish all the necessary machinery for a comprehensive system of rationing, and a Departmental Committee on Rationing and Distribution was appointed to prepare a scheme dealing both with the scales of rations and with the machinery for rationing all essential foods. The Committee was at the same time given the function of examining all distribution schemes prepared for various foods and of approving them before they were put into force.

On the other hand, the Food Control Committees were called on to deal in the first instance with the immediate problem of the queues for tea, bacon, and margarine. It had already become clear that an important factor in the creation of queues was the tendency of customers to go from one shop to another in search of supplies ; the numbers in the queues were thereby swollen ; the more active or fortunate shoppers obtained more than they needed, while the others got nothing at all. The obvious remedy for this lay in the registration of customers and the tying of each household or person to a particular retailer. Several Committees—of which the most important was Birmingham —set registration schemes on foot during November. At the end of that month Lord Rhondda commissioned Captain

THE GREAT UNCONTROLLED.

Lord Rhondda. "LOOK HERE, JOHN, ARE YOU GOING TO TIGHTEN THAT BELT, OR MUST I DO IT FOR YOU?"

John Bull. "YOU DO IT FOR ME. THAT'S WHAT YOU'RE THERE FOR."

Reproduced by the special permission of the Proprietors of " Punch."

Tallents, as the Assistant Secretary in charge of the Local Authorities Division, to formulate a model scheme for dealing with queues, which might be sent to Committees generally. This led up to the issue on December 22 of an order, which, while it was entitled a Local Distribution Order, in fact enabled Committees to introduce schemes of local rationing. Under this Order from Christmas onwards a continually growing number of rationing schemes for tea, butter and margarine, and other articles were introduced throughout the main industrial districts of Great Britain. For butter and margarine, indeed, the local schemes became almost universal, and remained in force till they were absorbed in July 1918 in the full national system with the new ration book.

The main course of events, however, received its direction not from the provincial schemes, but from the special circumstances of London and from the sudden development of the anticipated crisis in regard to meat. Both by the Food Committees themselves and by the Ministry of Food it had been well realised that London must be dealt with as a whole. It would be impossible to have twenty-eight distinct rationing schemes in the twenty-eight boroughs forming the Administrative County, to say nothing of the numberless districts of Greater London. Representatives of the twenty-eight Food Committees of Inner London met on January 4, and decided that the Ministry of Food should be asked to prepare a single scheme for all their districts. The Ministry undertook the task and decided to have a butter and margarine scheme applying, if possible, not only to London proper, but to Greater London and the whole of the Home Counties. Scarcely had this decision being taken when an even more difficult problem—that of meat—demanded instant attention. Calculations made in the middle of January showed that for some months to come not more than $\frac{3}{4}$ lb. of butcher's meat per head per week would be available. The decision to ration meat in London and the Home Counties was taken at once.

Meat was thus added to the London and Home Counties rationing schemes after the first memorandum, dealing with butter and margarine alone, had already gone to the Committees. Though the peculiar problems of meat rationing had been considered at various times in a general way little or no practical work on them had been done. Substantially, meat rationing was extemporised at the last moment in the greatest possible haste, and when it was only one among many complicated problems of the Ministry. Until the last possible moment for decision it was still undecided whether meat should be dealt with on the same cards as butter and margarine or not ; whether the card should have detachable coupons or spaces for marking ; whether all kinds of meat—including bacon, preserved meat, poultry and the like should be included or not ; whether all classes of meat or only some should be subject to registration of customers ; how hotels, schools, workhouses, and other establishments should be classified and should receive their supplies. One of the most characteristic and valuable details of the British system—the money value of the coupon for butchers' meat—was an eleventh hour suggestion, rather doubtfully accepted after consideration by Lord Rhondda himself.

The scheme prepared by the Ministry was adopted by a second meeting of the London Committees on February 4 ; the Home Counties Committees were convened by their Food Commissioner county by county, and were persuaded (for the most part quite readily) to fall into line. The date of beginning was fixed for Monday, February 25.

It is needless to say that the interval before that date was one of the greatest possible anxiety. Apart from the inherent difficulties of any rationing scheme, the shortness of time for preparation made it seem almost extravagant to hope for success. The mere printing and distribution of the millions of cards, instructions, forms, and posters were a severe task, and inevitable failures at one point or another seemed at times to endanger the whole scheme. I had an impressive experience of this myself at a meeting of London and Home Counties executive officers, which was convened two or three days before rationing was due to begin, so that the officers might receive final instructions and a few well-chosen words of encouragement before they ' went over the top.' The meeting did not take the course expected. It developed into something like an indignation meeting against the Ministry of Food for not printing and distributing its meat cards and other forms in time, and for then telling the public by press notice to go and complain to the executive officer if they had not received their cards. A large proportion of the officers present, and certainly most of those speaking, declared roundly that the scheme could not possibly be launched on the date announced ; neither the forms nor the food would be available ; they wished to move a resolution postponing action for a fortnight at least. A few took a contrary view, and felt confident that they could ' muddle through ' ; they argued also that none of the executive officers had authority to speak for their committees and to vote either for or against a postponement of the scheme. I had a hasty consultation with Captain Tallents. We decided to take a firm line and refuse to put any resolution. I added that I would naturally inform Lord Rhondda of the meeting, but that I was quite certain that he would not sanction postponement. Ninety-five out of a hundred of the public had received their meat cards and would be disappointed at any delay ; for the rest, emergency cards must be issued on demand. As for food to meet the ration, limited reserves at least of bacon and of margarine would be available, and would be sent down on receipt of a telegram or telephone message.

I do not think that, in fact, I was able to tell Lord Rhondda about this meeting and the views of the executive officers at that time, as he was out of London. The story, however, does directly illustrate Lord Rhondda's methods. There can be no question, having regard to the results, that the decision to go on with the scheme at all costs was right. It would have been difficult, however, in the circumstances, for any official to take such a decision with any less firm and loyal chief behind him than Lord Rhondda. I knew that so long as he retained the services of an officer at all he was prepared to support almost any action which that officer deemed it necessary to take.

Though, however, Lord Rhondda did not know of this particular meeting till long afterwards, he had, of course, his full share, and more, of the anxieties of the time. He was profoundly distressed by the inconvenience and suffering involved in the prevalence of queues, which during February had grown to portentous proportions ; and he feared the effects of malnutrition on the physique of the nation, and particularly of the children. It was doubtful whether the Ministry of Food could weather the storm. There is no harm in saying now that Lord Rhondda at that time was much pressed to make a reorganisation in his office and appoint, or agree to the appointment of, a ' Director-General of Distribution and Rationing.' He was far from anxious to do this, but, in view of the vital importance of the food problem both to the Government and to the country as a whole, felt unable to resist the proposal if a suitable man could be found. He spoke to me on the subject more than once in February. On the first occasion he regarded the making of such a fresh appointment as inevitable. A few days later I was able to bring evidence that outside London the local schemes were already rapidly abolishing queues for butter and margarine, and to point out how soon the London scheme itself would be in force. We were, indeed, at that time within ten days of the starting of the scheme. All the essential cards and instructions had long been prepared and issued or were in the press. No new ' Director-General ' could have done anything whatever to hasten or vary the scheme ; the only danger was that he might have delayed its operation.

As it happened, no suitable man was found willing to undertake at the last moment the apparently thankless task of rationing. The mind of the Government was much absorbed with other matters, and Lord Rhondda displayed a masterly lack of alacrity in the business. He told me with considerable satisfaction that he had failed to see the Prime Minister on the subject for three days ; that he was going off into the country without fail on that after-noon ; and that he expected by the time he returned (which would be the Monday before rationing actually started) to find the whole attention of the Government diverted to other problems. This expectation was realised : the War Cabinet found many other things to think about in the last days of February 1918, and rationing was allowed to be born without a ' Director-General.' If any one had accepted the post (I believe that it was definitely offered in at least one case) he would inevitably have appeared in the public eye as responsible for the subsequent success, and would have absorbed without labour the largest share of that gold mine of reputations which the rationing system has proved itself to be : the whole public estimate of Lord Rhondda's character might have been altered.

In these conditions of anxiety and uncertainty the London and Home Counties' scheme for rationing meat, butter and margarine came into force on February 25. Under the scheme every individual received a meat card on which he had to register with a butcher, and a butter and margarine card on which he had to register with a grocer. He could only purchase from the retailer named in each case, and that retailer was furnished with supplies according to the number of his registered customers and the demands made upon him by establishments and institutions. Statutory sanction was given to the scheme by a Special Order, the Local Distribution Order of December 22 proving inapplicable.

The scheme had a dramatic and almost instant success. In the period preceding its introduction there had been queues on every day in the week, following a more or less regular cycle. They were lowest on Monday, rose to a slightly higher level on Tuesday, Wednesday, and Thursday, and ran upon Friday and Saturday to a total of something like half a million persons standing in queues on the latter day in the Metropolitan Police District alone.

During the first four days of rationing, Monday, Tuesday, Wednesday, and Thursday—25th to 28th February—there were practically no queues in London at all. With the end of the week came a revival of anxiety ; on Friday and Saturday queues were to be seen again in many parts of London. They were, however, as the figures proved, infinitely less than in the previous week ; they were not due to the causes which had produced queues before—namely, uncertainty as to where food was to be obtained and the desire of each individual to be first in the field ; they represented rather the inevitable delay in shopping due to

R

the unfamiliarity of the public and the retailers with the system, and to the time occupied in presenting cards and cutting off coupons. The following week saw the success of the London system absolutely assured ; the queues to all intents and purposes vanished for ever.

In the week before rationing 1,339,000 persons were counted in queues in the London area during the six days. In the first week the number fell to 191,000 ; in the second week to 64,000 ; and in the fourth week to 15,000 (including queues for unrationed articles such as cheese, lard, and fish). Before rationing about 550,000 people stood in queues every Saturday in London. On the first Saturday after rationing the number was 110,000, on the next 24,000, and on the fourth Saturday under 7000.

The fortunes of the London and Home Counties scheme were decisive for the whole country. After a meeting with a number of Food Commissioners in the second half of February, Lord Rhondda had already decided to ration meat throughout the country on the London model, and so soon as the success of that model was assured by experience it became clear that it was only a question of time before matters should be put right everywhere. Butter and margarine queues, as has been stated, were already rapidly disappearing under the influence of local schemes. Though during March meat queues continued in most of the big provincial centres, it was realised that they were under sentence of death. Meat rationing (originally proposed for March 25) was introduced throughout the country on April 7. The success of the London scheme was universally repeated.

The London experience was decisive also as to the form which rationing should ultimately take in this country. It was to be a national system administered by local authorities. The vigorous controversy which had raged in the Department itself as between centralised and localised administration of rationing was in this way settled. When national rationing with a single ration book was introduced in July, sugar, which since January had been dealt with on a centralised basis, was brought into line with other food, and the authority of the Food Control Committees was restored. At the same time, the varying local schemes for butter and margarine were unified so as to form part of the single national scheme.

The successful introduction of rationing made Lord Rhondda's a household name throughout the country, even to the extent sometimes of overshadowing his work in other fields of food control. Yet while it is wrong to think of Lord Rhondda only in connection with the rationing system, there is a sense in which that system can truly be regarded as his crowning achievement, and, indeed, as summing up all that he did. Rationing did not and could not stand alone ; it depended upon that other main branch of Lord Rhondda's policy—the control of supplies—and would have been utterly impossible without it. Behind the books and coupons which the public saw and thought of as the rationing system, was a no less vast machinery for controlling and distributing supplies, so that the coupon could be honoured. Speaking departmentally, rationing was throughout the joint work of two divisions in the Ministry of Food—the Local Authorities and Rationing Division under Captain Tallents and the Supply Division concerned with the particular food in question—*i.e.* in the most difficult cases of meat and margarine, the Meat and Fats Division under Mr. E. F. Wise ; in the case of bacon, lard, and tea, the Provisions Division ; in the case of sugar, the Sugar Commission. In more general terms, the feat of securing week by week, to every man, woman, and child, in every town and village of Great Britain, their fair share of meat, fats, sugar, and the rest was simply the supreme manifestation of the power of the Food Control built up by Lord Rhondda. It was the visible sign of all else that he had done.

The introduction of rationing was also the closing achievement of Lord Rhondda's active career at the Ministry of Food. His last visit to the office was in the beginning of April. He went away for a brief holiday and never returned. For some time indeed, during April and May, he continued to get reports from the Ministry and to deal with important questions. He approved, for instance, the July ration book and the arrangements for combining all foods under one uniform system. He interested himself in the development of National Kitchens. His fatal weakness, however, grew steadily, He died on July 3, 1918, having held the office of Food Controller for just over twelve months.

Some account has now been given of what Lord Rhondda accomplished. It remains only to attempt some estimate of the personality of the Food Controller, and some indication of the qualities which made his success possible. I may perhaps begin by one or two quotations from what was said of him when his death was still recent.

The first is a brief passage from the report on Food Control in 1918, prepared for the Government's Record :

' He saved the country from much difficulty and disorder by his resolute control of prices and by the confidence he inspired. Few probably except those who worked under him are aware of his many varied qualities and of the devotion with which he applied them to his task. A fine balance of judgment harmonised with a readiness to accept responsibility and to make decisions. He worked strenuously himself and was well served by his staff, because he was generous of the loyalty which he expected from others. It is true of him that his interest and influence were felt in every branch of the huge organisation over which he presided.

This was actually written by Professor (now Sir) E. C. K. Gonner, who from June 1917 onwards acted as Director of Statistics in the Ministry of Food. Lord Rhondda, who had an almost insatiable love of economic argument, spent much time in discussing with Professor Gonner the economics of food control and prices. A convinced individualist in theory, he was much intrigued by his position as the Arch-Socialist in practice, conducting on behalf of the State world-wide trading operations of unimagined scale and complexity.

The second passage is taken from an address given by myself to the Grocers' Federation at Hanley on July 10, 1918, almost immediately after Lord Rhondda's death, and even before his successor had been appointed :

' It is, I think, generally agreed that Lord Rhondda's achievement has been one of the most outstanding of this war. In considering how he accomplished what he did accomplish, it is necessary, of course, to recognise first of all that he had great qualities—a keen brain, a vast experience of men and of matters, a strong will, and a balanced judgment. He might, however, have had all these and still not have done what he did. There are three special points to which I wish to refer briefly, as being perhaps the most important elements in Lord Rhondda's success. He was a man who knew better than almost any other, or certainly better than most others, how to get the best work out of those who worked for him and with him ; he was scrupulously fair, and he recognised the importance of keeping in touch with the opinion of those for whom and with whom he worked.'

The picture here presented is, I think, a true one. It gives the simple secrets of Lord Rhondda's success.

In his Ministry of Food days, at any rate, Lord Rhondda carried reliance upon his trusted officers very far. His policy had always been to leave as much work as possible to his subordinates. When he came to the Ministry he was already feeling the strain of years. He used to say that he would have given anything to have had a task of this size and difficulty twenty years before. Now he had perforce to confine himself to dealing with really important issues, and with the two or three branches of work—study and control of prices, meat supply, watching and guiding of public opinion—which alone he had time to master in detail.

Apart from these points, he did not wish to be troubled with details. Even on large questions of policy he was not content to have balanced alternatives presented for his selection. He expected any officer submitting a point to take the responsibility of making a definite recommendation thereon, and he always, if possible, accepted that recommendation. Once he had done so, he would defend the decision to the last as being his own.

Naturally he was exposed to the risk occasionally of sanctioning wrong policies or leaving mistakes too long without a remedy. Probably he would have repudiated altogether the view that a Government Department cannot afford to make mistakes. I have been told that in making a new business venture Lord Rhondda's practice was to embark a certain capital, arrange for sharing the profits, appoint a man to take charge, and then leave him to do exactly as he would. If two ventures out of three succeeded, he was content, for he gained on balance. I imagine that he was following out the same line at the Ministry of Food, and there can be no question that he succeeded, not twice out of three times, but nine times out of ten.

Another occasional defect of Lord Rhondda's qualities—if, indeed, it is to be called a defect—was his unwillingness to hurt the feelings of any of his staff. He was immensely appreciative of good work, and most reluctant to punish failure. It was exceedingly difficult to induce him to get rid of those who for any reason whatever were no longer rendering good service. This soft-heartedness led occasionally to embarrassment. On more than one occasion when Lord Rhondda had been worked up to the point of seeing an official for the purpose of securing his departure, the official returned from the interview with a new lease of life and hopefulness.

Lord Rhondda, indeed, was a very human person. As a consequence, though he was not ordinarily an impressive speaker, his speeches were at times extraordinarily successful. On one occasion he had to address a Committee of Retail Traders, and was as usual furnished by his department with notes for his speech and a warning at the same time that the notes were somewhat lacking in the personal touch. He reported afterwards with glee that he had supplied the personal touch by telling the Retailers' Committee that his own father had been a grocer ; whether for this reason or not, the Committee were certainly delighted by his visit.

Yet another very human characteristic was his love of conversation. Sometimes, indeed, he appeared to earnest officials seeking instant decisions on concrete points to be wasting a good deal of his own time—and of theirs while they waited—in interviewing journalists or discussing economic theories. Lord Rhondda's invariable accessibility to journalists and stray inquirers, however, was in no sense an idle taste. It was an essential part of his policy.

He was profoundly convinced of the importance of

securing a ' good press ' in support of the bold measures which the times demanded. As one of his officers put it, he set up a ' press barrage ' of favourable opinion behind which his department could work without disturbance.

In doing so he came perhaps nearer to reproducing in war-time the ordinary function of the ministerial head of a department than many, if not most, of the war-time Ministers.

Under peace conditions one of the main tasks of a Minister has been to keep his departments in touch with public opinion, which in those conditions is embodied in the House of Commons ; he must represent and explain his department there, and must in turn convey to the department the feeling of members ; he must often introduce Bills and defend estimates and regulations. His time is largely occupied in this, and he cannot, if he would, undertake the duties of his staff in direct administration. The virtual suspension of Parliamentary Government during the war left Ministers to a large extent shorn of one of their principal functions, and with time on their hands for departmental work. Sometimes, of course, where the Minister had special administrative experience or aptitude, and where public opinion was unimportant, this proved an advantage ; in other cases not. In the case of food control at least, the necessity for keeping the department in close touch with public opinion was no less in war than in peace. The decay of Parliament made attention to the press and to other means of contact with the general public even more important than before. Lord Rhondda made this his special and personal task. With a true instinct he devoted to press interviews, deputations, and general publicity, rather than to departmental detail, the time which in other conditions would have been absorbed by Parliamentary duties.

In the other main branch of a Minister's work—that of making decisions on important issues of policy—Lord Rhondda was equally strong. He had judgment and courage, a sense of proportion and experience of vast operations. The mere size of an undertaking did not frighten him at all. He looked at big questions from a broad point of view. Some of the main decisions which shaped his policy—the decentralisation of administrative responsibility, the full control of supplies, the preservation so far as possible of existing trade channels—have already been indicated. The same quality appeared in many minor decisions which he had to give from day to day. He reached a decision often with difficulty ; when he had reached it, he was imperturbable by any passing gust of opinion.

In conclusion, it may be said that Lord Rhondda's career as Food Controller was a striking illustration of two general principles.

The first is that, on the whole, and even at the risk of mistakes, bigger results can be achieved, and harder work can be got out of a staff by trusting and supporting them than by supervision and pressure ; by appreciation rather than by criticism, by hope rather than by fear.

The second is that of the two master-passions of democracy—the love of liberty and the love of justice—the latter is with the British people the deeper and stronger. Lord Rhondda, like others, sometimes doubted whether the restraints involved in rationing would ever be tolerated. When the test came, he found that the public were prepared to endure any and every restriction—upon the quantity which they should buy and the quality and the place and the price—so long as they felt it to be a necessary condition of fair play for all.

CHAPTER XVI

LORD RHONDDA AT THE MINISTRY OF FOOD

By Sir E. C. K. Gonner

THE description in the foregoing chapter of the organisation of the Ministry of Food under Lord Rhondda, and the work which it performed, gives some idea of the magnitude and intricacy of the task which confronted him on assuming office, and of the qualities which characterised his administration. In some measure too it explains the nature of his extraordinary achievement. In less than a year, for though Food Controller for a few days over that period his active life in the Ministry was only nine months, he sprang into the front ranks of British Ministers and won the confidence of the people whose food he rationed and whose liberty of action he curtailed. But no account can be complete without consideration of his personal attitude and exertions. The critical nature of the emergency and the desperate hurry in which the work had to be done made the individuality of the Minister of unusual importance. Lord Rhondda was the last man to claim any undue share in the credit due to his improvised Department. He was generous in his appreciation of the work of his staff, and always frank in the public acknowledgment of their efforts. But there is not one of those who held a responsible position under him who would hesitate in assigning such success as was attained in the first place to his personality and labours.

As has been said before, he accepted his new post with considerable reluctance, mainly, as it seemed, because he doubted, not his capacity, but his physical fitness for coping with the difficulties which he foresaw. Half in jest and half in earnest, he said that he knew the work would kill him. To some extent also he disliked the prospect of unpopularity, for he took it for granted that a Food Controller must be unpopular. How can he be otherwise, as he said, when he interferes with popular comfort and appetites? But after a short hesitation he accepted office with a full determination to do the work thoroughly.

While he was far too big a man to enter on his work with any rigid and detailed scheme, there were certain points on which his mind was made up. The rise in food prices, which was manifesting itself in an alarming way in the summer of 1917, had to be checked and prices if possible reduced, an efficient machinery had to be set up for controlling food, and the health and courage of the nation had to be maintained.

The rise in food prices, as Lord Rhondda was well aware, was due to shortage, and he knew as well as those who have criticised his policy on this point that the best remedy lay in plentiful supplies and economical distribution. While he did his best to secure these, he knew, however, that some degree of shortage would continue, and that in the more necessary foods even a small shortage reacts in an alarming way upon price. The attempt to meet the danger by constant increases in wages he viewed with suspicion, both as a present remedy, with regard to which he thought that the increases acted unevenly and started from a wrong basis, and also in view of the difficulties which would have to be encountered when the necessity was past. Hence it was that Price Control assumed its prominent place in his programme.

As to the organisation of an administration there was much more to be done than the public ever realised. In point of fact a real administrative office had to be created at a moment when serious shortages were already manifesting themselves and when action rather than preparation for action was called for. As Lord Rhondda said with regard to the control of Home meat, ' I am called on to act before I have an organisation through which to act.'

There was one further matter to be noticed in this connection. The courage of the nation had to be maintained, and here food played no unimportant part. Not the least part of the success of the Food Administration consisted in the sense of security which the maintenance of a reasonable supply of food and the justice of its distribution had upon the temper and so the lasting power of the people. At one time indeed it may have seemed that the absence of visible danger and the sufficiency of comfort, despite the losses of life with their attendant grief, were lulling the country into a false security ; on the other hand, as time went by and as the burden of the war came to rest more and more upon England, the capacity of endurance became a great asset in the struggle. To secure this was one of the tasks which Lord Rhondda set himself, and it was for this he desired the confidence of the country. It is perfectly true that he liked popularity and welcomed its signs with real delight. But there was something more than this in his attitude. He knew that the confidence of the people was essential to the adequate performance of his work. He had support from the Press and he sought it. He took the nation into his confidence in good times as well as in difficult times, and as a result it came to rely on his judgment. Rationing was accepted mainly as a relief from queues, but partly also because it was Lord Rhondda who deemed it necessary. When after the development of his illness he contemplated resignation, one of the most potent arguments urged against it was the popularity which he had achieved.

While no man was more accessible or more anxious to keep himself well abreast of the whole work of the Ministry, there were three subjects which, after the labour of building up the administration was over, occupied a very large share of his personal attention—Prices, the Home Meat Supply, and Health.

The reasons which led him to attach so much importance to the problem of prices have been indicated. His methods for ensuring careful supervision of them remain to be described. His first step on coming to the Ministry was to introduce the system of costings, and this was one, though only one, of the reasons which made him eager to secure the services of Mr. Wintour as Permanent Secretary. He was consulted as to the price of any large intended purchases, a matter in which his wide business experience made his advice of the greatest possible value to the various officers and trade committees concerned. The same was true of schemes of distribution which laid down the margins or percentages of profit allowed to the different classes of traders. The movements of retail prices and their comparison with wholesale prices were matters to which he attached great importance and with regard to which he showed an insatiable desire for information. Quite apart from incidental information on different foods, during the active nine months of his *régime* some ten or twelve full reports were drawn up on the whole subject, and it was the constant saying in the Branch charged with this work that if the Controller didn't want a special report on the position of cattle and meat he was sure to want one on the movement of prices. Sometimes the two subjects overlapped, and then the demand was more than usually detailed and insistent. It must not be imagined, however, that he welcomed the task of fixing and controlling prices. On the contrary, he detested it, and one member of the staff well remembers how at his first interview with his new chief he was greeted with the inquiry as to how he viewed the job of fixing prices and interfering with their normal adjustment by Demand and Supply. Lord Rhondda expressed straight away his strong personal distaste, but added that abnormal conditions warranted abnormal methods. Of course, he said, it is only feasible when accompanied with the absolute control of the supplies. This in most cases meant State purchase and ownership. But once having settled that prices must be fixed he was determined that the method adopted should be thorough. Prices must be fixed at every stage and throughout was his decision. Half measures, as he often said, were useless. His resolution and care had their reward. The upward rush of prices was checked, and, if the chief foods be taken together, the price index was kept almost level for twelve months.

The position and prospects of the Home Meat Supply, on which the civilian population depended, received constant attention. Here again he felt he could effect something, and on this matter he considered his own experience was of particular value.   During the week he was in frequent conference with the responsible officers of the Meat Division, and every Saturday afternoon there was despatched to him at home a file, which grew into bulky proportions, setting out the latest statistics, obtained sometimes by telegraph or telephone, as to market supplies of meat, cattle and sheep passing through the markets, the import of Irish beasts, the imports of foreign meat, and all manner of details both as to supply and prospects.   On one occasion in reply to the inquiry as to how he had spent his week-end, he replied with a laugh that the file in question had occupied him for ten hours.   Even during his illness the file went down regularly for several weeks, to be returned with equal punctuality and with comments which grew pathetically few as time went on ; and when owing to his weakness the despatch of this file was discontinued both his private secretary and the officers responsible for its preparation realised sadly how ominous this was.   It has been stated in the preceding chapter that one of his last official communications was a request for a careful opinion as to the causes of the meat shortage in the winter 1917–1918.   This had worried Lord Rhondda greatly, not only at the time but during the months which followed, and shortly before he left the office for the last time a full memorandum had been prepared for him on the subject.   Consequently it was with grave apprehension that the writer of the memorandum read the letter which showed how completely illness had wiped out the explanation from his mind.

Another matter which gave him serious concern was the effect of curtailed consumption and especially of rationing upon the health of the population and in particular upon that of children.   One day he enunciated the view that it was desirable that people like himself who could afford foods other and more expensive than those under ration should not eat rationed foods, and an amusing discussion ensued as to whether he was doing his duty better by abstaining from rationed food or by setting the example to others of taking his ration in the ordinary way.

His personal attention to the above by no means implied any disregard of other activities of the Ministry.   It arose in the main from two causes, his eminently practical nature which led him to give much of his time to matters where he felt that he personally was doing something, and his fear lest these aspects which he rightly deemed of great importance should be neglected. This was certainly the case with regard to the movement of prices and the state of health, and to some extent it was true of the home meat supply.

In what he did much depended on his attitude towards both the public and his staff.

Quite apart from his deliberate view that popular confidence was an essential element in the success of his administration, he both felt and liked to show trust in the public. Except in a few cases, when information had to be concealed from the enemy, he was in favour of telling the nation what he knew. But when he gave news he liked to give the whole news, and it annoyed him when information issuing from his own department was published in a partial or, as he felt, misleading form. Further than that, he really believed in the national sense of justice. When after some misgiving he adopted the policy of rationing, it was because it commended itself to him as just, and as has been said elsewhere he felt that he could appeal to the people on that ground.

In his relations with his staff there was the same sense of confidence. Officers whom he trusted felt that they had his entire confidence. On one occasion, detecting a shade of surprise on the face of one whom he had told to use his name as he thought fit, he said, ' You don't think I would go back on you ? ' It was explained that it was not apprehension but surprise at the fulness of his confidence. ' You can use my authority as you think necessary,' he said ; adding with a flash of humour, ' but do be careful to let me know exactly what you have said.' Intercourse with him was singularly free, and when he consulted any member of the staff, so far from resenting freedom of speech he demanded it. His view indeed was that he was entitled to the best opinion of those with whom he was in contact, even if that opinion was directly opposed to his own. In addition to the secretaries, certain officers, as the Financial Secretary and the Director of Statistics, had access to him at almost any time in order that he might discuss the general financial or economic position, quite apart from detail or any particular transaction. So great was the feeling of common loyalty engendered in the Ministry during Lord Rhondda's period that there was little or no difficulty in information going direct to him without passing through the secretary. It may be said without exaggeration that no Minister has been more loved by his staff and throughout his whole department. After his death one of the supervisors said that the typists worked with more zest when they knew that work was being done for Lord Rhondda.

His own work fell into three sections. First, there was the general view of the food position and prospects and the policy based on that view. Matters of this order fall on the Minister himself, and it was in connection with these that the secretaries and certain other officers were in singularly free and unfettered intercourse with their chief. Secondly, there were certain subjects, referred to above, which occupied a large part of his personal consideration. Lastly, there was the general work of the department affecting supplies, storage, transport, distribution and rationing of different foods, and also the organisation of the local committees and the conduct of a number of other committees. Included with the above were the relations with other Government departments and especially the Board of Agriculture. All these called for a host of decisions from the Food Controller and in many instances entailed personal intervention and interviews. The actual burden of work was enormous, and owing to the rapid rise of the Ministry and the part played by Lord Rhondda in its organisation implied a heavy strain. Fortunately he was an experienced administrator, accustomed to deal with large enterprises and able to turn from one subject to another with facility. He knew when and how to delegate and yet to keep himself in real touch with the multifarious activities proceeding under his aegis. But the task was hard and unremitting, even to one who was a hard worker and able to thread his way through masses of figures when such, as was sometimes the case, were essential and to discuss a question with reference to the broad issues involved.   While in this power to grasp a complicated situation he was assisted by his early mathematical training and his leanings towards statistical and economic studies, he was anything but a doctrinaire. He discussed the general economic principles involved in any large matter awaiting decision because he liked to feel that in deviating from normal methods and principles he was warranted in his attitude by the abnormal conditions in which he was called on to act.   But first and last he always faced facts.   He knew the dangers and difficulties attending the fixing of prices and personally disliked the task, though deriving some amusement from the irony of circumstances which imposed the task on him of all men and led to his discussion of the matter with one of his staff to whom it was equally distasteful.   But he fixed them all the same and the work was done thoroughly.   He was fascinated for a time by the idea of a central register for the purpose of rationing, but convinced of its practical difficulties he gave it up.   On one occasion, discussing in the light of new knowledge a particular scheme on which the Ministry was embarked, he said, ' If we had known what we know now, we should not be acting in this way, but we cannot change now.'

His position as an administrator is undoubted.   He was a big business man with remarkable powers of organisation and wide views, and under him the mechanism of administration ran easily.   Partly owing to the strong affection felt for him, but partly by reason of a peculiar sense of security due to his soundness of judgment and loyalty to the staff, unity and coherence were given to a huge department created in a hurry and composed of officers chosen from almost all ranks and professions.   In the circumstances sketched here and in the preceding chapter the wonder is not that some mistakes were made and that duties occasionally overlapped but that the mistakes were not much more serious and that the administration worked at all, and that this was so, was due more to the personality of the Minister than to anything else.

There was something more, however, than administrative ability in Lord Rhondda's brief tenure as Food Controller.   There was an element of statesmanship in his intuitive recognition of the practicability of particular lines of policy. His prescience was remarkable. He concentrated first of all on the problem of prices, and events proved him right. He had little or no doubt that supplies could be maintained even when many of his advisers were filled with gloomy forebodings, and here again he was justified in his belief. Outside departmental politics it was the same ; he singled out essential things. On one occasion when he had been speaking of his many relations with the Prime Minister and criticising his attitude with his usual frankness, he said suddenly to his hearer, ' Yes, it's all quite true, but we must back him for all we are worth. He is the one man who can win the war, he has plenty of drive and he's an optimist. No one but an optimist can win a war of this magnitude.'

In his personal character, he was essentially lovable and generous to those who surrounded him, with abundant humour and singular freedom from pettiness. Despite his obvious strength and decision, he was by no means an unmoved or reserved man. On the contrary his naturally buoyant temperament rendered him liable at times to depression, and this was more than once the case in the trying months of February and March, 1918. At other times, despite anxiety, passing events would call out the almost boyish glee which was part of his character. His private secretary will not forget the morning when a telegram arrived with the news that his Hereford bull which had taken second prize had sold for several times the price of the winner of the first prize. But this very human trait only threw into stronger relief the courage which was never wanting when risks had to be taken.

When Lord Rhondda assumed office in July 1917, he made two prophecies. He said he knew the work would kill him and also that he would soon be the most unpopular man in the Government. The first came true. The second was certainly false, for before he died in July 1918 he had won the unstinted confidence and regard of the nation.

CHAPTER XVII

A SKETCH OF THE FOOD MINISTRY

By the Right Hon. J. R. Clynes

My association with Lord Rhondda began with his acceptance of the post of Food Controller at the time of real national crisis in connection with our food supplies. Many years before that, during his membership of the House of Commons, I could claim but a slight acquaintance with Lord Rhondda, but knew him as one renowned for great business activities and patriotic interest in public affairs.

The management of a Ministry of Food, especially during the most anxious years of the great war, became a matter of supreme concern, not merely to any one of the Allied Powers but to them all. The country was fortunate, therefore, in securing so fearless and experienced a chief as Lord Rhondda, for at the stage when he began his work the service of an extraordinary man was required to deal with an extraordinary situation. Food shortage was being felt severely. Prices were ascending. Distribution of commodities had suffered some dislocation because abnormal conditions attracted a number of the evil spirits always on the lookout to exploit any unusual situation. It was not merely the case that things were bad. There was growing in the public mind the fear that they would be much worse unless new and far-reaching plans were immediately tried.

The Ministry of Food was that Department of State which in these fateful years had to carry a great responsibility in relation not only to the task of securing food for the fighting forces, but in providing regular supplies for a much larger body—the civil population. The Food Ministry, therefore, stood in close contact to all classes of the people. Its work touched intimately the personal interests and appetites of every individual not on rare occasions, but several times a day.

Lord Rhondda began his great work with the handicap of being called to it late in the period of the war. He had to work under unusual pressure, and improvise his instruments as best he could until a great organisation was built up which stretched from London through the provincial centres to remote and thinly populated parts of the United Kingdom.

Apart altogether from questions of efficiency—questions of purchasing great quantities of food in other parts of the world and delivering them safely to these shores—the immediate task of the Ministry was to convince ' the man in the street ' that he was being treated fairly and was being provided for like anyone else. It was around Lord Rhondda that this conviction began to grow. It was the growth of this well-placed idea which explained his strength and popularity and which rescued the Food Ministry from a position of being the butt of everybody's displeasure to being an object of popular approval.

No Food Ministry, however efficient or skilfully managed, could during war conditions supply food to masses of the population under conditions as to price and quantity as satisfactory as food traders could supply it during a period of peace. This central fact was not readily grasped. It was essential, therefore, to convince the people of the realities of difficulties to be overcome, and Lord Rhondda found that the best way to get people to appreciate difficulties was to convince them that every human effort was being made, always from the standpoint of just and equitable treatment for every class in the land.

Lord Rhondda knew that in the conduct of a task so stern as this he would have to show no concern whatever for political consequences to himself resulting from any action which he might be obliged to take. His great knowledge of affairs, and his intimate touch with the business world, gave him an enormous advantage over many with whom he had to deal. Having in any particular instance ascertained due information of what was needed, he was always absolutely fearless in deciding what should be done to meet the need. Just as he had no concern for his own fate, he wasted no words on the degree of inconvenience which a particular interest might suffer in his determined pursuit of the national well-being. It was rare that he had to revise a decision, and it was seldom that he was asked to do so when it became known that he was prompted by no consideration other than public welfare and the efficient management of the great organisation of which he was the Chief.

No one could do the work well who was not qualified by experience and temperament to take quick decisions which would stand the test of producing beneficial results without these decisions being merely guess work or based upon the assumption that things would turn out well in the end. Not only did the responsibility and the quantity of the business increase daily, but the organisation for coping with it had also to grow at a corresponding rate. It required ceaseless supervision and the attraction and enlistment for purposes of administration and executive duty of a large number of men of great and varied experience. The quality of the work done in an extensive though untried undertaking depended very much upon the choice of men and upon the commands given to them, and in these matters the value of Lord Rhondda's judgment cannot be overstated.

In spite of having to work under the pressure of a new problem every day, and of having to reach decisions without the guidance of precedent, Lord Rhondda succeeded in his great aim of making supplies secure to people of all classes by a policy which placed all upon an equal footing and which secured for each the same treatment in respect to the weight, quality, and price of food. This was no small achievement at a time when the Food Ministry as an improvised State department was exciting perhaps greater public interest than any other Ministry dealing with the affairs of the civil population.

British habits and character were not thought to be amenable to the new and sometimes irritating methods which the Food Ministry had to apply day by day. The public response, however, to the various measures of discipline involved in the control and distribution of food, was due very largely to the confidence created in the public mind that the Chief of the Ministry of Food could be trusted to discharge the duties which conditions of war imposed upon him without fear of consequences or favour to any section.

No Ministry called into existence by war conditions stood in a more close relationship to critical bodies of public opinion, especially during the early period of Lord Rhondda's service, and it is not too much to say that no Ministry survived contact with this criticism in the same degree. Numerous property and trading interests, commercial and business activities, the settled habits of shopkeepers and the long established customs of wholesalers, middlemen, and at times speculators, were all brought into immediate touch with the daily activities of the Food Ministry. In addition to consoling those whose interests were disturbed or so composing claims as to ensure the submission and at times the co-operation of these interests, Lord Rhondda found that a part of his daily work was a succession of interviews with deputations, discussions with conferences, and consultations with innumerable groups of men, suddenly faced with new situations involved in the creation and management of a novel form of feeding the people.

The serious losses sustained by this country at sea during the last eighteen months of the war intensified the difficulty of reassuring the population and deepened the problems with which the Food Ministry had to deal.   Provisions were made in face of uncertainties and at times intentions were frustrated either because of submarine disasters, or by dislocations due to impaired methods of transport and defects in distribution. A multiplicity of such troubles were in due course overtaken, and the Minister, who in the middle period of his work rightly believed that to him there fell the task of standing between his country and the discontent and anger of a distressed civil population, felt at the end of his service not only the sense of relief which his labours had produced, but saw that the work of the Food Ministry taken altogether had made a substantial contribution to the effective efforts of the country in the allied task of forcing a successful issue in the world war.

Lord Rhondda saw from the beginning that failure in the great service to which he set his hand would have meant failure in every other effort which his country was making in the war. He faced his service as a stern and solemn duty, and never thought to try and save himself in trying to save the nation.

The complete success of Lord Rhondda as Food Controller was due to a combination of varied personal qualities. He had a keen sympathy with the poor, who were not only suffering the common privations of the war, but who had their suffering much increased because of their difficulties in obtaining food in competition with richer people. These difficulties he hastened to reduce or remove.

He applied to his work a large human touch which evoked from his colleagues and subordinates all the better service. He did not conceal his contempt for old or formal departmental practices when changed circumstances demanded new practices and methods for which there was no departmental precedent. He did not conceal his impatience with trivialities when faced with the need for great deeds and unconventional Ministerial action. His warmth of character made him always approachable, but in showing fairness to every interest, firmness of treatment was never lacking when required. It is not too much to say that no Minister in a similar period of service better served his country than did Lord Rhondda.

[See also an account of the Food Ministry from the point of view of the general public by Mr. Leonard Rees (Editor of the *Sunday Times*), Appendix E.]

AT HOME.

CHAPTER XVIII

THE LAST YEARS

ON Wednesday, December 6, 1916, Mr. Lloyd George undertook the task of forming his Ministry. On Saturday, December 9, my father, who was at Llanwern (as always at the week-end) was summoned to the telephone to answer a trunk call from London. The man at the other end of the line was Mr. Lloyd George, who asked him if he would take office in his Ministry, as President of the Local Government Board. ' Is it in the Cabinet ? ' asked my father. ' There isn't going to be any Cabinet,' was the reply (it has always reminded me of the small boy and the apple : ' There ain't going to be no core '). My father accepted, though he remarked that he could not quite see why he was chosen for this particular office, of which he knew nothing. ' I shall be a round peg in a square hole there,' he said. ' Oh no,' was the reply, ' I have specially selected you for that post because you will be able to . . . ' at that point the telephone, which had been bad from the start, gave out altogether, the conversation closed, and my father never knew to the end of his life for what reason he was specially chosen as President of the Local Government Board.

At the age of sixty he had by the chances of war attained the ambition of his youth, all hope of which he had given up ten years earlier. It was an irony of fate, for in a sense he was conscious that it had come too late. Still full of abounding life and energy he yet seemed often half conscious in those last years that the cup of life was nearly drained. When one said to him that now he had at last passed inside the barrier he would do great things he would reply, ' No, I am too old now, perhaps when I was a younger man I might have . . .' He did so long for youth. ' If I were only thirty years younger,' he would say again and again. It was odd because it was difficult to believe when one talked to him that he could ever have seemed or even felt younger than he did. He told me that he would often look at younger people and say to himself, ' I would change places with them entirely if only I could have their youth.' At one time we had a very unattractive looking, crushed, and particularly foolish under-parlourmaid. One day as she was doing up his boots he took a look at her and said to himself, ' No, not even to be your age would I change places with you.' He chuckled at himself as he told the story, but I think she was the only exception he found.

It seemed an almost cruel irony that political success— the thing he had coveted more than aught else, the failure to secure which had to some extent embittered his middle age—should only have come to him when he realised that it was too late. Yet I do not know that had he lived he would have wished to have stayed in office after the war. ' Business is cleaner,' he would say, ' and one can do more : there is no red tape there.' [1]

If he was at first puzzled as to why he should have been chosen as President of the Local Government Board, it was not long before he began to take a vivid interest in his work. The idea of a Ministry of Health appealed to him enormously. From the moment when he first heard of it he seemed to realise its potentialities and threw himself into plans for furthering the scheme with all his accustomed energy and enthusiasm.

All the months of his tenure of office at the Local Government Board were occupied in trying to push forward the scheme for a Ministry of Health, which appealed to him because it involved unified control and avoided overlapping —it spelt efficiency. He went very carefully into the question of the infant mortality rate ; he took the opinion of many specialists on the matter, and was appalled at the conclusion which was forced upon him that something like 50,000 infants' lives were needlessly sacrificed every year.

I have heard people express surprise that he should

---

[1] He used to declare that his business as a Minister was to try to ' substitute elastic for red tape.'

have been so genuinely horrified—it has never seemed to me surprising, it was entirely in keeping with every instinct he possessed. He had a horror of unnecessary waste, he was more conscious than most of the sacredness of life, to him a gift of inexpressible value (in later years he disliked killing even a wasp, though he was a little ashamed of admitting it) : death to him was a very terrible thing, a person who had died was always ' poor so and so.' This was no conventional phrase, it expressed his genuine shocked pity that what was to him the one—perhaps the only—great misfortune, should have befallen them. Moreover, he had the imagination which to some extent at least could visualise what those 50,000 deaths meant ; all his life he had dealt in figures and statistics—they were live things to him. And he always built for the future : he had a special reverence for children because they represented the coming generation. It was the most natural thing in the world that his imagination should be seized by these figures.

Sir Thomas Horder, to whom I had shown this passage, asking him for his impressions, wrote :

' Not that his imagination was stirred by this matter alone ; there were other blots upon the national health records that Lord Rhondda longed eagerly to remove. There was a big, and largely controllable, death rate of mothers in labour. There were preventable diseases that we were not preventing. There was crying need for more extensive medical research, towards which a few miserable hundreds of pounds were paid per annum. There was the large question of medical education carried on (with almost incredible courage and efficiency) chiefly by medical schools in a state of bankruptcy, with no official cognisance given to them, still less official encouragement meted out to them by the State.

' These and other problems made a big appeal to the virile and business-like mind of Lord Rhondda. How to co-ordinate the health services of the nation, give them more cohesion, and give them power to deal with these very practical matters, became an urgent purpose in his life, and offered good material for his driving power to spend itself upon. He saw clearly that health was an invaluable asset, as much for the nation as for the individual. Without it the public weal must languish; with it crises and hardships could be endured and could be conquered. The lessons of the war doubly emphasised all these considerations.

' Lord Rhondda had clear thoughts, too, about the importance of co-operation between his proposed Ministry and the working medical profession, whose intelligent sympathy and help he proposed to set himself to acquire should he ever see the advent of his scheme. Exactly how he would have dealt with the thorny question of control within the Ministry, as between the experts on the one hand and the secretariat on the other, would have been a matter of intense interest to watch. It is safe to say that his house would have been kept in order, that every servant, whether medical officer or administrator, would have given him cordial and loyal service, and that he himself would have invited and encouraged all contributions to the public health, from whatever quarter they came. That he never lived to see the inauguration of the beneficent work his mind conceived is one of the tragedies of the country's history.'

January, February, March, April, and May of 1917 were occupied in trying to push forward the Ministry of Health. He was on the one hand in closest touch with all those interested in it, and in daily correspondence with them : on the other he was pressing his ideas on the Cabinet. There was considerable opposition to the scheme in certain quarters and things did not move as fast as he would have wished.

On March 27, he sent in a Memorandum to the War Cabinet on the need for such a Ministry :

' (1) Public opinion is now keenly aroused on the existing deficiency and inefficiency of our public medical services, especially for maternity and infant welfare. There is a widespread insistent demand for improvement. The working of the Insurance Act has shown what can be achieved by a systematic provision of medical services, but these are admittedly inadequate, particularly for the crucially important needs of women and children.' . . .

' (2) There are several other grave difficulties resulting from the existing chaos in our health services ;

e.g., in providing medical services for discharged soldiers and their widows and orphans, in the obstacles hampering the development of the needed specialist services for insured persons, large numbers of whom are discharged soldiers; in the constant drag on the improvement of tuberculosis services; and in the quarrelling over maternity and infant welfare schemes. These and other crying evils can only be remedied by the immediate establishment of one Central Ministry of Health, in place of the two or three separate and competing Government Departments, which at present separately supervise various elements in the national health problem.

' (3) . . . All that is wanted is a three-clause Bill establishing a " Ministry of Health and of Local Government," to supersede the Local Government Board and transferring to it the medical and sanatorium functions (but, for the present, no others) of the English and the Welsh Insurance Commissions, and giving to it the necessary powers coupled with provisions of adequate Exchequer funds (as was proposed by Mr. Lloyd George in his 1914 Budget), for making suitable grants to the local bodies so as to get the work promptly commenced and efficiently done.

' (4) The Bill would be popular and would raise no party controversies. It would be essentially a war emergency measure for making possible the immediate development of the maternity and infant welfare and other services above described, for which public opinion is already clamouring, and which have become doubly needed by reason of the war havoc, and doubly urgent if they are to be started before the difficulties of demobilisation render such an initial step both too late and impossible. It is, therefore, earnestly desired that this small but supremely useful step be sanctioned forthwith, so that the Bill may be introduced in the House of Lords at once, with the promise of substantial Exchequer grants.

' RHONDDA.'

' 27th March 1917.'

A letter to Mr. E. S. Montagu, dated April 20, is of interest :

' I am much obliged for your letter of yesterday, but frankly I am greatly disappointed and also disheartened at the action of the Committee in postponing a definite decision on the main question, for until I receive Cabinet authority to proceed all my plans of Health Reform are held up, and if, as you appear to suggest, it may be the " end of this year " before I am able to publish my scheme, I should have to consider seriously my position.

' Already my proposals for dealing with infant welfare have been quite unnecessarily blocked for over two months, and realising as I do the possibility of saving something like 1,000 lives a week you can understand my feeling of responsibility in the matter.'

When Mr. Lloyd George asked him to move over to the Ministry of Food one of the reasons which caused him to hesitate was his objection to giving up his schemes for a Health Ministry. As a condition of his acceptance of the Food Ministry, however, he extracted a promise from the Prime Minister that a Ministry of Health should be brought into being.

Mr. Lloyd George's comment on the situation made to Mr. Begbie is perhaps characteristic of the point of view of a good many :

' When I formed a Government I asked him to join it. I offered him the Local Government Board. He went there and contracted quite a passion for the health of babies— rather an unexpected passion for Rhondda. I mean, he was a man of business who loved big adventures, loved success, loved playing his hand well, the stakes at his side only valuable in his eyes as a sign that he was winning. And here was a passion for babies ! However, the call of duty was powerful enough to interrupt that passion.'

The Ministry of Health Bill as finally drafted was practically on the lines which he had approved, although he had of course regarded the passing of such a Bill merely as the preliminary step to action.

One Sunday in March 1917 (after he had been three months at the Local Government Board) we were walking along the

Bishton Road up a slight hill when he complained of a curious pain at his heart, quite different to anything he had ever felt before. It came again up every hill. . . . The next week he went to a great heart specialist, who told him he had a mild form of angina pectoris, but that there was no immediate danger. The words startled me, and without telling him I went off and saw the heart specialist myself to make sure he had told him the truth. He said : ' Your father can live to be ninety with that heart if he goes slow and takes care . . . but he won't.' It was not very easy to take care at that time : a few weeks later Mr. Lloyd George asked him to become Food Minister. At first, with the doctor's words fresh in his mind, he asked him to find some-one else, but in a month the Prime Minister came back saying he could find no one suitable, and the position was becoming exceedingly serious. That was in June. My father still hesitated. One hot summer evening we walked up and down the lawn discussing it. He felt that from the point of view of his life it was probably suicidal, and he was a man who valued life, and in a sense just because he so loved life, feared death almost more than anyone I have met. He always seemed to me to be living in a blaze of sunlight, made the more vivid by the fear of the dark shadows that lay around.

There was another reason, however, which made him hesitate. It seemed to him practically certain that the Ministry of Food must be the grave of any man's reputation. ' I shall almost certainly lose my reputation over it,' he said, and I think he valued that next to his life.

What then made him accept it in the end ? Mainly that he knew no man had a right to consider his own life and reputation at such a time : partly, too, that the idea of trying to pull off a ten to one chance appealed to him even then as anything which appealed to his gambling and fighting instincts always had appealed throughout his life

At all events he accepted.

I give Mr. Lloyd George's account of the facts as he described them to Mr. Harold Begbie :

' Devonport, shamefully treated by certain sections of the press, had given up the difficult, the *most* difficult, office of Food Controller. I offered it to Rhondda. I did more than that, I begged him to take it.

' He said, " It will kill me, but if you say there is no one else who will take it, I'll take it ; but I should like to see my doctor first." His doctor forbade him to accept. Rhondda came and told me so, but said again that if there was no one else to accept it he would do so. I saw Sir Bertrand Dawson, who told me that if Rhondda was careful he might survive it. It was a grave risk. There is no doubt now that he was not careful enough, that he did not spare himself, and that it killed him. I examine my conscience in this matter, and I think my action was justified. No one else could have saved the country in that peril. His name acted like magic. His work restored public confidence. In a few weeks a new feeling of security was manifest throughout the United Kingdom.

' And yet the success of his work hung on a hair. There was a time, only a few months before his death, when it looked as if he had failed. . . .

' This was the man I had fought, the man who had tried to throw me, and whom I had thrown in at least one big fight. He was splendid. He nourished certain resentments, he never quite forgave some of the chief Liberal Imperialists, but when there was a call for national service his heart knew nothing but duty, and he was ready to lay down his life for his country.

' I never quarrelled with a nobler man. I am glad that the quarrel was made up. We made it up before he went to America about munitions, but after that I like to think that we were friends.'

During the last year he changed more than during all the preceding years I had known him. It seemed as if he grew up : turned from a schoolboy playing the game for the fun of it, never really worrying over results, into a man no longer young, and conscious, very fully conscious, of the almost intolerable burden of responsibility that lay upon him. He was working as he had never worked before, and worrying as he had never worried in his life. He used to wake up at three or four o'clock in the morning and do a couple of hours' work at his papers—my mother would find him at it. That winter—the winter of queues—was a terrible one. ' You and I, Clynes,' he said one day when they were talking together in his room, ' stand between this country and revolution.'

His attitude towards religion changed considerably during that last year of his life. He who had always queried came very near to, perhaps achieved, definite belief. ' Luck is on our side,' he would say, apropos of some achievement of the Food Ministry, and then he would correct himself : ' Providence is on our side.'

It seemed to me that the shock of the war and the strain of that year had the effect of bringing to the surface that temperamental part of him which in many ways seemed to war so oddly with his intellectual side. The ' two and two make four ' side was, for the time at least, in abeyance. The other side, the mystical side, was for the time being in the ascendant. One cannot tell whether it would have lasted. . . .

One curious trait of his added probably more than we realised at the time to the strain he was bearing. All his life it had always been all or nothing with him. Fifteen cigars a day, or no tobacco at all. Twelve oranges at a sitting, or not an orange for months. ' Nothing in moderation ' might well have been his motto. Now it was his business to set the example in economising food. He refused to touch any of his ration of sugar ; from Monday to Friday he ate no meat at all, and it was all anyone could do to get him to touch a small slice on Saturdays and Sundays. That was a winter when the shortage of food told on many people, but he was going shorter than many, he was working harder, and he was a man with a definite weakness.

At the end of March he went down to Llanwern for Easter ; the night he arrived his temperature was up and he went off to bed with what appeared to be a slight chill. That was the beginning of the end. All through April and May he went on getting one week a little better (he was able to sit out in the garden during the best part of May), the next a little worse.

Early in May he wrote to Mr. Lloyd George offering his resignation. The rumour that he wished to resign leaked into the press, although he had himself told no one (not even his secretary or my mother and myself) that he had written, and there was an outburst of praise and friendly anxiety.

He had always wanted recognition, and the preceding winter, when it seemed as if he must fail and he had been severely criticised, had been a bitterly anxious time. I think if the outburst of praise had come when he was well it would have been very sweet to him ; even as it was he was pleased, but only languidly pleased ; it seemed during those last weeks as if outside visions of himself no longer mattered very much to him. He was still following the progress of the war with intense interest ; he was still, in spite of protests from his doctors, attending to a considerable part of his work, and he was intellectually as alive as ever ; it was only a week or two before the end that he chose Prescott's ' Conquest of Peru ' as the book he would like to have read aloud to him (sandwiched in amongst detective tales, which he always loved). But he was almost past caring whether the world thought that he personally had made a success or failure of his job.

On May 17 came Mr. Lloyd George's reply :

' My dear Rhondda,
        ' It would give me great satisfaction if you could continue as Food Controller.

' I have discussed the matter fully with Clynes, and I am quite willing that he should be responsible for the work until you can return, which I understand will be in a few weeks' time.

' It will be a great help to me to know you are retaining office.

' I need not say how glad I am to hear you are making such good progress, and I trust that, with a further short period of rest, you will be completely recovered.
                ' With all good wishes,
                        ' Ever sincerely,
                                ' D. LLOYD GEORGE.'

He answered at once :

' My dear Prime Minister,
        ' Many thanks for your kind letter.

' I am only anxious to help you in every way I can, and if you think I can be of service by retaining the office of

Food Controller I have no option but to accede to your request.

'Clynes has proved himself to be an exceedingly capable administrator and loyal colleague, and you could not trust the work of the Department to more competent hands.

'The food position is easy and distinctly better than it was a year ago. The outlook for the next few months need cause the Government no anxiety. At the same time it will be very necessary for us to maintain our stocks of the principal articles of food for the coming winter.

'In falling in with your wish I assume that there will be no important change in food policy during my temporary absence.

'I have made considerable progress during the last week, and my doctors tell me that within a few weeks I may hope to be as well and even better than when I first undertook the work of the Food Ministry.

'With very best wishes for your continued success,

'Yours very faithfully,

'RHONDDA.'

On June 3 he was made a Viscount. He had wanted this step largely because he had always hoped that if it came it would be possible to have attached to it the privilege of passing the title on to me, a matter to which he attached considerable importance. Even at the very end he was still pre-occupied over this. The title was made to pass as he wished, and I think the letter he received with it was even then a big pleasure to him :

'June 18th, 1918.

'My dear Rhondda,

'I am very glad to be able to tell you that at the audience which the King has just given me, he agreed that the Remainder of your Peerage should be settled upon your daughter. He is always very reluctant to make these special arrangements, and as he explained to me yesterday, he only assents in cases where the service rendered to the State is very conspicuous. That is the reason why in your case he was prepared to depart from precedent.

'In my judgment there has been no case during the King's reign where it was better justified than in yours. You undertook the most difficult and thankless task which

T

could be entrusted to a Minister. To undertake it required great courage. It required not merely courage, but great ability and especially judgment and untiring effort to carry it out. There is but one opinion about your efforts—that they have been one of the most distinguished triumphs of the war. No Food Controller in any belligerent country has won such unanimous encomiums and no one has better deserved them.

' I am sincerely sorry that the very hard work and the constant anxiety through which you have passed have temporarily affected your health, but I am glad to learn that with some weeks of rest your medical advisers are confident that you will be able to continue your valuable labours for the State.

' Yours sincerely,
(Signed) ' D. Lloyd George.'

All this while he was constantly seeing the Food Ministry officials, and insisted on attending to his papers. The official bag was sent down every day, though he was often so tired that he would drop asleep whilst he was reading, and it was easy to see that it cost him a great effort to go through it. Towards the end of May I went to see his secretary at the Ministry of Food, and made him promise that he would discontinue the official bag. When it failed to arrive, however, my father was most indignant, and it had to be sent once more.

Early in June things took a turn for the worse, and he was thenceforward confined to his bed. I think he realised better than we did what was happening. ' I must be the strongest man on earth by now,' he remarked one day ; ' every day for the last three months I've grown stronger— everyone has told me so.' At the very end the doctors took complete command, and at last the official bag was stopped.

It is easier for some one less close to him to give some account of those last weeks. I am indebted to Sir Thomas Horder, who was with him at the end, for the following account :

' It was not my good fortune to know Lord Rhondda when he was free from the trammels of sickness. When I first met him he was full of bodily discomforts, and his mind was perplexed by a problem that involved himself in an intensely intimate fashion, and yet seemed to be for once outside his own power to solve : during the whole of the time I spent with him he was either struggling against the increasing difficulties imposed by the failure of vital functions, or, none the less harassing, he was enduring the necessary hardships imposed by his treatment ; and when we parted it was with the bitter yet clear knowledge that the last strenuous fight was over, and that the battle was lost.   Sick-room, doctors, nurses, attendants, ceaseless ministrations, frequent periodical examinations, and all the wearisome processes that encumber the slowly ebbing strength of a very ill man—with such a background and such a setting, it would be readily understood if the central figure on the stage had left but a blurred outline in my mind. But it was quite otherwise.   The man's genius shone vividly against and amongst all these dull and tiresome things, and has left a radiance which is likely to burn brightly so long as memory lasts.   Some souls are vital to the end even when the last days are clouded by pain and weakness ; his was one of these.   This vitality was the feature that struck me most ; so dominant, so forceful was it, even in that room into which the Shadow crept so slowly and yet so remorselessly, that it was quite easy for me to realise from my own brief experience, quite apart from all I knew and heard, that this man was of the spirit of him who declared, " Give me health and a day, and I will make the pomp of emperors ridiculous."

' With such a spirit life is not generally relinquished without a struggle, nor without regret, and though he might truly say that he had " warmed both hands before the fire of life," Lord Rhondda never assumed the sentiment necessary to declare " it dies, and I am ready to depart." Life was a good thing : *there was still so much to do :* this disease was a challenge ; the challenge must be accepted ; issue must be joined ; Medicine was on its mettle and must show its power ; he would co-operate ; " Tell me what you want me to do to help you "—nothing must be allowed to interfere with the chances of success.   In short, though the body was sorely hit, though the heart (" the life of the blood ") was hard put to it to keep going, the mind was healthy and would only yield if, and when, it was assured that all efforts were unavailing and met with no further response.   " Is that now ? " " No." " Then go ahead ; I will fight with you on condition you tell me when that time comes " ; and right loyally and manfully was the promise kept : nor was the condition omitted when it became all too certain, as well to the sufferer as to his physicians, that further efforts must be fruitless, and to stretch out his noble soul any longer " upon the rack of this tough world " was both vain and void of purpose.

' " Still so much to do." The best thing of all yet to do. And in the quiet intervals between the bouts of breathlessness, during a week in which the patient's native optimism revived with the feelings of increased physical vigour due to the careful husbanding of his strength and to the remedies employed, Lord Rhondda discussed the Ministry of Health—even then too long in embryo—and his purposes in regard to it. He sketched his plans and talked confidentially of the men he had already chosen in his mind to aid him in the work that was to crown his busy life, if he were spared to launch his scheme. Compared with this achievement his organisation of the Food Control, magnificent in the eyes of the world, seemed to him rather a little thing. He was almost ashamed of the enormous reputation it had brought him, and he valued the kudos chiefly as a powerful lever that might be used in order to lift his new Ministry into the confidence of the nation and give it a send-off that would ensure success. This fresh endeavour was the thing that lay nearest to his heart. It was a constant source of conversation with his doctors, whose presence tempted him to more talking than could be allowed in his weakness.

' Two problems in connection with the public health were uppermost in Lord Rhondda's mind : infant mortality and medical research. Lord Rhondda's concern about the care of the infant, and his efforts in the direction of checking the terrible sacrifice of infant life in this country, are familiar to all. His interest in research as applied to the advance of medical knowledge, though equally keen, is not so widely known. He was much attracted by the suggestion that research into the causes of any disease could be closely co-ordinated with the treatment of the patients suffering from it, and a discussion of the benefits likely to accrue from such a co-ordination aroused no little degree of enthusiasm in him. He actually proposed to incorporate such a " Research Hospital," or a number of such hospitals, with the work of the new Ministry. Or, if this were not a feasible proposition, then he would start such an institution himself, attaching to it the best experts that he could find. This institution would demonstrate to all and sundry the method of advance in medical science which, he was quickly convinced, promised the best results.

' Alas for these schemes, these visions, and these ambitions ! The Fear that stalked in the background of all our deliberations for the physical welfare of the race came nearer and nearer even as we talked. But its presence never led to a revocation of these very practical ideas—it only led to the expression of the hope that, if he himself were denied the work, this might fall into the hands of some one who would " make good " For some men made good and others didn't, and Lord Rhondda was never shy of indicating to which category he thought so-and-so belonged. Brilliance made very little appeal to him, and for the political adventurer he had nothing but scorn. He judged men by results. He was sceptical as regards his own genius, but never as regards his own power. He was pleased when I reminded him that Napoleon showed his genius by displaying common sense in emergencies—probably because he felt instinctively that here lay the secret of his own successful life.

' That Lord Rhondda was a most lovable man, surely all who came very near to him, and who had the gift of loving, must have felt. That one *was* allowed to get so near to him was a part of the man, that which seemed to perpetuate his boyhood into man's estate and even to the grave. How could affection hold back when, once he chose his friend or his colleague, entire confidence was placed in him, by one possessed of such a generous spirit, such an expansive mind and such a gentle mannner ? '

The outside world was full of his praise during those last few weeks, and he who had loved praise cared little for it. I spoke to him once of what they said, and how much they needed him to live. I thought it would be sweet to him, as it always had been, but he just turned from it. He died on Wednesday, July 3, 1918.

CHAPTER XIX

His Philosophy

By Harold Begbie

In the spirit neither of the pedagogue nor the alarmist Lord Rhondda contemplated in the spring of 1918 the idea of laying before those of his countrymen willing to heed him a statement of his political philosophy.

It was his wish to appear before his countrymen as a simple citizen, who had made faithful effort to serve the community, and who addressed them in no professional robes and with no assumption of pedagogic solemnity, certainly not as a dogmatist, but as a fellow man engaged in the main business of life, and ready to share his experiences with other people.

He recognised that the end of war would be the beginning of strife, and in that strife of man's soul he desired to play a part, just as he had played a part in the war of men's bodies. This part, as he saw it in the spring of 1918, would lie in suggesting one clear and very definite idea to the mind of British democracy, an idea which, if clearly seized, at the outset of political strife, would tend in his opinion to avert violence and to abate intemperance. It is this idea which I shall now endeavour to formulate in language as simple and direct as that in which Lord Rhondda conveyed it to me.

Selfishness is an enemy of mankind only when mankind is unable to control it. But under the control of men, so that it is unable to run riot, selfishness is a great servant of mankind. This was his thesis.

'Let us admit' [he would say] 'that Providence has distilled into the heart of man a drop of selfishness. I say Providence because I have got no other term for the mystery which lies at the back of phenomena. But, in any case, this is quite certain—that in the heart of every man there is a force called selfishness which urges him to regard his own interests and which drives him into activities for his own advantage. It is folly to ignore the presence of this selfishness, or to denounce it. It is more reasonable to regard it as a force intended for use, and to try to see how it may best be used.

' Now, all my political thinking has been governed by the conviction that selfishness is an essential part of the plan for working out humanity's destiny, and I have never been moved an inch from this conviction by the obvious disadvantages which accrue from uncontrolled selfishness. Everything in socialism is founded upon the spectacle presented to the world by the working of uncontrolled selfishness ; but socialism, as I understand it, would get rid of selfishness altogether, and in that way would land humanity in stagnation. I have always set my face against socialism because it goes against human nature. I am perfectly certain that you have got to take human nature with you to whatever millennium you may be seeking. And one of the essentials of human nature is this force of selfishness. I regard selfishness as one of ' the most powerful instruments we possess for improving human conditions. It is wisdom for the State to interpose its will between the selfishness of the individual and the community only when the latter is endangered by the former.'

He was born and cradled in the strongest form of individualism, and he told me that nothing in his experience, though he had kept his eyes wide open, had modified his faith in this ancient gospel. When I pressed him a little, saying that surely the war must have produced some effect on his earlier opinions, he confessed that he was now prepared not to object to the nationalisation of railways, canals, minerals and land. My surprise at this confession, which he made with frankness and without hesitation of any kind, seemed to stimulate his desire to express more decided opinions than ever on the side of individualism.

' But do not think for a moment,' he said, ' that if I am willing to nationalise these things I am therefore weakening in my individualism. First of all, I would have such prizes and rewards in the national management of these undertakings that men would strive with all their might to win them, just as now the best men in railways rise to the top often from quite the lower grades. I am quite certain that without great prizes and rewards there would soon be an end to progress in those directions. But in any case I should leave the whole field of industrial enterprise outside these particular interests to the play of individual forces. I do not believe that any good would come to this country from the nationalisation of the cotton trade, for example, or engineering, or agriculture, or wool. Nor do I think that any of our great industries could be managed by committees. I am as much opposed to management by committees as I am to control by the State. I am opposed to them both because they would paralyse the action of the individual, whose self-regarding interest urges him along the road of progress. The State has a perfect right to prevent this individual from treating badly those whom he employs, and it has an equally perfect right to take from him in the shape of taxes a part of the wealth he earns by his energy and his daring. But the State has no right to control his creativeness; and if the State would not impoverish itself it should do everything in its power to encourage that creativeness, which cannot possibly enrich him without enriching the State. Here, you see, I stand firm in my old individualism, quite unshaken by the war.'

We spoke of some later forms of socialism, and at the end of this discussion he summed up his opinions of socialism in these words :

' Socialism has always been a theory. No country in the world has yet dared to put it to the test of practice. It gains sympathisers and adherents, but it produces no operator. The operations of socialism remain to be seen ; and I can conceive of no greater disaster to socialism itself than to put it into practice. Even our very wealthy trade unions in this ˌcountry, with capital enough to buy up industry after industry, have been wise enough to spend their time in the abuse of capitalists. Socialism would never work, they know that well enough. You must have captains—captains or anarchy. I dare say there are many concerns in this country which might continue in prosperity for a certain number of years under the management of a committee ; but I am perfectly certain that they would sooner or later collapse under the competition of rival concerns directed with a single mind.

' Socialism is a fallacy because, in building its dream cities, it leaves out of account the factor of human nature. It asks us to contemplate a social organism from which every particle of human nature has been extracted. It is a social organism composed rather of archangels than men and women. But we have the whole experience of history to warn us that the affairs of this world are in the hands of erring men and women, that over and over again the fortunes of the human race have been saved by individuals, and that without the driving spur of necessity it is very easy for mankind to sink towards its original savagery.

' Socialism does not so much suppose a new state of things as a new human creature. It would substitute the committee for the creative mind, and it believes that the collective virtue of the committee would be of greater service to the State than the courage and enterprise of the creative mind. Well, they are trying some such theory of existence in Russia. It is a theory of existence which is doomed to failure. It will produce nothing but a mess. You cannot dethrone intelligence to gratify the average man without causing very great suffering to the whole organism. The secret of a nation's progress lies in the State's encouragement of its remarkable men. This encouragement is simply the recognition of extraordinary talent. It means that having found those capable of advancing its progress, the State gladly gives these men as free a hand as possible in developing its resources. There must be restrictions, of course, and a toll taken of their wealth ; but there should be no antagonism to their labour, the fruits of which in a variety of ways go as much to the State as to themselves. I do not see how any dispassionate student of human history can deny that progress in every direction, industrial progress, political progress, scientific progress, has been the work of individuals.'

It amused him to see those who condemned conscription among the loudest advocates of socialism. He regarded socialism, not only as the worst form of conscription, but as its only complete expression. So far, the principle of military conscription afflicts the freedom of a man only for a few brief years, and does not prevent him at the expiration of his military service from choosing any career to which his inclinations lead him, or from abandoning that career for another whenever he is so minded. But logical socialism is conscription from the cradle to the grave. It is the negation of individualism and therefore the negation of freedom. A man could not possibly enjoy a real freedom in a socialistic State. He would be as continuously subject to the orders of the State as were our munition workers during the war. The State would be his master from whose service he could not depart at will, a master owning him body and soul.

Lord Rhondda's instinct for freedom, which made him abominate every form of despotism, inspired his antagonism to socialism. It was not to safeguard his treasure that he opposed himself to the socialist, but to safeguard the liberties of his fellow-men. The platform socialist is fond of sneering at the rich man's opposition to his gospel as a sign of both guilt and fear ; he never seems able to acquire the natural modesty which we look for in one who advances a new and untried theory of existence ; on the contrary, he is so in love with his idea that all who presume to argue with him must be denounced as knaves or fools. But I am persuaded that in opposing himself to socialism Lord Rhondda was entirely unselfish : and that in advocating individualism he was thinking far more of the happiness and prosperity of his fellow-countrymen than of protecting his own interests. It may be difficult for a socialist to believe in the morals and intellectual honesty of a capitalist, but until socialism has made more converts it is only prudent, as it is certainly fitting, that its advocates should listen with respectful attention to arguments on the other side, even when they proceed from a capitalist.

Is socialism compatible with individual freedom ? This is the question Lord Rhondda desired democracy to ask itself. He said that he could not conceive of any form of socialism which would leave the individual as free as he is now under our present system. Freedom, whether a good thing or bad, must be sacrificed if socialism is to reign. A socialistic state could no more do its work without despotism than a military State. The same discipline which exists in an army would be essential to a socialistic State, and the same punishments would be necessary to enforce that discipline.

As to whether freedom is a good thing or a bad thing, as to whether the democratic form of government is better on the whole than the autocratic, he would say that no man worthy of the name would elect for despotism in whatever garments of illusion it might appear before the tribunal of public opinion. Freedom for him was the very breath of existence ; so completely did he feel freedom to be a part of man's dignity that he never once questioned the right of workmen to use their liberty to combine against their employers. But he acknowledged that there were many evils existing in a free democracy which might inspire scepticism as to the virtues of freedom. These evils, however, could be removed by sensible legislation ; despotism could but aggravate their nature and multiply them a thousandfold.

He said that no man could argue in favour of a socialistic State without shutting his eyes to the manifest shortcomings of human nature. For those who did so argue always supposed that the committee in charge of the fortunes of the State would be men of unerring judgment and flawless virtue. They never contemplated the social organism in the hands of blunderers or rascals. Always virtue was to reign. But, he asked, who is to guarantee the wisdom and honour of a Soviet ? If governments may err why not a committee ? And if the mistakes of a democratic government are serious, how much more serious must be the mistakes of a socialistic committee charged with the whole management of industrial and social life ? As for the newest forms of socialism, he found himself on exactly the same grounds of opposition. The most recent form of all, Guild socialism, seemed to him even more pernicious than the old-fashioned thesis of State socialism. It introduced the dangerous principle of separation into the body politic ; its tendency could not be in any other direction than that of anarchy ; it placed the community at the mercy of single interests ; it magnified the part till it was greater than the whole. But here too the old objection stood firm. Guild socialism strikes at the root of individual freedom, and is inspired by precisely the same heresy which maintained State socialism in the middle years of the last century. It is an unjustifiable deification of human nature.

' It is a fashion in revolutionary circles,' he said, ' to denounce the capitalist, and even among those who are not revolutionary there is a disposition to apologise for the capitalist, as if he were a difficult factor in the political problem requiring defence and explanation. But really and truly the matter is quite simple. We have only to be honest to see the facts. The man who brings an industry into existence, or develops and extends an industry already existing, is not an enemy to the State but its good friend. Instead of being ashamed of our captains of industry we should be proud of them ; and instead of being silent when they are attacked we should carry the war into the enemy's camp. What has the socialist orator done for the State ? Is he a parasite on the social organism or one of its enriching benefactors ? Who is the better off for such a man ? How many people does he provide with a living, what is the value to the revenue of his exports, and what is his contribution to the national expenditure in the way of taxes ? Socialism says that its benefit is to come. It is a bird in the bush. The nearer we approach to it the more disposed it seems to spread its wings. It is very difficult to get near enough to socialism to examine its features. But the capitalist is a bird in the hand, and very much in the hand. His liberty is more and more under the control of the State. He is the organiser of the State's wealth, the captain of the State's in-dustrial armies, he cannot enrich himself without enriching thousands of others, and he is very little more than a tenant for life of that part of his wealth which escapes taxation during the years of his activity. We know what capital has done. It has opened up the wide field of the British Empire, and advanced civilisation by leaps and bounds. There are evils which may fairly be attributed to its action, but they are insignificant in comparison with the great blessings it has brought mankind, and even outside that comparison, dark and bad as those evils may appear, they are not incurable.

' What I would like men to see is the advantage which

comes to them from the activity of even the most selfish capitalists. One has to look at this matter without emotion, if you will a little cynically. What is most necessary to the happiness of men? It is wealth: that is the opportunities of comfort to people in general. To divide up the actual wealth in existence would make small difference to the happiness of the most poor. Population increases at an enormous rate, and to provide happiness for men it is necessary to produce more and more wealth. Our only question, then, is—What does experience teach us to be the best way of producing wealth? The answer is—that wealth is produced, not by political committees and not by religious altruists, but by selfish men seeking their own fortunes. It has always been so, and it will always be so. The great reward is the great spur. Man is by nature a lazy creature. He is only active and energetic when he has something to gain. Our soldiers could not fight as they are doing if their courage were not spurred by a great purpose. The bravest man in the world would fight badly for an ill cause. I am sure man is so constituted that he never does his utmost for nothing. There is a passion in man to excel. It has many forms, and none of them need be injurious to the State. A poor man struggling to be rich may give an exhibition of ridiculous vulgarity at the end of his struggle, but if his trade is an honest one he must have enriched others as well as himself. All the evils of selfishness may be cured by education. The higher type of man does not use either his capital or his energies for the sake of a vulgar display; he uses them for the pleasure afforded by industrial creation. Democracy is perfectly safe against the excesses of the selfish man; and the more educated democracy becomes the safer it will be. But democracy will be exposed to great perils if it seeks to eliminate the industrial activity of the selfish man. On that activity depends its fortune. The wise thing for democracy to do is to give every child in the land an equal opportunity for making the best of its talents, so that where there are now hundreds of industrial organisers there may one day be thousands.'

It was characteristic of him that he always pointed to the more obvious and practical aspects of this matter, never turning his gaze to the complex subtleties of economic theory; in any question vitally affecting the daily bread of many people he never allowed his wits to be enskied by the idealist. He asked men to study the facts of economics, and to see how simple this difficult and abstruse science became when attention was fixed upon its direct bearing on the common business of daily life.

Wealth is provided by industry. The revenue of a State comes to it by the industrial activity of its people. There is no other way of earning revenue. Therefore it is a simple question for democracy to decide whether this wealth can best be earned by the co-operation of capital and labour or by the dominance of the State over labour. Labour must always work under direction. It must work either under the direction of an individual employer or under the direction of State officials. And always a part of its earnings must go to the revenue of the State. The wages of labour are a part of the price of the product ; the profits of the employer are another part of the price of the product ; and the taxes paid to the State by the employer are another part of the price of the product. Eliminate the employer, and his profits would be taken by the State to pay for the costs of management.[1]

Let democracy think it over and decide which system is most serviceable to its own interests.

Lord Rhondda was neither a hard-hearted man nor a covetous man ; but in this matter of capital and labour he clung as tenaciously as the most tyrannical and selfish of employers to the economic facts. He believed that democracy imperilled its own happiness by ignoring those facts. The modern socialistic notion of attacking profits as the central evil of our industrial system seemed to him a convincing proof that socialists were blind to economic facts. Profits there must always be.

[1] Mr. Vernon Hartshorn, a thoughtful Socialist, said of Lord Rhondda many years ago :

'It would not be difficult to write an article to prove that though Mr. D. A. Thomas is generally regarded as merely a capitalist he is first and foremost a labourer, a producer. His function as a capitalist is very much inferior to his function as a worker, and he is really as much an exploited producer as any manual labourer in the country. It is a tragic anomaly that this competent labourer, this efficiency-promoting brain is compelled by force of circumstances to take up a false position and pay toll on his brain to a motley crowd of shareholding dividend-mongers.'

The State may interfere to control profits, but national bankruptcy would result if the State attempted to do away with profits. The profits of capital are nothing more mysterious or evil than wages ; they are as honourable to the man who has risked his money in an undertaking as the wages of the workman employed by his capital. Labour can never do without capital. In one form or another capital will always be necessary to labour, and a part of the earnings of labour will always have to go to capital, whether that capital is represented by the money of a bank or an individual, or by the credit of the State.

Here, again, Lord Rhondda returned to his favourite thesis. He asked democracy if the selfishness of the man with capital did not in sober truth minister to the well-being of labour. Was it not better, he asked, that the services of labour should be requested by an individual seeking his fortune, than that they should be commanded by a Government Department with no incentive to make money ? Could democracy hope for a greater increase in wealth from the control of industry by the State, or by a committee of working men, than from the co-operating toil of an individual seeking to enrich himself in every quarter of the globe ? Democracy must look at the facts and decide for itself. The facts were plain enough. To increase the general wealth of a community there must be labour ; to organise and direct that labour there must be management ; to secure the best brains for management there must be great rewards.

He did not believe that idealism in trade was possible. The man who would give his services to labour as a manager or director was the man most likely to wreck an industry. The man contented to work as a manager or a director for a small reward would be a small man. What industry wants if it is to prosper is the tremendous labour of individual men seeking with all their might and main for personal advantage. Such men as these, taxed heavily in their lifetime, are made to deliver up a great part of their savings when they come to die, and the industries which their genius has either created or brought to a state of perfection remain to serve the interests of the community.

It was Lord Rhondda's conviction that democracy is led astray into the dangerous fields of emotionalism by losing sight of this central economic fact in industrialism, that the selfishness of an employer is an advantage to the State.   He desired to place this fact clearly before the eyes of the people.   He thought if they once could realise that a rich employer is only a tenant for life of part of the wealth his talent for organisation brings into existence, they would be less disposed to listen to the socialist's wild and sweeping abuse of capital.   The knowledge that in certain parts of the United Kingdom a form of Bolshevism was obtruding itself, if it did not dismay him, certainly disturbed him. He did not, I think, suppose that Bolshevism would ever triumph in a British community, but he seemed to fear that the thesis of Bolshevism might influence British socialists in a direction leading more and more to the State's control of industry.   It was to guard against this danger that he contemplated the idea of publishing a statement of his political philosophy.   He was convinced that the working classes would suffer from the State's control of industry ; and he also thought that the increasing propaganda in this direction would have a paralysing effect on industry just at the very moment when confidence would be most necessary to repair the ravages of war.

I have purposely refrained in this chapter from speaking of Lord Rhondda's character.   Kindly, cheerful, and quite boyish as was his disposition, he never for a moment allowed anything but the strictest logic to govern his political opinions.   He was good-tempered enough in argument with socialists or idealists, but he was inflexible in his convictions.   The one central seriousness of his life was respect for the laws of political economy.   He never played the fool in business.

He was without any kind of sentimentalism.   He died without any dogmatic faith in God, and he lived almost entirely without a definite religion.   His attitude in politics was that of a fellow man who found himself in the midst of a universe not yet explored by knowledge, and governed by laws which, whether moral or immoral, were dangerous to break.   It was his conviction that men must pay great attention to those laws, must press on with their exploration of the universe, and that the mysteries of existence, which a wise man will respect, should be left out of count in dealing with the business of daily life.

This main business of daily life, as he saw it, lay in the steady progress of humanity from ignorance to knowledge, from weakness to power, from poverty to wealth. In his view the chief servant of humanity was commerce, for it was only by the operations of commerce, in the widest sense of this term, that the general fortunes of humanity were advanced. Nothing so much engaged his political affections as the prospect of enriching the soul of commerce by all the forces of knowledge and breeding. He hoped that men of culture and refinement would come more and more to feel the spell of trading, and that gallant and adventurous spirits who had hitherto looked to Army and Navy for a career, would see in trade the opportunities for all the daring of their dreams. He believed that we are now only fumbling with the blessings of commerce and that in time we shall turn it to so great an advantage that the whole face of existence will be transformed. He regarded trade as man's great central life of adventure, and the fruits of trade as the politician's only means for social reform.

Coldly and cynically as he regarded the idealist *quâ* economist, he was friendliness itself to the idealist as politician or social reformer.

As he advanced in knowledge and experience, he turned his back more and more squarely on the amateur philanthropist and gave himself with a strangely increasing devotion to the idea of State action in social reform. He believed that in the hands of honest and single-minded men, Government might perform miracles of social betterment, using to that end the enormous revenues accruing from successful individualistic commerce, and employing to that end the services of the best minds in science. I believe that his passion to live, his almost terrible shrinking from the destruction of death, came in no small degree from his great desire to serve humanity in his way, to serve it as a statesman who saw his way at least as far as the foothills of millennium. This earnest desire to govern was a part of

u

his love of life. Everything that was difficult attracted him. He could not conceive of life as any form of idleness, and the more difficult life was, the more it authenticated and confirmed his definition of human existence. With all his heart and mind, he desired in his last sad months at Llanwern to rescue social reform from the hands of the politician and to entrust it to the man of science. He believed that science working in collaboration with disinterested statesmanship could give democracy better health, happier cities, lighter toil, higher wages, and a far nobler conception of culture. He longed to serve the State in the capacity of statesman, and he looked back on his work as Food Controller only to see it as an apprenticeship to this end. Few men of our generation were so purely, honourably, and whole-heartedly impassioned by the idea of national reconstruction. But fundamental to all his plans for social reform was the bed-rock of economic fact. This whole superstructure of social reform which he desired to build was based in his mind upon an iron individualism. The revenue which it demanded could come only from commercial prosperity, and he saw no smallest chance of raising that huge revenue except from a commerce which was inspired by all the driving forces of individualism.

CHAPTER XX

A Character Sketch

' A happy man or woman is a better thing to find than a five-pound note. He or she is a radiating focus of good-will; and their entrance into a room is as though another candle has been lighted. We need not care whether they could prove the forty-seventh proposition; they do a better thing than that, they practically demonstrate the great Theorem of the Liveableness of Life.'

STEVENSON.

. . . souls whom some benignant breath
Has charmed at birth from gloom and care

. . . .

The world to them may homage make
And garlands for their forehead weave,
And what the world can give they take;
But they bring more than they receive.

MATTHEW ARNOLD.

THERE can be no more difficult task than the attempt to give any clear picture of a man. In my father's case I have found the difficulties intensified for a number of reasons. In the first place, I can imagine no more difficult character to sum up, he was so many sided; it does not really seem to me possible that any one person could come to an end of him, or see the whole of him. In the second place, to try to give any picture of a bigger person than oneself is to attempt to show a quart measure through the medium of a pint pot, and can never be entirely successful. In the third place, I knew him too well, I was too close to him. It is easy enough to take in the whole of a distant view, to appreciate its varying values, to analyse its general effect. But if you stand close underneath a hill you can only see one patch of it at a time.

I know also that the reader must feel that I am a prejudiced witness. I will only ask him to believe that all through

291

the book I have tried to be perfectly honest, to set down the good with the bad, or rather to give the man as I saw him without attempting to judge between the good and the bad, the big and the small. I have recognised that when it comes to opinions I must necessarily be a prejudiced person, and I have therefore so far as possible throughout this book avoided giving opinions, setting down so far as might be simply the facts, and allowing the reader to form his own judgment. In a chapter such as this that is not possible. I am bound to give opinions. I can only ask the reader to believe that I have tried to make them honest and just. Nor do I myself believe that I saw my father any less clear-sightedly because I loved him—indeed I do not know how I could have attempted to understand him otherwise. I know that it is not easy to be just, but at least I have tried very hard to stand upright, even at the risk of leaning over backwards.

The keynotes of his character have always seemed to me to be his intense vitality, his spontaneous joy of life, and his absolute simplicity. He was interested—enthrallingly interested—in whatever he took up, simply because he would never have looked at it had it not attracted him ; never in his life because it was the correct thing to be interested, nor because other people were, nor because it was the fashion. Whatsoever his hand found to do he did it with all his might. The things which were not worth so doing he simply ignored. In fact, whether work or play, it was done for the same one simple reason, because he enjoyed doing it. Therein lay half the secret of his success.

He might be searching for an owl's nest in the Decoy Pond woods, reading ' Pepys' Diary ' or some new book on economics, playing bridge, walking round his cattle with his bailiff, concluding a business deal, or discussing his affairs at home ; whatever it was he was absorbingly interested in it. If he wasn't interested he wasn't doing it. He wasted no time whatever either in talking to people or doing things which bored him.

Like most people he believed himself to be a first-class judge of character. He certainly had a considerable know-ledge of the workings of human nature. I remember when

I was a child of fifteen he and I had bicycled down to Llandrindod together, and there we met an acquaintance of his. The two of them fell into conversation, and my father, taking him by the arm—as was his wont—confided some business tale in his ears. ' Of course, my dear fellow, I don't want this to go any farther, but I am telling you confidentially,' he explained. I was slightly troubled : the man did not strike me as the type to whom I should feel I could confide with safety my innermost secrets, and I said as much to my father as soon as we were alone. ' He is the greatest chatterbox in Cardiff,' said my father, ' that is why I told him.'

Sometimes, however, he was singularly blind : he always found it difficult to understand or to believe that a man could not see what was to his own *ultimate* advantage. Instinctively he took the long view himself, and he found it difficult to suppose that there were people who would snatch the present at the expense of the future ; he did not overrate their altruism or their honesty, but he did overrate their intelligence. An instance of this recurs to me. When we travelled in Southern Europe we used to find in most of the big towns agents of some colliery company or exporting firm in which my father was interested. These gentlemen (usually foreigners of course) were very *empressé* in looking after us, and were known in the family as ' Father's Ambassadors.' On one occasion in Southern Italy we were met by a newly appointed agent whom my mother and I with one voice acclaimed as a rogue of the first water. ' Don't trust him, David,' said my mother. My father's retort was typical. The man might be a rogue (though he disliked thinking such a thing of an employee without any definite reason), but the agreement between him and the firm was so drawn up that it paid him to be honest, therefore of course he would be honest. I don't doubt that it did pay him—ultimately—but he was of the kidney that prefers pocketing £1 to-day by devious means to making £2 next week by straightforward ones, and he acted up to his instincts shortly afterwards. His point of view was one that my father was constitutionally unable to grasp.

He was certainly, I should say, a better judge of character than most men, but his success lay almost more in his knowledge of how to treat folk than in his power of selecting them. He had a wonderful gift for managing people. It used to seem to me that he made them fond of him and the rest was easy. But I don't think it was only that. He could somehow always get the best out of them, keep them up to concert pitch, straining to please him. In a way he was apparently easy to please, he did not criticise much, and never very severely, he assumed that the man who had failed would be sufficiently upset at knowing he had failed without his rubbing it in. So he did not rub it in. But one always remembered his lightest criticisms, there was somehow a sense of the things he had refrained from saying behind to make them hurt. He seemed to me to praise very little. I used sometimes to try to get him to praise a man more. Just as he felt that the man was sufficiently punished by failure, so I think he felt that he was sufficiently rewarded by success. He did not quite realise how much a word from him would add to the sense of success. At least I suppose it was that. I think he would have thought it almost impertinent to praise too much, it would have been patronage. ' Of course, you've succeeded; why not ? You and I are really clever fellows, between us we'll go a long way ' ; that was the attitude—it was the ' you and I ' that was so intoxicating. I think it was the fact that he never thought of people as working to please him, but only to succeed, that made them work as they did. In one sense he praised; he always gave credit where credit was due; he always told every expert how much more he knew about the subject in hand than he himself, and listened whilst they talked. Whether it were the manager of a colliery, a lawyer, a stockbroker, or a scientist, the method was the same. Also, he never took anyone else's credit : he often got it of course, the head must continually in the public mind get the credit that is due to some subordinate ; but he never took it, he always explained that that was due to ' so and so.' He had no sort of use for credit which did not rightfully belong to him, it gave him no pleasure.

He was, I think, vaguely aware that his great strength lay in his management of men. I remember his giving me some advice once. ' It's not only a question of finding the right man, the great thing is to know how to use him when you have got him.' And again, ' Never use the big stick.' He despised heartily the man who was in the habit of using the big stick. He did not tell one to trust people, on the contrary he would say that no person was completely trustworthy. The breaking place, he believed, came in every person at some point. ' You cannot trust anyone entirely.' But that always seemed to me to be the result of precept and experience rather than instinct. He was theoretically of the opinion that no one was completely trustworthy, on the ground that human nature was not so built as to bear more than a certain amount of strain, and he repeated the fact to remind himself. But in this instance theory was divorced from practice. His instinct was to trust, and he usually followed it, sometimes with what seemed to me a magnificent courage. It was part and parcel of his talent for delegating. The power to delegate, a singularly rare one considering its value, is after all founded on the ability to trust. He had a very strong sense of his obligation to subordinates, or indeed to any one he worked with, and would have considered it disloyal not to trust them. I remember his once looking troubled and hurt about a man he was working with. ' The little beggar doesn't trust me,' he said. ' I don't know how you can expect him to trust you or anybody else when he can't trust himself,' I replied. He said nothing : I think he must have agreed with me, but he was working with the man and would not criticise him.

He had not a high opinion of human nature. He always assumed that self-interest would be the ruling motive, certainly in the bulk and probably in the individual. Only he expected it to be ' enlightened self-interest,' a quality for which he had considerable respect.

His relations with other people were sometimes complicated by the fact that he had very strong likes and dislikes, and he found it next door to impossible to work with a man whom he really disliked. He had a vivid way of summing such a person up. I remember one of his political colleagues whom he described as ' The kind of man who would steal a saucer of milk from a blind kitten,' and yet I am not sure that he could have really been said to have entirely disliked that man for he was intelligent, and intelligence was always a passport to my father's favour. ' A dull drab mediocrity,' the sentence which he used to describe a well-known Cabinet Minister of the day, was an even more damning indictment so far as he was concerned.

A man with such strong antagonisms and such a picturesque method of describing those whom he disliked was bound to have many enemies. He had. Especially in his youth. Not that this ever disturbed him. ' A man who never makes enemies never makes anything else,' he would declare, and go happily on his way. I don't think he ever in his life went out of his way to do harm to any one, nor did he ever allow his personal feelings to prevent him from admitting and even advocating their just claim to any post. Quarrelling was in fact a luxury—it must not be allowed to stand in the way of doing justice, which was a necessity. In later years, however, with heavier responsibilities, he came to realise the importance of avoiding making enemies. So he changed his habits if he did not change his tastes. ' Quarrelling,' he said, with something of a regretful sigh, ' is the luxury of youth,' and— reluctantly—he gave it up.

If he disliked a man or thought him a fool (which came to much the same thing so far as he was concerned) he disliked to have him in the room ; it gave him, I imagine, the same kind of feeling as a cat did. In later years he learned, however, to conceal his feelings fairly well. There were several cases in which men who were working under him were quite unaware that he disliked them, though his secretaries had orders to admit them as seldom as might be.

The reverse side of this was his enthusiastic, wholehearted, and frank appreciation of those whom he liked. Whether they were the older men he revered in his youth or amongst the small group of younger ones who surrounded him during his later years, his admiration was generous and unstinted. He never feared youth, he loved it.

I should say that his strong likes and dislikes had been a disadvantage to him in many ways. A man with strong selective instincts cannot hope for universal popularity amongst the unselected, always the larger group of the two. And yet I do not know that this gives a fair picture of him. In a sense he was the friend of all the world, for he had the American knack of being friends with his acquaintances, and of these latter he had the most surprising number : a heterogeneous collection of men of every sort and condition and of every possible point of view, in every possible walk of life from Bishops to pub-keepers.

He gave one very little definite advice, though his discourses on life in general (always given in the vein of a boy who is ever making fresh discoveries in which he is enormously interested and which he desires to share) were wonderfully instructive. He would often talk about the best way to do things and to manage people, partly to tell one, partly to tell himself. One thing he always said was ' Never threaten,' by which he really meant never threaten unless you mean it. He never could stand threats himself, or even the faintest hint of them. If he was considering some business proposition and was told by the men who wished to interest him that other people were after it too, he would cry off immediately. 'Let them have it then,' he would say. ' I make it a rule never to touch anything that anyone else is after.' Another favourite theme was the need for imagination in business, and indeed everywhere else. ' No man,' he declared, ' can succeed in business without imagination.' It was a quality by which he set great store. Probably he was conscious of possessing it.

It was perhaps part of the simplicity I have spoken of that he never patronised. The idea of patronising intelligence, however inexperienced, would never have occurred to him, and the unintelligent or the pretentious he simply avoided, they bored him (he had a capacity for avoiding bores and boredom which amounted to genius). For some reason which I do not quite follow, it never fed his vanity to patronise, as it does most people's. He was as fond of having his vanity stroked as any other man—but patronising just didn't do it. This made him a very pleasant companion to those whom he liked. If a child of twelve was worth talking to at all, he or she was worth talking to as an equal, his or her opinion was listened to as something worth hearing, and even considering. This was not in any way conscious tact. He valued intelligence very much more highly than experience, and was honestly impressed by any intelligent opinion. Curiously enough, those whom he regarded as boring were usually a little frightened of him —though he was the least frightening of men—and were for their part only too anxious to avoid him. He had a way of being rather silent when bored which may perhaps have been a trifle disconcerting to his neighbours at dinner. ' I saw you doing the strong silent man,' remarked a friend of his after some big function he had had to attend in America, at which he confessed that he had been terribly bored.

I have never met a man so free from all priggishness and tendency to pose. It would have been utterly impossible to imagine him belonging to a clique, or even indeed realising that such things existed, or what their atmosphere was like. He never posed to anyone, not even to himself. This is not to say that he was not interested in himself, he had his full normal share of vanity and was indeed always delighted at praise, provided it was genuine (it was no use laying it on with a trowel, he knew the false from the true better than most men do), and would repeat it at home with immense satisfaction. My mother used to declare that he was really a very modest man, he was always so frankly and surprisedly pleased at appreciation which one would have supposed he must have felt that he had a right to expect, and never seemed to grow used to it. I am inclined to think she was right. Modesty was certainly not, however, a virtue at which he aimed (if he ever consciously aimed at any virtue except loyalty and straightness). ' Remember,' he used to say ' that people always take a man at his own valuation.' He had no use for a man who was always apologising for his own stupidity : he usually assumed that such an one was probably right.

His morality used to strike me as being rather pagan, in fact he was rather pagan altogether. One always felt as if it were quite impossible to shock him, but as a matter of fact it was easy enough if one went the right way about it. His code, like everything else about him, was a very simple one. In fact, it was the merchant's code. (He had a high opinion of business and was very fond of quoting Napoleon's saying, with the emphasis on the last half, which is usually forgotten, ' The British are a nation of shopkeepers, *and the odd thing is that they are ashamed of it.*' Business, he would say, is much cleaner than politics.) A bargain or a promise once made must be kept, whatever the consequence. There must be absolute loyalty to those one worked with, whether alongside, above, or below. He gave it, exacted it, and got it. One must never in any way abuse hospitality or criticise one's hosts, that was bad form. In a word one must ' play the game.' That was his code, he did not say much about it, but he kept it to the letter, and looked puzzled and troubled if any one he liked fell short of it.

On the other hand, he often spoke of his philosophy of life. He said it could be put into a nutshell—it was : ' Take as much happiness for yourself as you can get without interfering with other people's, and as a corollary to that give as much happiness to others as you can without inter-fering with your own.' That was one of his favourite sayings, and he lived up to it. Others were less suitable for copy-book maxims and were a considerable puzzle to those—and they were many—who never could decide whether to take him seriously or not. ' Reputation is better than character,' he always declared, and ' The eleventh and twelfth commandments are the ones to keep, " never get found out," but " confess freely what is already known."'

I have heard him called a cynic. I should not have used that word. For cynicism is based upon sentimentality— a cynic is just a frost-bitten sentimentalist—and of senti-mentality he was entirely devoid. He was, however, most certainly a realist, and when he talked would often un-consciously shear off some of other people's cherished illusions : for himself he had no use for illusions : all he asked was to know what the truth was.

He avoided most carefully hurting people's feelings, but that was I imagine on no principle except that he disliked it almost as much as they did. He had the Celtic instinct, was very sensitive to atmosphere, and knew in an instant if he had said the wrong thing. He did not always, however, avoid hurting feelings, since he loved to tease wherever he was, and I never saw the person he could not reduce to a state of crimson speechlessness if he had a mind to.

More than any other vices he disliked cant, false senti- ment, and hypocrisy.

His complete absence of pose had several results; it meant that he was curiously ignorant of a number of things most people know something about because they would feel out of it if they did not. Take reading for instance— He was a great reader : he would often sit up reading far into the night. He read occasionally biographies, more usually books on economics, or coal, or heredity, or farming with which his shelves were chiefly stacked. In his youth he had read more widely. For instance, he was fond of quoting from Shakespeare, Byron, and Gray ; he had come across them when he was young, and they had appealed to that imaginative side of him which never really slept. He was fond of the ' Ingoldsby Legends ' (he gave me 10s. as a youngster for learning the ' Jackdaw of Rheims ' by heart). He liked Dickens and Stevenson. He loved Macaulay's ' Lays.' (I remember that he and I both shed tears over a parody of one of Macaulay's ' Lays ' which appeared in *Punch* during the war. I tremble to think what we should have done if we had happened to read the original just then.) But I should say that he barely knew of the existence of any writer who had chanced to come into fame after the early eighties. Kipling was an exception to this rule. He admired him immensely, and I once took him to ' Man and Superman,' which he much enjoyed. But it would never have occurred to him to find out who were the fashionable writers of the day because most people knew ; still less to admire them when found. ' The correct thing ' was just left out of him. His taste, such as it was, existed for his own pleasure, and for nought else.

Have I given the impression of a man entirely unin- fluenced by others ? He was not that. Up to a point he often seemed to be very easily influenced by those whom he trusted, and he owed a good deal of his popularity to that fact. But it was a purely surface influence they wielded. He used to remind me of a field of corn that sways to the wind, but continues to grow in its own way. On the other hand, if he did not choose to be moved no man on earth could move him. It was his complete certainty of this that made him readily consider and often adopt other people's suggestions when he did choose.

He was the very opposite of inconsequent. Whatever he was at he had always a definite aim in view. I don't suppose he ever drifted in his life.

It was his habit to take life philosophically. He said once that no one who was not ' a bit of a philosopher ' could be really intelligent.

He was strictly logical : he refused to accept or believe anything that he could not prove ; that was one side, the intellectual side, the result of precept and training on a naturally sceptical and clear-sighted brain. The other side was quite different—he had a thousand superstitions, convictions, and rules of conduct which had no basis in facts at all. If he had been asked to square them with his intellectually held beliefs he would have replied that he did not believe them—but he acted on them.

He was a curious blend of the intellectual and practical type of man, and he really despised complete specimens of either. It was his capacity for blending theory with practice that was the secret of a great part of his success. It meant of course that he was continually trying experiments. ' I don't expect more than one venture in six to succeed,' he would say.

He was naturally frank and truthful, but it would be an exaggeration to suggest that, so long as he himself told the truth, he minded other people deceiving themselves if they chose to do so. ' To tell the truth,' I have heard him declare, ' is the best method of deceiving people, they can never believe it is true.' It was a method which he sometimes enjoyed using. He could act, of course. I remember on one occasion a business associate made him an offer for small coal. My father snapped out one or two questions to get the offer clear, and then apparently somewhat bored turned the conversation on to some schemes in which he was at the moment immensely interested. Half an hour later when the man had left, I made inquiries— the contract was a big one at a very good price and I knew he was keen to get rid of his small coal—why hadn't he fancied it ? Fancied it ! he had been thrilled over it ! He went about chortling for days afterwards at having deceived me as well as the man.

I have scarcely ever seen him really lose his temper. In his younger days he was very sweet tempered, and in later years he can scarcely have been said to have had a temper, but there was at times a certain intense, though usually well suppressed irritability about him, especially when he was overworking. To the sensitive it was all the more unbearable because so well controlled, it gave the sense of so much more behind. On the other hand, many people were unaware of its existence. I have seen a thick-skinned man who had been working with him all day, totally unaware in the evening that he had been cross at all, though it was obvious that he could have bitten the man's head off with pleasure a dozen times.

If he was—as he certainly was—sensitive and highly strung, there was a strong balanced sanity about him which kept the other side so well in check that many meeting him casually can scarcely have noticed that it existed.

He was a great faddist. He had a dozen varying theories as to how to keep perfectly fit and live to be eighty. At one time he would be an ardent vegetarian, at another he would declare that he could do better work on meat, which made him, so he said, feel more alive and more combative, and would indulge in an unrestricted meat diet. Sometimes he would live almost entirely on bananas, at another he would dine off sardines ; I have seen him eat a dozen oranges at a sitting. There was no end to his food fads. Nor did he confine his efforts towards perfect health to food questions only. He was a great believer in fresh air and exercise, which he took in the form of walking and bicycling. At one time he used to get up at six and walk round the farm before breakfast, and always he took a very considerable amount of regular exercise. He believed

WITH A PRIZE BULL

also in sun-baths, and on warm days we used to be warned off a portion of the roof where he was taking his sun-bath. He loved the sun and would always sit in it for choice.

He gave almost every one who came closely in contact with him a sense of being still a boy, and although as a matter of fact he shouldered all his responsibilities with a very sensitive conscientiousness, he could somehow give one the impression that he hadn't a care or a responsibility in the world.   I used sometimes to call him 'Peter Pan.' But I think he was slightly doubtful of the nickname : as a matter of fact he probably did not know in the least who Peter Pan was.   It seemed to me typical of him that to the end of his life he used occasionally to tell himself stories about himself—just the sort of blood-curdling stories of a school-boy's days they were.   And during the war, when he was at the Food Ministry, he would sometimes picture himself fighting in France.   I daresay most people do this, only one does not usually chance to know it about them.

One of the things which makes it difficult for any one person to judge him was his capacity for being all things to all men.   Take for instance this :

I have spoken of him to many of those who were with him during the last years of his life, and I find that each one holds—and holds with complete conviction—an entirely different view of what he intended to do after the war had he lived.

Politicians and press men believe that he wished to stay in politics and make good there.

Doctors believe that his great aim was to have the building of the Ministry of Health.

Business men believe that he was only longing for the moment when he could shake red tape and political dust from his feet and return to the enthralling schemes of big business.

Americans believe that his future life would have been spent more on that side of the water than this.

His bailiff believes that what he really yearned for was to cut off all outside interests and live at peace on his farm with the Herefords.

Men of a labour complexion incline to the theory that

had it been possible he might have liked to continue in politics as a free-lance representing the point of view of Labour in the House of Lords.

The fact is probably that he wanted to do all these things, and instinctively, unconsciously and most typically dilated in each different case upon the one with which his hearer was most in sympathy. But which did he want to do most ? Heaven knows !

I am sure that his bailiff was wrong ; and I think I know which were the two favourite dreams, but as to whether he would really rather have gone back into big business or built up a Health Ministry I do not know in the least. Perhaps he did not know himself.

In looking back, it seems as if it were the joy in life that stands out most. He was the happiest man I have ever known.

APPENDICES

APPENDIX A TO CHAPTER I

PROFESSOR R. J. Knaggs of Leeds writes the following description of his college life :

'It happened that towards the end of their first year (1877) a few men, nearly all keenly interested in rowing, found themselves inviting one another to their rooms for tea after Hall. In this way a little circle was gradually formed, and those informal gatherings continued daily for the rest of their college life.

'The friends who belonged to this coterie always looked back upon these evening meetings as perhaps the most enjoyable of their many happy times. William Ridgeway, R. F. Cobbold, D. A. Thomas, J. W. Welsford, and the writer formed the nucleus, and they were joined, but less frequently, by George Riven, G. F. Welsford, Walter Winslow, and H. Jervis-White-Jervis.

'The party would break up just before nine, and then Thomas and the writer would take an evening walk for a mile along the Trumpington Road before settling down to work. This, as also a morning walk through the " Backs " before breakfast, was part of our method of training, which was very seldom intermitted ; but it is needless to say that during these strolls there were many talks on many and various subjects, and our knowledge of one another's characters grew apace. Looking back, I can see how the determination he then showed in everything he set his mind to, and the level-headed way in which he looked at things, and his scorn of everything that savoured of crookedness were the same qualities which helped him to achieve in later life his great success.

'Thomas was one of a rowing family. When he was a freshman his elder brother and a cousin (T. W. Lewis), who was also the President of the C.U.B.C., rowed in the Caius four, and another member of it afterwards became his brother-in-law (A. W. Haig). Under these circumstances it is not to be wondered at that he was clearly impressed with the call that the river makes upon its devotees.

' In due course in his second term he earned a place in the third boat, and from this time his delight in rowing and sculling never left him, and resulted in his becoming one of the most familiar figures on the Cam.

' In his third year Thomas won the College Sculls and the Pairs, and we were looking forward to the " Varsity Pairs " in the May term, when the illness and death of his father kept him at home till about ten days before the May races.

' Just after his return Mr. Bazelgette, who was rowing bow in the first boat, broke down, and, fortunately, Thomas was available to take his place. The boat, which was second on the river, was bumped by *Lady Margaret*, and ended third.

' In his third year he had quite a successful time at regattas. He won the Junior Sculls at Burton and also at Tewkesbury (I believe), whilst at the former place we won the Pairs. In the October term he forsook the river, except for occasional exercise, in order to work for his Tripos.

' He had never been a hard worker at his books, but in this term he did his best to make up for lost time. He obtained a place sufficiently high up in the Senior Optimes (fourth) to prove that if he had worked consistently throughout his time he would have been well up in the Wranglers.

' It is needless to add that a man whose nature will be guessed by what I have written had not only good friends but a nickname. And it was as " Tights," and not Thomas, that he was always known, and is still thought of, by his contemporaries.'

APPENDIX B TO CHAPTER VIII

Miss Evelyn Salusbury speaks in the following note of some of D. A.'s interests :

' During D. A.'s Parliamentary days, I remember he was very keen on chess, and often at week ends used to organise a match for " The Chess Championship of Llanwern,"—lasting most of the day—played out in the garden—weather permitting—in order to combine the fresh air cure. I recollect playing many games, specially about the time of the yearly Chess Tournament in the house, to practise up for that event. D. A. played a very plucky attacking, but rather unorthodox, game. He never would resign—even when the game was obviously lost—always playing on till actually checkmated—on the off chance of his opponent making a slip. He was also fond of solving chess problems, and was a very good hand at them. He always used to work them out on the printed diagram, and rarely set out even the most intricate position on the chess-board.

' Before the days of motoring, D. A. used to like bicycling trips, and often got up expeditions to some place of interest—everybody carrying some lunch to eat out of doors. I remember one ride to the ruins of Llantony Abbey ; we overhauled the old Abbey, D. A. reconstructing the old scenes most vividly, then we climbed the mountain at the back of the Abbey. On that day our luncheons seemed quite inadequate—Mr. Thomas had only brought half a dozen protein biscuits (protein biscuits were just newly invented)—and though he explained to us on the way up the mountain that six biscuits really contained enough nourishment to sustain a person for several days, yet in that keen mountain air the six biscuits and our light luncheons failed to keep the wolf from the door ; and when we descended to the Abbey Inn we ordered a glorious lunch of ham and eggs. D. A. was greatly disappointed when the ham turned out to be only bacon.

' He always enjoyed everything, however simple, just like a schoolboy ; and often made us feel quite ancient and blasé, though we were a good deal his juniors.

' When he retired from the House, and his time became so taken up with business, he chartered me to look after his bees. Till then he had always tended them himself. He instructed me thoroughly in the routine of bee-keeping—demonstrating every detail. " Never handle anything twice, if you can possibly help it," was one of his sayings which he applied to bee-keeping. For instance, when one opens up a hive one should complete operations as far as possible in order to avoid disturbing the hive oftener than is absolutely necessary.'

APPENDIX C TO CHAPTER VIII

I am indebted to Mrs. M. E. M. Walker for the following account :

'It was here in his home he loved so well that I first met D. A. Thomas. It was luncheon time on the day after my arrival. I had heard that he was unwell, and had not gone to business in Cardiff, but as he walked across the long hall from his study,. with his firm, quick step, talking so eagerly to the friend who was with him, it was difficult to imagine that this man, whatever his bodily health, was not feeling in the best of all possible spirits. One had only to look at him to be aware of his strength, and my first impression was one of his great vitality.

'I remember he asked me what I thought of the country, and when I had nothing more enlightening to say than that it was my first visit to Wales, he caught me up quickly and said I was not in Wales yet, although the dividing line between Monmouth and Wales is hardly perceptible outside the map. I watched him and listened with accumulating interest. He tilted his chair on two legs and balanced himself with the tips of his toes on the bar of the table, and in this precarious-looking position, which I was soon to learn was his normal attitude at meals, he discussed politics, the Cardiff Exchange, the prospect for the harvest, and the bees in his garden ; and into everything he said there entered that amazing vitality and eagerness of tone which was one of the great charms of his personality. He talked very quickly, and to one unaccustomed to his voice sometimes indistinctly. I remember the lively interest he took in his vegetarian lunch, about which he asked his wife many questions, and his giving an order to the parlourmaid to send one of the farm boys to the cider press for some of his special brew of cider. I noticed with what alacrity his slightest behest was obeyed.

'After this luncheon I did not see him again until the

following morning. At half-past eight he came down to breakfast. On the table there lay an enormous pile of letters, and beside him sat his secretary, a quick-moving little man whose every action reminded me of a well-plied needle. He sat, pencil in hand, the while Mr. Thomas ate his bacon, drank his coffee, opened his letters, and dictated answers, the parlourmaid meanwhile lacing up her master's boots. In less than ten minutes the secretary had gathered up an armful of papers and was following hurriedly in the wake of his chief to the car which awaited them at the front door. The parlourmaid, standing in the hall, held his overcoat, umbrella, and hat. There was less than five minutes to catch the train at the little station of Llanwern, and as they whizzed off gaily to the tune of some forty-five miles an hour I caught a last glimpse of the secretary and the pencil still writing furiously. It was amazing, and I thought surely to-day they must have got up late. But on the contrary this was the ordinary every day procedure. Mr. Thomas liked to do things thus, and he never wasted a moment of his time.

' Once he had gone the house lost its air of activity—that electrical atmosphere that surrounded and vitalised us all, for one could not be in his presence without feeling it. In the evening the hoot of his motor horn in the drive would as suddenly turn on the current again.

' I remember he told me I must go to see his office in Cardiff. He said he believed in having a pleasant place to work in, and that his room was filled with fresh flowers every morning. Business was to him a recreation that he loved. He said it was not the acquisition of the money that appealed to him, it was the making of a success of anything to which he put his hand. He had a firm belief in his own luck—" I usually come out top "—luck being his wonderful gift of foresight and imagination and his ability of putting a new idea to the test of the concrete. He was a lover of quick actions, and immediate results pleased him more than anything else. " Imagination," he would say, " is what we want in business—imagination and University men." He wanted to see scholars in the world of business ; he was ambitious and zealous for the repute of business, and I think one of the chief reasons why America and the Americans appealed to him so much was the esteem in which a business man was held in that country.

' I used to say to him that it was success in business that

the Americans worshipped, and that an unsuccessful man was nowhere in America. But he maintained that they were right in their valuation of success—by which, I think, he meant the will and energy necessary for the carrying out of a successful enterprise. He liked an enterprising man with plenty of pluck to take risks. Later, when I became his personal secretary and went with him to the Ministry of Food he would discuss most of the people we came in contact with there, and those he picked out as specially appealing to him from a business point of view, and on whom he said he " must keep his eye on after the war," were always men who made quick decisions and got things done. The one thing that irritated him more than anything else in official life was departmental delay.

' On one of the rare holidays he took from his business in Cardiff I remember a picnic party to Pen Ithon in North Wales—a motor drive of eighty miles. We started at the cold hour of seven o'clock in the morning. He was in the gayest spirits, and pointed out the landmarks on the journey, recalling tales of former times. At three o'clock in the afternoon he had an appointment to meet his agents at Pen Ithon to settle some business matter in connection with the estate. I had brought the papers and had hoped to get everything fixed in a short interview. But three o'clock came and the agents did not appear. Mr. Thomas began to get restive and ordered the car to start on the return journey at 3.45, for we had eighty miles ahead of us. He was very annoyed at the unbusinesslike attitude of the agents, and just as we reached the avenue gates we met their car approaching and I asked him if we should stop, but he signalled impetuously to the chauffeur to proceed at top speed and we left the agents to chew the cud of remorse in solitude. He was always impatient of delay. Coming home I remember how kindly he insisted that I should take his seat, because sitting with my back to the engine had not agreed with me, and he was quite annoyed when we compromised by my taking Miss Haig's seat beside the chauffeur. The atmosphere of the journey home was just a little electrical, but six or seven miles from home he got out and walked with a friend and arrived at Llanwern in the best of spirits. He was very fond of walking and exercise.

' Sundays, I think, were his happiest days at Llanwern. He usually spent the morning with his farm bailiff inspecting the Herefords, of which he was so proud. I can see him now with his thick boots, his short covert coat, his Tyrolese hat, and a burly walking-stick, setting out on a Sunday morning for his tour of the farm, while the car waited at the front door to take Mrs. Thomas to church. He would explain that there was " no church of his denomination within reach," but as a boy his mother had seen to it that he went to chapel regularly on a Sunday. I never once heard him mention his parents or his home at Aberdare without a tone of warm affection coming into his voice. Of his other relations he had little to say, unless it were Arnold Thomas, his cousin, for whom he maintained the very highest regard and affection to the end of his life.'

APPENDIX D TO CHAPTER XIII

(By David Evans)

IN 1911 he visited South America, in 1912 Germany and France, and in 1913, 1914, and 1915 the United States and Canada. He was tremendously impressed by the scope for enterprise provided by the gigantic scale on which production, distribution, and finance were carried on in the United States and by the undeveloped resources of west and north-west Canada. The outbreak of the war in 1914 and the subsequent entry of the United States into the European conflict prevented the materialisation of schemes for the acquisition of collieries in West Virginia, the establishment of a mammoth barge goods transport service on the Mississippi, the exploitation of the mica resource of one of the American provinces, the inauguration of a great oversea service between New York and Europe, and the development of the virgin soils of north-west Canada.

Of these, perhaps, the two which appealed to him most were an Anglo-American combine for the shipment of American coal to Europe, and a gigantic corporation for the development of the Peace River District of north-west Canada. The following notes were written soon after his return from the United States in the spring of 1913 :

'April 4th, 1913.—Found D. A. in a communicative mood concerning his American ideas. He made it clear that they had not yet assumed practical form. Since his last visit to America he has had several offers of properties situated in the Pocahontas district of Virginia West, and he is favourably inclined to participate in a scheme for the purchase of some of them. His main idea is an Anglo-American concern with a capital of between five and six million sterling, half of which he states an American capitalist is prepared to find, and the other half of which has to be raised in this country by D. A. He sees no inherent impracticability in the scheme. The coal supplies in the

States are obtainable at so low a cost as to make a systematic sale of American coal in the Mediterranean practicable. He mentioned cases where the cost of bringing the coal to the wagon was about 2s. 6d. per ton, but he calculated on a 4s. per ton cost at the pit, and an extra 6s. for carriage to port of shipment, at which price he considers it possible to market the coal in Europe at about 20s. per ton at a profit. He would build his own steamers for the trade. In the long run he was of the opinion that this control of his own tonnage would enable him to avoid the risks of freight, and mentioned a case where a contract of 130,000 tons with a South American firm had involved the combine in a possible loss of £30,000. His primary notion is that these steamers shall be used as colliers for the purpose of the business of the Anglo-American Combine. Among other advantages it would enable the combine to guarantee delivery to a far greater extent than is possible under existing conditions, but would necessarily prevent it from taking advantage of booms in freights. I observed that a great economic factor in favour of such a proposal was to be found in the fact that the coal in this country had permanently reached a figure that was likely to accelerate the operation of the law of substitution. He agreed, but added that the same causes which had led to the increase in the cost in this country might, and probably would, operate in the States, although not perhaps in the immediate future. He also foresaw that the present conditions in regard to non-unionism in the American mines would not continue indefinitely, and repeated with belief the statement of the late Pierpont Morgan that the greatest danger to American industrial and commercial interests was Lloyd George, meaning, of course, what he considered the socialistic tendencies of the Chancellor of the Exchequer's legislation. Of his American partner he said he knew nothing of coal, " which is just as it ought to be," but added that he was an exceptionally shrewd person and enormously wealthy. Among other things he told me that he had just completed the formation of a coal distributing agency in Spain, and he expressed the view that the future of by-product production was great. One of his ideas was the carriage of coal to continental centres and the production of electricity by-products, such as gas, etc., but the main difficulty was the disposal of coke. He believed it possible to reverse the currents of trade in many directions, pointing out that the economies accomplished in the production of coke, and the increasing cost of coal in South Wales would have a tendency to carry coal to iron ore centres instead of carrying ore to coal centres.'

In the far west province of Canada he found a new potential empire which appealed irresistibly to his imagination. In 1913–14 he obtained charters from the Dominion Government granting powers to build boats and tramways and to navigate the lakes and rivers of the north in the name of the Pacific, Peace River, and Athabasca Railway Company with powers to construct a railway from the sea-coast in British Columbia, to Prince Albert in the province of Saskatchewan. The plans of these companies, as well as of the Thomas Syndicate which he had formed, provided for the construction of a railway extending over 1500 miles between the points already named, the building of steamships for lake and river service, the development of oilfields, coalfields, and other mineral areas, and the provision of facilities for the encouragement of forests, agricultural, fishing, trapping, and other enterprises. These plans alone were estimated to involve a capital expenditure of at least twenty millions.

The reports of the experts employed to investigate the resources of the districts, stated that the mineral wealth of the Peace River Valley included petroleum and coal in great quantities. It was stated that 'a great oilfield has been discovered outcropping over a district 1000 miles long and 200 miles wide. The "blowers" are among the largest in the world. In some cases the flames attain a height of 35 feet, and native Indians assert that at certain points of the Slav River they never can recollect a time when the river was not "on fire." For a distance of 100 miles in the Athabaska country the proposed new railway will run over a bed of tar and sand 200 feet thick. From this originally rich oil-bearing area all the volatile parts have escaped ; it has been estimated by the geological survey of Canada that the oil thus evaporated must have amounted to 8,000,000,000 tons, or a larger quantity than has yet been taken for commercial use out of all the oilfields of the world. An analysis of the oilfields which it is proposed to develop has been made for the Thomas Syndicate showing 16 per cent. gasolene, 9 per cent. kerosene, and 25 per cent. cylinder oil.'

The outbreak of the war and the premature death of

Lord Rhondda prevented the carrying out of any portion of this grandiose programme for the creation of a new vast agricultural and industrial empire. But in the distant future when the resources of older countries have been exhausted, and when the great seats of population and enterprise have shifted westwards to what are now the virgin provinces of Western Canada, his name will be remembered as that not only of a man of vision, but also as that of a business genius who was at any rate capable of imagining and planning for the developments which time and opportunity prevented him from executing.

In the United States he obtained partial control over a small mine in West Virginia ; he liked to see a great river barge, christened under his own name, launched on the Mississippi ; and he became one of the principal partners in the shipping firm of R. Martens & Co., which during the period of the war acted as agents for the Russian Government for the purchase and transport of war material and for other services.

APPENDIX E TO CHAPTER XVII

(By Mr. Leonard Rees, Editor of the ' Sunday Times ')

FEW men in any period of our history have so fully won the public confidence as did Lord Rhondda in those dark days of the war when the food supplies of the country were running perilously short owing to the depredations of the enemy submarines. He had as Food Controller to make an unprecedented interference with the domestic economy of the nation, to restrict within narrow limits its consumption of essential foodstuffs, and he won the cheerful consent of all classes in the ordinance, because they were convinced of his capacity for his task and his singlemindedness of administration.

His success was the more remarkable because till the war brought him his great opportunity for public service Lord Rhondda was not well known to the majority of people. To be sure, in his native Wales, and especially in the South Wales colliery district, his name had been a household word for many a year ; the miners to a man respected his expert knowledge of their industry, and implicitly trusted the man who had fought their battles as well as his own. But though he sat in Parliament for twenty years, he was instinctively averse from the methods which make for prominence in the political world, and public attention was not really riveted upon him till he accepted the Ministry of Food.

This acceptance was a signal act of courage that at once evoked the admiration of the country. Brief as had been its existence, the Ministry of Food had already been the grave of one reputation. One after another of our public men had declined a post which seemed to promise only failure, and the unpopularity and discredit which almost inevitably have followed failure. Lord Rhondda might well have refused a thankless task, for he had found a congenial post as President of the Local Government Board, and was in the way of revitalising its hitherto somnolent activity. But with the same strong sense of duty that, after his terrible experience on the sinking of the *Lusitania*, sent him back to America to complete his work of organising the supply of munitions on the other side, he yielded to the Prime Minister's urgent representations and migrated from Whitehall to Grosvenor House, where the Ministry of Food was then housed.

How great the sacrifice he was making, how brief his span of life must be, even if he went dead slow, few knew at the time, but our public reacts to courage, and instinctively it gave him sympathy and goodwill. It was soon to find that he brought much more than courage to his task. One of the experiments of the war was the requisitioning of our successful business men to ginger up the public departments, and it proved in the main disappointing. Their success had usually been won in a groove, and when they were taken out of it and put to a fresh job, they frequently failed to sustain their reputations for super-efficiency. Lord Rhondda, however, had never been circumscribed in his interests, and his genius for organisation had been given constant variety of play. It functioned as readily and as effectively in the administration of a public department as it had done in the co-ordination of the supplies of munitions from America, and as, before that, it had done in the building up and consolidation of the South Wales coal industry. It was to be put to a stern test at the Ministry of Food, for not only was the problem presented there of an unprecedented character and difficulty, but the staff of the Ministry was a scratch team hastily got together, and for the most part without official training. Add to this that it was inconveniently housed in a quarter of the town equally remote from the business centres and from Whitehall, and it will be seen that the situation demanded a superman.

Food had become the dominant concern of every household, and the work of Grosvenor House was watched with anxious attention by the public. Lord Rhondda welcomed and encouraged their interest, for he felt that the surest way of enlisting their support and co-operation in the measures he might be called upon to propose was to take them into his confidence. He had as little use for the traditional reticence of a public department as he had for its red tape. No Minister was so accessible as he, nor so free from Whitehall ' side.' He would not let you waste his time with trivialities, but he gave a ready hearing to men with practical knowledge and experience, and they came away from his room impressed both by his readiness to grasp new ideas and suggestions and his unfailing courtesy of manner. He had always a welcome for journalists, whom he regarded as amongst his coadjutors, able to give information as well as to receive it. 'What are they saying?' he would often ask. 'I can't succeed if I don't carry public opinion with me. You've got your ear to the ground and can tell me.'

Soon the public became conscious of a change at Grosvenor House. Order was being evolved, and the left hand of the Ministry was no longer ignorant of what the right hand was doing. Instead of a haphazard succession of 'orders' often contradictory and sometimes inept, there was evidence of a definite policy based on a scientific examination of the situation and of the resources of the country.

Lord Rhondda saw that if there was to be effective and equitable control of food supply it must be exercised at every stage, and that he must begin with determining prime cost. He had always been a sure judge of men, and he set the best brains he could find to probe out the data he required, with the result that the decisions he took commanded general approval as much by the merchant and trader as by the consumer. 'This man knows his job,' said the public, 'and we'll stick by him.'

But what confirmed the public confidence in Lord Rhondda was the rigid impartiality of his administration. He was determined that when the restriction of food consumption became imperative it should be enforced all round without regard to class or position. And so when he found that the orders against food-hoarding were being disobeyed, he set the law in motion without distinction. Quite a number of the hoarders were well-known people, one of them an M.P., and both social and political pressure was brought to bear on him to spare them the ignominy of prosecution. His answer was peremptory. There was, in this matter at least, to be the same law for the rich and the poor, the castle and the cottage, the West-end flat and the workman's dwelling, and if there was to be any interference with the prosecutions, any shielding of offenders in high position, he would throw up the Ministry and let the public know the reason why. That was an alternative that no one was prepared to face, and so the prosecutions went on, and to their bitter wrath a number of the more important culprits were heavily fined. It is impossible to exaggerate the effect of this even-handed justice. It was not only an assurance to the country that the Minister would give it a square deal in the restrictions he might lay upon it, but it was a wholesome deterrent from an unpatriotic and selfish practice. Hoarding came to be regarded as a dangerous risk, and people who had secretly prided themselves on their prudence in providing for days of scarcity, made haste to unload on their neighbours and friends.

And so when the food position became more perilous, and the Government gave a reluctant assent to the policy of rationing the community, Lord Rhondda was enabled to launch his scheme with the general consent. The public were convinced by his straight dealing that he only asked what was essential to the safety of the country, and that the scheme would be administered with an equality of incidence. Rationing was the most irksome of all the war-time limitations of personal freedom, and could not be endured gladly, but it evoked remarkably little grumbling or resentment, and remembrance of the hoarding prosecutions curbed any inclination to wangle illicit supplies. And though there were inevitable hitches in the machinery, it worked in the main with such smoothness that few people realised how tremendous was its achievement. Rationing had been tried before in other countries, and had always failed. Germany preceded us in the experiment and gave us an object lesson in how not to do it. Lord Rhondda succeeded because he had the trust and support of the public, and also their active participation, in their several localities, in the administration of his scheme.

Though by this time in precarious health he strictly confined himself to the prescribed rations, and as much for the force of example as for considerations of health avoided public luncheons and dinners. I remember meeting him on Lord Mayor's Day 1917, and asking him if he was going to the Guildhall banquet at night, to which as a Minister he had of course been invited. 'No,' he said, 'I've made excuse. I felt my presence there would make a bad impression. I don't suppose I should have eaten any more there than I shall at my own table, but the visibility of my dining at the Guildhall would have been very much greater than the actuality.'

The public confidence in him surprised him as much as it

delighted him, for he felt when he went to the Ministry of Food that he must expect more kicks than eulogies. And when he was preparing his rationing scheme he predicted that ' in six months' time I shall be the best hated man in the country.' Yet even when, in the winter of 1917–18, the queue difficulty presented itself to abate the faith in him, men felt that the development could not have been foreseen, and that anyhow he would put it right, which indeed he did. All the same, it gave him acute anxiety and distress at a time when he badly needed quiet and rest.

Gradually the public regard for him ripened into a warm affection. People grew familiar with his face—for his portrait was now to be seen on the screen and on picture-postcards in company with the heroes of the war—and they were intrigued by the kindly smile which offset the handsome but rather severe features. They were emboldened to address him personally, and the oddest communications reached him from persons of all classes. Not all of them were concerned with food control, and in one case he was asked to give advice in a delicate matrimonial problem.

And then, in the early summer of 1918, when the end of the great war was beginning to come into sight, death, which ever loves a shining mark, stepped in and claimed him. It was a good ending—to have come at long last to the thing he had ever strongly desired—service to the State ; to have done that service so signally as to deserve and win a nation's gratitude ; and to have left a memory of fine statesmanship untarnished by self-seeking or subservience to fear or favour. Only for the country there was this melancholy reflection, that till he was in the autumn of life his great capacity never found the national outlet it needed, and only the accident of war saved it from total neglect.

APPENDIX F TO CHAPTER XVIII

THE following notes on Lord Rhondda's work at the Local Government Board and his methods are taken from a letter written by Mr. F. L. Turner, C.B., who acted as his official private secretary both while he was President of the Local Government Board and Food Controller :

'Lord Rhondda was perhaps a little disappointed in coming to his first office of State to find it a department of long standing, largely ruled by precedent, restricted by innumerable Acts of Parliament and Regulations, and hedged in by forests of Case Law. Hence his progress as a reformer was always slower than he wished.

'He knew what he wanted to do and was always in favour of the most direct methods of reaching the end. When he found his way blocked he was willing to adopt drastic means to get through. Thus when he discovered that pig-keeping, which he regarded as a valuable asset on the side of food production, was being hindered by the byelaws in force in many parts of the country he issued a direction for their suspension. Opposition always encouraged him to greater effort.

'He quickly came to the conclusion that the most important part of his duties was the preservation of the public health, and that it was up to him to do his utmost to repair the ravages of war. He threw himself whole-heartedly into the work of child welfare, being convinced that there was an opportunity of saving thousands of children's lives every year. And when he found that the care and control of health were scattered among several departments of State who did not move in the same way he decided that it was necessary for success that all these health powers should be in the hands of one department— a Ministry of Health. The establishment of such a Ministry, able and willing to take all necessary action for the betterment of the public health, became his ideal, and to secure this he worked unceasingly.

'His six months at the Local Government Board were full of action, and many schemes of health reform were carried through, often in face of opposition. He realised fully the need of better housing conditions, and to help him to prepare a scheme did not hesitate to ask the advice of critics. One of his acts was to set up an advisory body containing representatives of all sides on this housing question.

'He took little interest in the Poor Law as such. He visited Poor Law institutions, it is true, and expressed his appreciation of the admirable arrangements made by the Boards of Guardians, but he regarded the Poor Law rather as a dying concern. His view was that there he had no chance of doing much and that it was more useful to devote himself to the preventive side.

'He left the Local Government Board with much regret, for he was deeply interested in the work and his schemes were unfinished. He felt it, however, to be his duty to accept the office of Food Controller, though he did so with some reluctance as, his health was not good and he doubted whether his strength would stand the strain. On the other hand, he saw that the problems of food control were in the main business questions with which as a business man he felt qualified to deal.

'He was impatient if things did not move as quickly as he wished. He was always wanting progress. "A trading concern," he used to say, "or an office is either progressing or going back : it cannot be stationary. I do not want to be associated with a concern which is not going forward."

'He was a great organiser and he applied his business methods to his official work. He had the faculty of being able to use people of all descriptions and to get the best out of them.

'A great charm was his directness—almost bluntness at times. He went straight to the point and did not mince words. He was a plain-speaking, plain-thinking man and believed in talking straight to people and putting his cards on the table. His great success at interviews was due to this frankness : he used to take his audience into his confidence, tell them his plans, and if need be ask their advice.

'He never seemed dogmatic but always gave the impression of being practical, sane and fair. But if he made up his mind that a thing was right he said so without hesitation, and the look of his jaws sometimes warned his hearers that there was no hope of change.

'It was noticeable that persons went away satisfied after their interviews with him even if they did not get what they wanted. He did his best to persuade his audience to accept his decision : he was always ready to argue with them, and he would take immense pains to remove their doubts. He sometimes said, "It is no good allowing me only an hour for an interview like this one. I found they did not agree with me and I had to argue them out of their views. I would rather give two or even three hours to the interview and satisfy them than let them go away unconvinced."

'He was a great believer in the power of the Press, and knew that he was much more likely to carry out his plans if he had its active support. Therefore he made it his business to interest the Press in his schemes. This was especially the case when he was Food Controller. He realised how necessary it was that the public should be kept calm, and should be encouraged to accept willingly the restrictions he had to impose on their food supply. He was ready to trust the Press : and when he had explained his proposals and invited criticisms he generally got their assistance. Throughout his official career he found the Press most helpful.'

APPENDIX G TO CHAPTER XX

For the following notes I am indebted to Mr. H. O. Hughes, who was for many years his private secretary :

'Lord Rhondda did not, as far as I can remember, mention a favourite author. Such novels as the "Adventures of Sherlock Holmes" strongly appealed to him, and he never travelled by rail without sampling the contents of the bookstalls. All kinds of books and periodicals were found in his study after a journey ; among them the leading London dailies and reviews, together with recent novels. Some of the bookstall attendants had so many opportunities of studying his requirements that they knew his wants, and it was amusing to see the bundle accumulating under the deft hands of these attentive men, while the purchaser stood watching the pile grow, scarcely uttering a word.

'"Jevons on the Coal Trade" was a book he took greater interest in than any other during the whole time I was with him. In his own work, "Coal Exports, 1850–1900," the authority of Jevons is frequently quoted. He had several copies of this work in his study. About eight or nine arrived at one time from Quaritch's, some much the worse for wear. Of these a few were presented to friends who shared his enthusiasm for the coal question, but his study was never without copies of Jevons.

'He was deeply interested in the *Journal of the Royal Statistical Society*, and insisted that his copies of it should be always at hand. I fancy the *Economist* came in a good second : and any book, pamphlet, or periodical on statistics was always welcome.

'Lord Rhondda simply loved statistics, and would spend long hours in the night preparing figures for some scheme or other, generally in connection with the Coal Trade. When I discovered one morning the immense work done on the previous night and remonstrated with him, as I feared that his health would suffer, he replied, "My dear fellow, why can't I enjoy myself ? If I like it, what does it matter to anybody else ? "

' He took immense trouble with anything he had on hand ; for instance, his scheme for the prevention of under-selling in the Coal Trade. He visited, consulted, and ex-pounded the matter to the principal colliery owners of Cardiff, but he could not prevail upon them to adopt it. The late Mr. Edward Davies of Llandinian, the father of the present M.P. for Montgomeryshire, he informed me, thoroughly grasped the scheme, but as for the others, " I don't think anybody can drive it into their heads."

' The scheme did not " catch on," but Lord Rhondda never wasted time over the disappointment its rejection caused him. He turned his mind to something else and never grumbled or referred to the matter which had cost him untold labour, and which he had very much at heart.'

INDEX

ABBOT, Mr. F. W., 207
'Abernant, Dai,' 73
Abraham, Mr. W., see Mabon
Admiralty Collieries, 139, 140, 189
Alberta, Northern, development, 56, 191
Albion Steam Coal Co., Ltd., 132
Allgood, Mr., 159
Allied Provisions Export Commission, 231
America and the War, 195, 313; New York in 1915...195
American aspect of the Munitions Mission, 208
American. character, the: Lord Rhondda's high regard for, 31, 56, 193, 194, 211, 310–11
American coal in Europe, 313–4
American interests of D. A., the, 191 et seq.; investigation of the American coal business, 191 et seq.; plans for Anglo-American combinations, 56, 192, 193, 313–4; Mississippi barge service, 193, 194, 313, 316
Anglo-Continental Guano Co., Ltd., 141
Anglo-Spanish Coaling Co., Ltd., 136, 314
Anson, Sir William, 79
Asquith, Rt. Hon. H. H., 62, 65, 66, 68, 77

BAILIE, Mr., 211
Balfour, Rt. Hon. A. J., 79, 80
Ballot Act, 60
Barry Urban District Council, 79
Bazelgette, Mr., 306
Beer Restriction Acts, 219
Begbie, Mr. Harold, on Lord Rhondda's philosophy, 278 et seq.; mentioned, 201, 268, 269
Belgian Refugees, 195
Bell, Mr., 166
Berry, Mr. H. Seymour, 56, 57, 141
Bethlehem Steel Works, 207
Beveridge, Sir William H.: account of the Food Ministry under Lord Rhondda, 218 et seq.
Beynon, J. W., 134

Board of Trade, the, 126, 141, 219, 220
Boer War, the, 31, 77, 196
Bolshevism, 288
Borden, Sir Robert, 208, 210, 212
Brand, Hon. R. H., 210
Bread subsidy, the, 226, 229
Brewing, restriction of, 219
Bridge, Sir John, 61
'Bridgend policy,' the, 78, 79, 80
Britannic Merthyr Coal Co., 132, 134, 136
British and American combinations: D. A.'s interest in, 56, 192, 193, 313–4
British Columbia development, 191, 315; investigation of coal reserves, 192
British Munitions Board, 207
Burt, Mr., 166

CA' CANNYISM, 124
Caius College, 14, 28 n.
Callaghan, Mr. T. J., 131 and n.
Cambrian Collieries Ltd., 130, 133; original starting of, 45–8; sales agency, 51–2, 136; not in the Coal Association, 99, 103; attitude of management in the Sliding Scale controversy, 103; strikes at Clydach Vale, 110–3, 123, 152; at work during strike at the Associated Collieries, 114, 127, 131 n., 167–8; strike in 1901...153; the Cambrian Combine, 132, 133, 142; strike in 1910–11...122; profits, 168–9; increase in number employed by, 171; increase in average wage, 171–2; effects of Syndicalist policy on, 172; criticism of, by Mr. T. Richards, 173 et seq; Mr. Hartshorn's suggestion, 170
Cambrian News, 137, 215
Cambrian News, Ltd., 137
Cambrian Trust, Ltd., 130
Cammell Laird & Co., 210
Campbell-Bannerman, Sir Henry, 55, 77, 83

Canadian aspect of the Munitions Mission, 208
Canadian Cartridge Co., 210–11
Canadian interests of D. A.: North Western Canada development schemes, 56, 191, 193, 212, 313, 315
Canadian Pacific Railway Co., 210
Canadian Shell Committee, 205, 209-10
Capitalism *versus* Socialism, 284–6, 288
Cardiff Business Club, 186
Cardiff Liberal Association, 158, 161
Carr, Mr. R. H.: account of the Munitions Mission, 204 *et seq.*
Carson, Sir Edward, 169
Cattle prices scale, 229–30
Cawdor, Lord, 79
Chamberlain, Rt. Hon. Joseph, 58, 60, 61, 77, 80
Child welfare, 264–5, 266, 267, 268, 276, 322
Churchill, Rt. Hon. Winston S., 158
Clwyd, Lord, 63
Clydach Vale, 110–13, 123, 127, 152, 153, 154. *See* Cambrian Collieries
Clynes, Rt. Hon. J. R., 258, 270, 271, 272
Coal Owners Association, 99, 152 ; action in Sliding Scale controversy, 102–9 *passim*, 117
Coal by-products, 314
Coal conservation, 169–70
Cobbold, R. F., 14, 305
Commerce, 289, 290
Compensation Act, 119
Conciliation Board, 118, 119, 120
Connaught, Duke and Duchess of, 208
Conscientious objectors, 31–2
Consolidated Cambrian, Ltd., 133
Co-operative Wholesale Society, 231
Cox, Mr. Harold, 80
Crawshays, the, 2
Cyfartha, 2 *and n.*
Cymru Fydd movement, 31, 69 *et seq.*
Cynon property, the, 134

Davey, Sir Horace, 59
Davies, David, 46, 59
Davies, Edward, 326
Davis, D. & Sons, Ltd., 140
Davis, Thomas, 71
Dawson, Sir Bertrand, 270
Democratic government, 125

Devonport, Lord, 269
Dillwyn, Mr., 60
Dowlais Iron Works, 2 *n.*
Duffryn Rhondda property, the, 134
Du Parck, Mr., 69, 70, 78

Ebbw Vale Steel and Iron Co., 135
Economist, The, 87, 325
Edison, Thomas Alva, 204, 207
Edwards, Frank, 64, 65
Edwards, Principal, 74
Edwards, Roger, 59
Eglwyslan Churchyard, 36
Elder Collieries, 140
Elias, John, 59
Ellis, T. E., 59, 62, 64, 65, 66
Evans, Mr. Beriah, 69, 70, 73, 75, 76, 77
Evans, Mary Hamilton, 3
Evans, Sir Samuel, 59, 62

Fenianism, 185
Fenwick, Mr., 166
Ferndale Collieries, 140, 142
Fernhill Collieries, 134
Fitzgerald, Mr., 210
Food Ministry, The. *See under* Ministry
Fowler, Mr., 65
France, 313
Free Trade and Tariff Reform controversy, 80 *et seq.*
Fry, Sir Edward, 117

Gee, Thomas, 59, 66
Gee & Sons, Ltd., 137
George, Rt. Hon. David Lloyd. *See* Lloyd George
Germany, 313, 320
Gladstone, Herbert, 158
Gladstone, Rt. Hon. W. E., 41, 58–64 *passim*, 165
Glamorgan Collieries, the, 122, 126–9, 130, 136, 171 ; by-product recovery at, 132–3
Glantawe, Lord, *quoted*, 81
Globe Shipping Co., 137
Gonner, Sir E. C. K., on the Ministry of Food under Lord Rhondda, *quoted*, 244, 249, *et seq.*
Government War Contracts Committee, 139
Grace, Mr., 207
Grey, Sir Edward, 77
Griffith, Mr. R. A., 72
Grocers' Federation Meeting, 1918, 244–5
Gueret, Mr. Louis, 131
Gueret, L., Ltd., 131, 132, 136

Gueret's Anglo-Brazilian Coaling Co., Ltd., 132
Guest, Mr.(Lord Wimborne), 158–62
Guild Socialism, 283–4
Gwaun-Cae-Gurwen Anthracite Colliery, 141

HAIG family, the, 16, 27
Haig, A. W., 15, 306
Haig, George Augustus, 15–17, 22
Haig, George Augustus, Mrs., 15, 17
Haig, Lotty, 16
Haig, Rose Helen (Mrs. J. H. Thomas), 3, 15
Haig, Sybil Margaret, 15 et seq., and see Thomas, Mrs. D. A.
Hall, Mr. R. N., 73
Hammond, Mr., 51
Hardie, J. Keir, 54 n., 156 and notes 1 and 2
Hartshorn, Mr. Vernon, 170–1, 182, 286 n.
Hester, Inspector, 205
Hichens, Mr. W. L., 210
Hiraethog, Gwilym, 59
Hodges, Mr. Frank, 186
Home meat supply, 250, 251, 252–3
Home Rule, election of 1886, 58
Hood family, the, 127, 128, 130
Horder, Sir Thomas, quoted, 265–6, 274–7
Housing question, the, 323
Howell, Frederick Robert, 3
Hudson, Dr. C. T., 7, 8, 11–12
Hughes, Edwin, 9
Hughes, Mr. H. O., 325
Hughes, General Sam, 205, 208
Hughes, Sir Thomas, 78

IMBRIE & Co., 192
Imperial Munitions Board, 210
Imperial Navigation Coal Co., Ltd., 136
Individual freedom, 282–3
Individualism, 279–80, 282, 290
Industry, State control of, 286–8
Infant mortality, 264–5, 276, 322
Innes, E. A. Mitchell, 128
International Coal Co., 141
Investment banking organisation, 192–3
Irish Disestablishment, 60, 62
Irish Food Control Committee, 229
Irish Nationalism, 30, 71

JAMES, Mr. C. H., 53, 58
Jameson, Miss Nina, 204, 205
Japp, Mr. Henry, 207

Jervis-White-Jervis, H., 305
Jevons, W. S., The Coal Question, 29 and n., 325
Jones, Major, 63, 64
Jones, Mr. Lester, 152, 153
Joseph, Morgan, 2
Joseph, Rachel, 3
Joseph, Thomas, 4, n. 2
Josephs, the, 2, 6, 8
Journal of the Royal Statistical Society, 325

KITCHENER, Lord, 205
Knaggs, Professor R. L., 14; account of Lord Rhondda's college life, 305–6

LABOUR and Capital, 286
Labour Bargain, the, 186
La Compagnie Chargeurs Française, 136
Laurier, Sir Wilfrid, 212
Lawrence, Lord Chief Justice, 79
Lawrence, Mr. Joseph, 155–8
Leigh, Rev. John, 36
Lewis, Mr. Herbert, 54 n., 63, 64, 65, 73
Lewis, Sir T. W., 8–9 and n., 10, 305
Lewis, Sir W. T. (Lord Merthyr), 99, 100; Sliding Scale controversy and the coal strike of 1898...100–20 passim, 146, 150–3; reconciliation with D. A., 120
Liberal Imperialist League, 77
Llanwern, 52, 84, 215; home life at, 84 et seq. passim, 263, 309–12; guests, 85, 91; the study, 90; D. A.'s favourite week in May at, 94
Llewelyn, Sir Leonard, 128, 134, 154, 164
Lloyd George, Rt. Hon. David: in Welsh Disestablishment controversy, 59–77 passim; account of D. A.'s acceptance of the Munitions Mission, 57, 201–3; offers Lord Rhondda the Presidency of Local Government Board, 57, 263, 268; on Lord Rhondda's acceptance of the Food Ministry, 268, 269–70, 272; an American view of the tendencies of his legislation, 314
Lloyd Morgan, Judge, 59, 63, 78
Llwynypia property, the. See Glamorgan Collieries
Local Government Board, 221, 264 et seq., 317, 322–4

Lusitania, torpedoing of the, 196 *et seq.*; the German warning, 196-7; the landing at Queenstown, 199-200
Lysberg Limited, 129-30, 136

MABON (Mr. W. Abraham), 60, 107, 118, 147, 148, 149, 153, 166
Mahon, Major-Gen. R. H., 205
Mannesmann Tube Co., 141
Marstons, the, 204
Martens, R. & Co., 316
Martin, John : case of, 164-6
Maternity welfare schemes, 265, 267
Meat and Fats Executive, 223
Meat rationing, 237-8, 242, 250
Medical research, 276
Merthyr, 2 *and n.*
Merthyr, Lord. *See under* Lewis, Sir W. T.
Merthyr Express, the, 137
Merthyr Tydfil representation, 53, 54, 58, 59, 155, 156, 168
Mica resources exploitation, 313
Military conscription, 281
Mill, John Stuart, 28
Minimum Wage Act, 125
Ministry of Food, the, under Lord Rhondda, 218 *et seq.*, 249, 258; unification and organisation, 219-20, 250, 251, 259, 318; blending of governmental and business experience in, 220; policy, 220 *et seq.*; 243, 250; 318; programme, 221-2 ; control of supplies, 222-4, 231; the 'disappearing rabbit,' 224-5; control of prices, 224-6, 250, 252, 256; distribution and rationing, 226-7, 231 *et seq.*, 243, 320-1 ; national rationing system 234, *et seq.*, 251, 256 ; queues, 233, 234, 240-2 ; Local Distribution Order, 237, 241 ; press support, 247, 251, 319, 324 ; public confidence in, 251, 254, 259-61, 270, 317-21 ; punishment of food hoarders, 319-20 ; difficulties intensified by losses at sea, 261, 317 ; yearly total turnover, 223
Ministry of Health, 264 *et seq.*, 276, 303, 304, 322
Ministry of Health Bill, 268
Mississippi barge service, 193, 194, 313, 316
Mitchelson, A. & Co., 137
Mitchelson, Mr. A., 141
Monmouthshire and South Wales Coal Owners Association, 124, 137

Montagu, Mr. E. S., 268
Morgan, David, 73
Morgan, Col. Fred, 154, 155
Morgan, Sir George Osborne, 60, 63, 73
Morgan, J. Pierpont, 204, 206, 314
Morgan, Messrs. J. P. & Co., 203, 205, 206, 207, 213
Morgan, Rev. J. V., 9
Morgan, Thomas, 36
Morgan, Mr. Watts, 163 *et seq.*
Morgan, W. Pritchard, 53 *n.*, 54 *n.*, 64, 155, 156
Muir-Mackenzie, Lord, 174
Munitions, Ministry of, 202, 209, 210, 214, 216, 219
Munitions Mission, the, 201 *et seq.*; D. A.'s acceptance of, 201-2 ; ' Hansard ' his only visible authority, 202-3 ; account of, 204 *seq.*; American and Canadian aspects of, 208 ; Canadian Shell Committee, 209-10 ; tour of the Eastern Provinces, 211 ; relations with the press, 212 ; humours of the work, 213

NATIONALISATION, 279-80
Nationalism, 30, 31
National Kitchens, 244
National Miners Strike, 1912, 122-3
Naval Colliery Company, 122, 130, 131, 132, 136
New York, in 1915, 194, 195
Nicholas, Mr., 51
North's Navigation Collieries (1889) Ltd., 141
North Wales Liberal Federation, 64, 74
Norton, Derwent, 11

OCEAN COAL CO., 46
Oil Seeds Executive, 223
Oppenheim, Mr. August Rust, account of Lord Rhondda's American plans, 191-3
Ovendon, 50-1
Owen, Mr. V. Lloyd, 205

Pall Mall Gazette, 138
Passive resistance, 185
Peace River Development Corporation, 191, 313
Peace River enterprise, the, 56, 191, 193, 313, 315
Pearson, Messrs. S. & Co., 207
Pease, Lieut.-Gen. L. T., 207
Penrhiwfer Colliery, 132
Perry-Herrick property, the, 215

Philipps, Wynford (Viscount St. Davids), 74
Philps, Rev. W. F., 187
Phipps, Col. C. E., 207
Pig-keeping, 322
Pilgrims Club Dinner, 207
Pitwood Consumers Syndicate, 130, 139
Pitwood imports into South Wales, 129
Plisson & Co., 136
Plisson-Lysberg Insurance Co., 137
Pontypridd, Lord, 63, 72, 73
Pontypridd newspaper series, 137
Poor Law, 323
Port Talbot Railway and Docks Company, 135
Princeton, motor car journey to, 194

RADCLIFFE, H., 54 n.
Randell, David, 59, 64
Rationing, 222 et seq., 243, 251, 256, 320
Reed, Sir Edward, 63, 64, 160
Rees, Noah, 166
Rendel, Lord, 60, 62
Rhondda Valley Urban District Council, 41, 171, 217
Rhondda, Lord. See under Thomas, David Alfred (Lord Rhondda)
Rhondda, Viscountess, 130
Rhys, Professor, 61
Richard, Henry, 58, 59, 60, 61
Richards, Mr. T., 173–82
Riches, John Osborne, 3, 45–6, 47
Riches, Osborne Henry, 45, 46, 47, 50, 51
Ridgeway, William, 305
Riven, George, 305
Roberts, Bryn, 63, 78
Roberts, Herbert (Lord Clwyd), 63
Rockefeller, John D., 204
Rosebery, Lord, 65–8 passim, 75, 77
Royal Statistical Society, 120; Journal of, 325

ST. DAVID's, Viscount, 74
Salusbury, Miss Evelyn, account of D. A.'s interests, 307–8
Sanatogen, Ltd., 141
Schwab, Charles N., 207
Selfishness, 278–9, 285, 287, 288
Shaughnessy, Sir Thomas, 210
Shopping : American and British shops, 194
Sliding Scale Agreement, 101–20 passim, 146, 150–3
Smyth-Pigott, Capt. B. C., 207
Sneddon, Mr. J. P., 207

Socialism, 280 et seq.; D. A. accused of promoting, 187
Social Reform, 289–90
South America, 313
Southney, H. W. & Son, 137
South Wales Printing and Publishing Co., Ltd., 137
South Wales Coal Annual, quoted, 2 n., 45
South Wales coalfield in the 'nineties, 100–1, 146 ; organisation of the mining industry in, 101, 134–5 ; wages in, 101, 123, 146 ; Sliding Scale controversy, 101 et seq., 146 150, 168 ; the strike of 1898...100, 109, et seq., 122 n., 131 and n., 168 ; strike settlement, 118
South Wales Daily Telegraph, 157 and n.
South Wales Journal of Commerce, 137
South Wales Liberal Federation, 64, 66, 76
South Wales Miners Federation, 172, 176, 189
Spain, coal distributing agency in, 136, 314
Spender, Mr. Harold, 69
Spring-Rice, Sir Cecil, 206
State control in war and in peace, 190
Stettinius, Mr. E. R., 206, 207
Stewart, Lord Ninian, 162, 167
Sugar Commission, the, 218, 220
Sugar Distribution Scheme, 231–3
Swansea Corporation, 79
Syndicalist movement in Wales, 125, 172

TAFF Vale Railway Co., 135
Tallents, Captain, 237, 239, 243
Tarian, the, 137
Tarian Printing and Publishing Co., the, 137
Tariff Reform controversy, 80 et seq., 158
Temple, Sir Richard, 68
'The Miners' Next Step,' 125, 172
Thomas, Alfred (Lord Pontypridd), 63, 72, 73
Thomas & Davey, 54, 126, 136
Thomas, David Alfred (Lord Rhondda) :
    Ancestry, 1–2 ; parents, 4–5, 7, 312 ; birth, 4 ; brothers and sisters, 2–3 ; home life, 6 ; early years, 6–7 ; school-days, 7–13 ; nickname, 8 and n., 306 ; ill health, 13–14 ; foreign

travel, 14 ; life at College, 14,
15, 28 *and n.*, 305–6 ; studies
law, 15, 41 ; and mining, 15,
17 ; engagement, 15–27, 30 ;
his baptism, 19–20 ; marriage,
27, 49 ; views on economics,
28–9 ; attitude to Nationalist
idea, 30, 31 ; sympathy with
the American character, 31,
56 ; religious views, 18 *et seq.*,
32–3, 96, 271, 288, 312 ; early
views on life, 34–9 ; views on
children, 35, 95, 96 ; early
ambitions, 40–1 ; takes up
public duties, 41, 42 ; becomes
a Freemason, 41 ; death of his
father, 41, 46–7

Business :
Determines to succeed in his
business, 45 ; partnership in
Cambrian Collieries, 46–8, 49,
50, 51, 54 ; Cardiff, 50 ; de-
cides to go on London Stock
Exchange, 50, 51, 52, 137 ;
birth of his daughter, 50 ;
life at Ovendon, 50–1, 52 ;
Llanwern, 52, 84 ; home life
at Llanwern, 84 *et seq. passim*,
263, 309–12 ; combines politics
and business, 54, 58 ; business
life at Cardiff, 87 *et seq.*, 93, 310 ;
his theory regarding inter-
views, 88 ; interest in new
patents, 89 ; views on organisation of the coal industry, 101,
102, 142 ; scheme for control
of output, 102–3, 146, 326 ;
regulation of coal prices policy,
101 *et seq.*, 120, 128–9, 131,
142 ; attitude to the speculative
middleman, 101, 120, 135–6,
142 ; opinion of the Sliding
Scale agreement, 101, 119 ;
originally not a member of the
Association, 102, 122 ; attitude
to Sir W. T. Lewis's control
scheme, 103, 108, 109, 117, 146 ;
sympathy with the miners in
1898, 103, 105–8 *passim*, 110 ;
on the action of the Associated
Owners, 104–9 *passim*, 117 ;
attitude to Clydach Vale
strikers (1898), 110–3, 122 ;
his part in the strike of 1898,
114, 117, 118–9, 167 ; views on
the industrial unrest in the
South Wales coalfield, 122–6 ;
devotes himself entirely to
politics, 54–5, 126

Politics :
D. A.'s political ambitions, 40,
42, 54, 263–4 ; disabilities for a
political career, 42–5, 55, 68, 317 ;
stands for Merthyr Borough,
53, 58, 59 ; views on canvassing for votes, 53 ; Merthyr
Tydfil results, 53–4, 66 ; in the
Welsh Disestablishment Controversy and the Tithe War,
61 *et seq* ; the 'Welsh Revolt,'
65–7, 78–80 ; D. A. and Lloyd
George, 66–70, 75, 76, 77–8 ;
elected President of South
Wales Liberal Federation, 64,
66 ; the Cymru Fydd move-
ment, 31, 69 *et seq.* ; a loyal
follower of Campbell-Bannerman, 77 ; Welsh Education
Revolt, 78 *et seq.* ; the Free
Trade movement, 80 *et seq.* ;
political failure in 1906, 55,
83, 264 ; retires from Parliament in 1910, 169. (*For*
Political Views *and* Political
Philosophy *see below.*)
Returns to the Cambrian Board
in 1906...55, 126 ; becomes
immersed in new schemes, 56 ;
acquires Glamorgan Collieries,
122, 126–9, 130 ; views on his
duty to shareholders, 129, 138 ;
acquisition and consolidation
of coal interests, 129 *et seq.*,
140–3 ; creation of the Cambrian Combine, 133 ; centralisation of sales agencies, 135–6,
142 ; directorships of joint
stock undertakings, 135 ; insurance business, 136–7 ; acquires control of newspapers
and printing firms, 137–8 ;
profits from coal enterprises,
138 ; positions on committees,
139 ; American and Canadian
interests, 56, 191 *et seq.* ;
schemes Anglo-American combinations, 56, 192, 193 ; in-
vestigates American coal business, 191 *et seq* ; Mississippi
barge service, 193, 194, 313,
316 ; Canadian development
schemes, 56–7, 191, 193 ; relationships with newspapers,
88, 137–8, 324 ; prolific contributor to the press, 100, 138,
144 *et seq.* ; views as to London
newspapers, 138 ; devotedness
of his servants, 89–90, 93 ;

respected and trusted by the miners, 100, 317.

In the early years of the war, 56, 57; journey in the *Lusitania*, 196 *et seq.*; effect of his experience in the torpedoed vessel, 199-202, 318; the Munitions Mission, 57, 201 *et seq.*; receives a peerage, 57, 216-7; becomes President of Local Government Board, 57, 217, 263, 264, 317; work at Local Government Board, 322-4; accepts post of Food Controller, 217, 218, 221, 244, 249-50, 257, 268, 269, 270, 317, 323; leaves Local Government Board, 218, 221, 323; interest in project for a Ministry of Health 218, 221, 322; his work at the Food Ministry, 243, 254 *et seq.*, 262, 290; factors in his success, 254-5, 262; example in economising food, 271, 320; illness, 271; offers resignation, 271-3; receives a Viscountcy with Remainder to his daughter, 273; continues his work as Food Minister when lying ill, 274; temperament in the last year, 270-1, 272; attitude towards religion, 33, 271; death, 244, 277, 321

Appreciation of:
Coalowner, as, 99-100, 118-9, 122, 143
Food Controller, as, 244 *et seq.*, 255-7, 259-62, 269-70
On 'Change: D. A. as We Know Him, 184-5
Characteristics, 7, 8, 15, 31, 38-9, 42-5, 55, 90, 100, 193, 246, 257, 277, 288-90, 305, 308, 309, 320, 323-4; in the last year of his life, 271; character sketch, 291 *et seq.*
Adaptability, 97
Character, judge of, 292-4
Class-consciousness, devoid of, 32
Code and philosophy of life, 299
Constructive ability, 63
Controversialist, 100, 144-5
Conversationalist, as, 91-3, 95
Correspondence, in, 23, 30, 87, 144
Death: attitude to, 265, 269, 289

Delay, impatient of, 310, 311, 323
Delegating talent for, 295
Dress (as a young man), 26
Duty, sense of, 317-8
Faddist, 302, 307
Figures: fascinated by, 12, 14, 213, 325
Frankness, 56, 323-4
Imagination in business, 297
Individualism, 29
Intelligence: appreciation of, 298
Joy in Life, 86, 87, 263-4, 292, 304; longing for youth, 263-4
Loyalty, 164, 299
Management of people, aptitude for, 33-4, 294-5, 323
Organisation, genius for, 318, 323
Patronising, dislike of, 37, 294, 297
Pedantry in use of words, 23, 87
Pose, freedom from, 298, 300
Realist, 299
Relations with other people, 32, 42-3, 294, 295-7, 299-300
Simplicity, 98, 292, 297
Superstitious, 33, 301
Temper, 89, 302
Theatres, taste in, 194-5
Thoroughness, 292, 326
Trust, 295
Vitality, 139, 275, 292, 309
Waste, horror of, 265
Habits, 36, 86 *et seq. passim.*
Letters and Press Controversies, 144 *et seq.*
Clydach Vale strike, 1901...153
Coal Combines, 188
Coal conservation, 169-70
Coal output, control of, 147 *et seq.*
Colliery profits and colliers' wages, 173-82
Election campaign: South Monmouthshire, 154 *et seq.*; Merthyr (1901), 156; candidature of Mr. Guest (Cardiff, 1904), 158 *et seq*; of 1910...167-9
Labour Bargain, 186
Labour Leaders, criticism of, 147 *et seq.*
Llwynypia stoppage, 166-7
Syndicalist movement in Wales, 171
Woman Suffrage; Women's Work, 185-7

Maxims, 6, 12, 264, 295–9 *passim*, 308

Motto, 217

Political views and political philosophy of, 29–31, 35, 55, 63, 68, 77, 80, 121, 278 *et seq.*, 288

Capitalism *versus* Socialism, 284–6, 288

Commerce, 289, 290

Free Trade, 80–3

Guild Socialism, 283–4

Individual Freedom, 282–3

Individualism, 29, 279–80, 282, 290

Industry, State control of, 286–8

Labour and Capital, 286

Military conscription, 281

Nationalisation, 279–80

Nationalism, 30–1

Selfishness, 278–9, 285, 287, 288

Socialism, 30, 280, *et seq.*

Social Reform, 289–90

Trade, Idealism in, 287

Recreations :

Bee-keeping, 51, 308

Birds'-nesting, 6, 13, 94, 95 ; favourite week in May, 94

Cattle breeding, 93, 311–12

Chess, 307

Cycling, 307

Games, not cared for, 35 ; his game of ' Bridge,' 90–1

Reading, 29, 87, 272, 300, 325 ; favourite books, 325

Rowing and sculling, 14, 305–6

Walking, 6, 35–6, 86, 94

Works by :

The Growth and Direction of our Foreign Trade in Coal, etc. (Coal Exports, 1850–1900), 120–1, 325

Some Notes on the Present State of the Coal Trade, etc., 101–2, 120

The Coal Trade, contributed to the volume *British Industries under Free Trade*, 80–3

Thomas, Mrs. D. A. (*née* Sybil Margaret Haig) [wife], 15 *et seq. passim*, 44, 73, 84, 85, 89, 91, 92–3, 97, 205

Thomas, Rev. Arnold [cousin], 11, 13, 312

Thomas, Rev. David [uncle], 2, 5, 11, 13, 40

Thomas, John [grandfather], 1, 2

Thomas, John, Howard [brother], 3, 6, 7, 8, 15, 152, 166

Thomas, Mary [sister], 3

Thomas, Mima Williams [sister], 3

Thomas Samuel [father], 3, 4–7, 13, 14, 29 *n.*, 45

Thomas, Mrs. Samuel (*née* Rachel Joseph) [mother], 3, 4–7

Thomas, Samuel Moreton [brother], 3

Thomas, Riches & Co., 46, 51, 133

Thomas Syndicate, the, 315

Tithe War, the, 60

Toronto, 216

Trade, Idealism in, 287

Trades Disputes Act, 126

Trade Unionism, 124, 126

Tredegar, Lord, 155

Turner, Mr. F. L., notes on Lord Rhondda's work at Local Government Board, 322–4

ULSTER Rebellion, the, 185

United States coal, 82, 313–4, 316

United States : D. A.'s visits in 1913, 191 ; in 1915, 194 ; the Munitions Mission, 201 *et seq.*

Upward, Allen, 54 *n.*

VON DONOP, Sir Stanley, 207

WALES :

Disestablishment in, 59 *et seq.*, 71, 75, 78 ; Nationalist movement in, 31, 69 *et seq.* ; Tithe War in, 60

Walker, Mrs. M. E. M., *quoted*, 309–12

Walkers, the, 128

War Bread, 219

Warren, Mr. Algernon, account of D. A.'s schooldays, 8–11

Warren, Mr. Edward, 10, 11

Warren, Sir Herbert, 10, 11

Welsford, G. F., 305

Welsford, J. W., 13 *and n.*, 14, 305

Welsh Army Corps Clothing Committee, 139

Welsh Disestablishment, 59 *et seq.*, 71, 75, 78

Welsh Nationalist movement, 31, 69 *et seq.*

Welsh National Liberal Federation, 72

Welsh Parliamentary Party, the, 64 *et seq.*

Welsh Education Revolt, the, 79–80
Western Fuel Co., 192
Western Mail (Cardiff), 137, 168
Wheat Commission, the, 218, 220, 223
Wheat Executive Agreement, 218
Williams, Benjamin, 3
Williams, B. Francis, 53 *n.*
Williams, Jane, 2
Williams, Mr. Lewis, 159
Williams, Mr. Llewelyn, 75 ⅃ account of D. A.'s political life, 58 *et seq*
Williams, Thomas, 73
Williams, Judge Watkin, 60, 64

Wilson, John, 166
Wimborne, Lord, 158–62
Winslow, Walter, 305
Wintour, Mr. U. F., 220, 251
Wise, Mr. E. F., 243
Woman Suffrage, 185–6
Women's Work, 186–7
Wood, Mr., 211

Y Baner, 137
Y Tyst, 137
Young Wales, 59
Ysgyborwen, 4 *and n.* [1]
Ysgyborwen Colliery, 4 *n.* [2]
Ystradyfodwg Local Board of Health, 41

Printed at THE BALLANTYNE PRESS
SPOTTISWOODE, BALLANTYNE & CO. LTD.
Colchester, London & Eton, England

ImTheStory.com

Personalized Classic Books in many genre's

Unique gift for kids, partners, friends, colleagues

Customize:

- Character Names
- Upload your own front/back cover images (optional)
- Inscribe a personal message/dedication on the
  inside page (optional)

Customize many titles Including
- Alice in Wonderland
- Romeo and Juliet
- The Wizard of Oz
- A Christmas Carol
- Dracula
- Dr. Jekyll & Mr. Hyde
- And more...

CPSIA information can be obtained at www.ICGtesting.com
Printed in the USA
LVOW01s1801130214

373595LV00025B/1411/P